HOSPITALITY AND TOURISM CAREERS:

A Blueprint for Success

Carl Riegel

Melissa Dallas

Prentice Hall
Upper Saddle River, New Jersey 07458

Library of Congress Cataloging-in-Publication Data

Riegel, Carl D.
    Hospitality and tourism careers : a blueprint for success / Carl
Riegel and Melissa Dallas.
        p.   cm.
    ISBN 0-13-228545-2
    1. Hospitality industry--Vocational guidance. 2. Tourist trade-
-Vocational guidance.   I. Dallas, Melissa.   II. Title.
TX911.3.V62R54   1998
647.94'023--dc21   97-21990
                                                              CIP

Production Editor: *Eileen M. O'Sullivan*
Managing Editor: *Mary Carnis*
Acquisitions Editor: *Neil Marquardt*
Director of Manufacturing and Production: *Bruce Johnson*
Manufacturing Manager: *Ed O'Dougherty*
Marketing Manager: *Frank Mortimer, Jr.*
Editorial Assistant: *Rose Mary Florio*
Cover designer: *Miguel Ortiz*
Printer/Binder: *Banta-Harrisonburg*

©1998 by Prentice-Hall, Inc.
A Simon & Schuster Company
Upper Saddle River, New Jersey 07458

Printed in the United States of America
10   9   8   7   6   5   4   3   2   1

ISBN 0-13-228545-2

Prentice-Hall International (UK) Limited, *London*
Prentice-Hall of Australia Pty. Limited, *Sydney*
Prentice-Hall Canada Inc., *Toronto*
Prentice-Hall Hispanoamericana, S.A., *Mexico*
Prentice-Hall of India Private Limited, *New Delhi*
Prentice-Hall of Japan, Inc., *Tokyo*
Simon & Schuster Asia Pte. Ltd., *Singapore*
Editora Prentice-Hall do Brasil, Ltda., *Rio de Janeiro*

CONTENTS AT A GLANCE

DETAILED CONTENTS

PREFACE

WARNING: THIS IS NOT A TEXTBOOK!

The world of hospitality and tourism is huge! It offers an almost unlimited array of satisfying and exciting career opportunities for those who have the interest and qualifications to succeed in it and who prepare properly to attain that success. However, developing qualifications or making preparations is a complex and highly individual matter. Successful careers require a lot more than dumb luck. They require careful attention! If you keep waiting for that lucky break, it *may* happen but chances are much greater that you will just drift along.

The purpose of this book, therefore, is to serve as a guide for **defining**, **planning**, and **managing** your career to achieve the maximum fullness and richness from your career that can be obtained from careers in the world of hospitality and tourism.

This book grew out of years of discussion about how best to advise hospitality and tourism students on career search strategies and career management. Between us, we have over 15 years of management experience in several industry segments including hotels, contract foodservice, full-service restaurants and airport concessions. In addition, we have spent over a quarter of a century (between us, of course!) advising and teaching hospitality and tourism students at the community college, university, and executive education levels. During that time we have been in a position to observe both career successes and career failures, as well as career paths that defy conventional notions about how people should manage their professional lives.

Furthermore, in our capacity as teachers and advisers we have had the pleasant opportunity to work with our students to help them develop resumes and cover letters, and to offer advice on other job search strategies including interviewing techniques, researching companies, and planning their work experience so that they can get the job they want when they graduate. It also seems that our relationship with our students doesn't end at graduation because our alumni frequently consult us on such matters as how to handle organizational politics, when to change positions, whether or not to pursue an advanced degree, or what appropriate salaries are for particular positions.

We enjoy this aspect of our jobs tremendously and feel a great deal of satisfaction when we see the tangible results of our efforts – when people produce resumés they are proud of, or students obtaining their dream jobs, or an alumnus successfully turning around a sticky political situation. However, we have found that there were also frustrations in doing this work. Often, we could dispense advice or rattle-off facts simply based on our experience.

But, equally often, we didn't have the answers and were forced to consult other resources such as resumé books, salary surveys, or industry contacts. Sometimes we simply had to refer our students and alumni to other sources because we couldn't come up with an answer or didn't have the time to find the answers needed. Wouldn't it be nice, we thought, if someone were to develop a comprehensive source of information regarding job search and career management strategies which would enable us to find the answers we needed quickly or to which we could refer those we serve so that they could find their own answers. We kept waiting and such a work never materialized.

Then it occurred to us that if this resource wasn't available, maybe we should do it ourselves. After all, we had been doing this work for a long time. As we began to discuss it, we decided that was *exactly* what we should do, and we approached our task with interest, enthusiasm, and a great deal of thought about *who* we were writing for and what their needs were.

Career management, as we will say later, actually begins the minute you commit to an intention, and one sign of this commitment is deciding on a major. In other words, your career management process began the day you decided to enroll in your hospitality and tourism program or the day you decided to pursue a career in this field.

With that in mind, we designed the content of this book to cover career management from the time you seriously commit to building a career in the hospitality and tourism industry, either by enrolling in an academic program or by following some other route, until well after you have landed your first professional or managerial job.

We cover the basics such as career opportunities and preparation for a career and job search. We also provide information about how you can manage your personal affairs such as making it on your own and taking care of your health and emotional well-being in a fast-paced and sometimes stressful field of work. Finally, we attempt to provide practical and useful information about how to manage your career *after* you have ventured out into the professional business world.

We have thought long and hard about our reading audience and have tried to make this book both appealing and useful to the audience. **It is not intended to be a textbook!** Rather it is designed for students and others to use as a reference to guide them in both preparation for and the management of their hospitality and tourism career for some time to come. Our perspective is not theoretical, or, for that matter, even idealistic. We approached our work with a sense of realism and the advice we give is intended to be practical and achievable. Our hope is that you will find the book to be both *engaging* and *useful*.

Recognizing that prospective readers will come from a variety of backgrounds and have varied ambitions, we have been mindful to cover topics which pay attention to our diverse readership. Examples and topics have been carefully selected to be of use to university students, community college and vocational students, non-traditional as well as traditional students, and for those who simply want information about careers in the hospitality and tourism industry. You may not find that everything applies to you, but there is a relatively good chance that you will find a substantial amount of information which you can use. You may not find each chapter to be relevant to your personal situation, but, as the saying goes, "Take what you need and leave the rest."

Another goal is to *involve* our readers as they progress through the book. To accomplish this, we write in a conversational style and we include checklists and self-assessment exercises in almost every chapter to help you clarify your values and needs in selected areas as well as to help you formulate plans and strategies for career development.

In addition, throughout the book, you will find charts and tables which summarize useful data about a variety of areas which will be of concern to you now and in the future. Things like cost of living indices, salary surveys, and national employer listings are included.

This book is divided into three sections and each section discusses a different area of career management or development. The first section is concerned with preparation for professional employment. As such, it provides information about employment opportunities in many of the segments in the hospitality and tourism industry and discusses and illustrates career paths which you might choose to follow. It also guides you through the mechanics of identifying potential employers and writing resumés and cover letters. Finally, Section One provides practical advice on interviewing and follow-up etiquette. In addition, throughout the book, you will find charts and tables which summarize useful data about a variety of areas which will be of concern to you both now and in the future – things like cost of living indices, salary surveys, and national employer listings.

The second section focuses on the transition from school to career. We talk about the realities of organizational life including your relationship with subordinates, co-workers, and superiors, as well as organizational politics. We stress the need for you to determine performance expectations and to stick to them. We also provide some useful information on life skills such as budgeting, apartment hunting, and making friends in a new location. It also includes an important section professional development as it relates to your career and to your ultimate job-related success.

The final section extends beyond your first job in this industry and is designed to help you **manage your career and your entire being**. It covers a wide range of topics which include personal development and the future of the hospitality and tourism industry. Our purpose here is to point out that change will occur and your success depends on how well you can manage and adapt to change.

In each chapter, we also present commentary from senior managers and executives as well as from managers at all levels. All have made the transition from school to the managerial or professional arena and have made mistakes and had successes, and are now fully engaged in the process of managing their own careers.

To gain maximum benefit this book **should not be read**! It should **be worked**. That is, you should think about how each topic applies to *you*. Use the resources we have provided to assess things for yourself or to guide you through the process of finding the right job and managing your career so that you can gain **success**, however *you* might define it. GOOD LUCK!

Carl Riegel
Melissa Dallas

ABOUT THE AUTHORS

CARL RIEGEL

Carl Riegel, Ed.D., is the Associate Director of the Hotel and Restaurant Administration rogram at Washington State University; Director of the Seattle Center for Hotel and Restaurant Administration; Director of Professional Development for the Hotel and Restaurant Administration Program; and Co-Director of the Hospitality and Tourism Institute (that's a lot of ways of saying that he works for the state of Washington).

He is the author of numerous papers, monographs, and chapters in books and teaches courses in operations management, strategy, financial analysis, and whatever else interests him at the moment.

Carl lives near Seattle with his loving wife, his spoiled rotten Persian cat named Muffin, and with Gus, his rowdy and obnoxious Rottweiler.

MELISSA DALLAS

Melissa Dallas, J.D., serves as the Assistant Dean of the Hospitality and Culinary Arts Division at Seattle Central Community College, Adjunct Associate Professor with the Hotel and Restaurant Administration Program at Washington State University; and Co-Director of the Hospitality and Tourism Institute (that's a lot of ways of saying that she works for the state of Washington, too).

She is the author of numerous papers and chapters in books, and teaches courses in foodservice management, hospitality law, and whatever else interests her at the moment.

Melissa lives near Seattle with her loving husband, her sweet and gentle Persian cat named Muffin, and with Gus, her sensitive and well-behaved Rottweiler.

ACKNOWLEDGMENTS

Writing this book, or any book, is not an easy task unless you are Stephen King or John Grisham. These guys probably write one before breakfast everyday and store them in their garages for future publication. However, that's beside the point.

We had a great deal of support and help, and would like to acknowledge those who helped along the way. First, we would like to thank A. Gayle Sullenberger, Dean of the College of Business and Economics, and W. Terry Umbreit, Director of the Hotel and Restaurant Administration Program at Washington State University. Along with them, we extend our sincere thanks to Ron Hamberg, Vice President of Instruction, and Myrtle Mitchell, Dean of Professional Technical Education, at Seattle Central Community College. These people encouraged, supported, and believed in our work. Not only that, but they are our bosses and we thought that by ingratiating ourselves to them, we could get a nice raise next year.

We also extend our appreciation to the reviewers who took the time to read and comment on early drafts, and to our Acquisitions Editor, Neil Marquardt, who bought a lot of dinners and drinks without being sure we would really finish this thing!

We appreciate the support of Gordon and Jody Dallas for their comments and insights; to Judy Dallas for listening to our complaining and helping us to keep the faith; to Tom Powers and Hazel Dallas for serving as inspirations; and to Marguerite and Ted Tucker for their love and support.

Thanks, also, to David and Sarah Riegel for their love and understanding, and to Gus and Muffin who spent a lot of time on the office floor messing up piles of discarded papers.

Finally, we thank God for his or her making this possible to happen.

INDEX TO APPENDICES, FIGURES, AND TABLES

PREPARATION FOR PROFESSIONAL EMPLOYMENT

Congratulations! Your decision to pursue a career in the hospitality and tourism industry is just the beginning of an exciting, challenging, and satisfying work life in one of the largest and most important industries in the new global economy. Career possibilities in hospitality and tourism are almost limitless, and the rewards and satisfactions you will experience cover a dizzying range – from financial success to rapid advancement to the satisfaction of helping to the rewarding experience of introducing young people to the world of work.

CONTRIBUTING TO THE GLOBAL ECONOMY

Not so long ago, the hospitality and tourism industries were viewed as two separate and distinct entities. Because of that, government agencies, educational authorities, and even the general public tended to underrate the significance of this field as a major source of jobs and an important contributor to both domestic and world economies.

This prejudice, however, is rapidly disappearing. Millions of people, including young people just beginning their careers as well as people in the middle of their working lives, are looking to the hospitality and tourism industry for an opportunity to fulfill a variety of both personal and professional goals.

Did you know that the hospitality and tourism industry in the United States alone employs 10.5 million, or one in twelve, workers and the United States Bureau of Labor Statistics predicts that this number will grow to 12.4 million employees by 2005? Not only that, but the industry is one of the top employers in a majority of the individual states. To put this in perspective, the hospitality and tourism industry contributes in excess of 5% of the gross domestic product in the United States and employs more people than the agricultural, auto, electronics, steel, and textile industries combined.

States and employs more people than the agricultural, auto, electronics, steel, and textile industries combined.

On a world-wide basis, the industry generates in excess of $3.5 trillion in annual revenues and employs over 112 million people. Plus, the hospitality and tourism industry contributes, on average, about 5.5% of the gross national products of countries around the world.

So you can see that ours is a large industry and an important one because of its economic significance. In addition, the travel and destination activities that are a part of the hospitality and tourism industry are frequently a necessary first step in the development of emerging nations. Adequate transportation, lodging facilities, and even restaurants are part of an infrastructure which makes it possible for other types of enterprises to develop and grow.

Furthermore, having an appropriate infrastructure attracts foreign investment and generates tax revenue which can be used to train and educate a satisfactory labor pool. This increases employment and boosts the economy of developing nations even more. So, in addition to being important because of size and financial contribution, the hospitality and tourism industry is often the forerunner of overall economic development.

LATE COMING BUT PERMANENT SIGNIFICANCE

The significance of the hospitality and tourism industry wasn't always appreciated. In fact, as recently as a decade ago, many people could not understand the rationale for college level programs to prepare people for careers in this field. There were probably several reasons for this.

First, many people tended to view the hospitality industry in terms of its functions – of what the customer saw occurring in a hospitality business. Therefore, cooking, checking people into hotels, carrying luggage, washing dishes, and the like were the primary identifiable characteristics of the industry.

The logic about a restaurant career may have gone something like this: If people are good dishwashers, they will become cooks; if they are good cooks, they will become managers. Why would you need college training for this? If you have any experience at all in the hospitality industry, you know that this simplistic view of it is far from accurate.

A second and more important reason probably had to do with economics. The hospitality and tourism industry, along with other service-related businesses, were viewed as providing services to a variety of other "mainstay" sectors including manufacturing and agriculture. This may or may not have been the case, but today, service businesses account for over two-thirds of the U.S. gross domestic product. The service sector includes banking, retail, and information services to name but a few. It is important to note that the hospitality and tourism industry is one of the largest subdivisions of the service sector!

Third was the notion that service was somehow a less prestigious vocation than others. However, a changing view of what service is and an emphasis on quality in service, be it medical, express mail, customer service, or food service, have raised the prestige of those who work in the service industry. The recognition that the service sector of the economy provides most of the jobs and the new view of service as an honorable profession combine to increase the importance of a college-level education for developing service managers of the future.

Finally, the classification of hospitality and tourism as one industry, or at least as a closely intertwined industry, has done a lot to increase the general recognition of its significance. Take, for example, the People's Republic of China (PRC). The PRC is often referred to as a sleeping economic giant. However, to realize its full potential as a major economic power, the PRC has to trade with other countries, and this means that people from other countries must be able to conduct business there as well.

Thus, international and domestic airline routes must be developed, hotels built, and western style restaurants and other facilities constructed. It's simply not enough to cater to the business traveler. It's important to realize that leisure tourism is *also* necessary to share the cost burden of developing this complex infrastructure.

A RATIONALE FOR A SINGLE INDUSTRY

Because of this interconnectedness between hospitality and tourism, the Council on Hotel, Restaurant and Institutional Education (CHRIE) has chosen to recognize tourism and hospitality as one field.[1] CHRIE believes that the

---

[1] Carl D. Riegel, *A Guide to College Programs in Hospitality and Tourism* (New York: John Wiley & Sons, 1995), p. 3.

industries share the same mission and heritage – serving the guest – and that they possess a common future.

CONCERNING THIS SECTION

By now, you should be aware that your chosen career field is a major industry, important to the economy, and widely varied in terms of career opportunities. This section is about planning your career in the hospitality and tourism industry.

Chapter 1 will introduce you to the notion of careers and career development. You will learn about career opportunities and starting salaries, and you will be able to test your suitability for a career in this field.

Chapter 2 discusses career paths and how to make plans for your career. It places special emphasis on the steps you should be taking now to make sure that you get off to a good start.

Finally, Chapter 3 is dedicated to the nitty gritty of job hunting. We talk about developing resumés, writing cover letters, and interviewing. In addition, we'll show you how to launch a job search and discuss the importance of preparation, appearance, and etiquette.

CAREERS IN HOSPITALITY AND TOURISM

"Only the educated are free."

Epictetus

This book is about careers! You might be tempted to equate a career with a job, a series of jobs, or moving up the ladder. While this may be true in part, a career is much more than that. In many respects, the main focus of a career is your *life*. Why? Because besides being a way of making a living, a career gives us the satisfaction that we want to receive from work and determines the time we have available to do other things. It also partially contributes to our vision of ourselves.

So, while for some, a career may be more about advancement than anything else, for others a career is about meaningful work and a balanced lifestyle. For example, many professionals such as engineers, architects, and lawyers decide, in the middle of their careers, to pursue training in fields such as culinary arts. They do not do this to find a job, but rather because they have evaluated their life and want to change its direction or pace. For some, culinary training may provide an opportunity for self-expression; for others, an opportunity to please people; and for others still, an opportunity to use undiscovered talents. The point of this is that neither point of view regarding careers is right or wrong. Rather, the point is that careers are what *you* make them, and that even the best laid plans can and probably will change as you progress through your life.

Your career plans will be influenced not only by your interests and values, but by a number of external factors including politics, the economy, social and environmental factors, and technology. As a result of this, your beginning is important. You need to have a good understanding of the industry you are about to enter and you need to take care to match your talents, expectations, and values with whatever job you initially choose. Hopefully, this chapter will help you sort these matters out.

In this chapter, we address the topic of career development with an eye toward the 21st century. Our industry is one of the brightest of the future, along with other service industries, technology, and health care. We also discuss the skills required by the modern manager and explore career opportunities as well as the realities of a career in the hospitality and tourism industry. As you will find throughout this book, there are some self-assessment tools, and we include a national salary survey as well.

CAREER DEVELOPMENT

We will go into the "hows" of career development in Chapter 6. In this section, however, we are going to explain how career preferences develop as well as how they can change. Our purpose is to help you develop self-insight regarding *how* you chose the hospitality and tourism industry and, from that, assist you in making an initial job choice.

Earlier, we said that a career was more than a job because it had more to do with a wide range of satisfactions you expect from your working life than it did with the benefits that go hand in hand with salary and advancement. The reason for this is fairly complex. For one, what you do, the industry you do it in, and even where you do it results directly from what you have come to expect from work – that is, which rewards you value, what satisfies you, and your lifestyle choices. Second, what you expect from your worklife and your beliefs about careers started from the day you were born. Third, you may find that your career choice and your identity are not as separate as you might think.

How often have you heard people identify themselves as doctors, engineers, or hotel managers? They may also be mothers, joggers, members of a particular religious denomination, or even students, but they choose to identify themselves by their careers. Also, how many conversations have you had with total strangers when, after a few minutes, the question, "What do you do?" comes up?

We offer these observations to enhance your awareness of:

- ✓ the notion that careers are much more complex than mere jobs; and
- ✓ the probability that your career will more than likely become a major source of personal identity.

Now, let's explore the ways in which careers develop. Most likely, if you are reading this book, you have already made a preliminary commitment to a career in the hospitality and tourism industry. Why? Take a look at Figure 1.1.

FIGURE 1.1
A Model of Career Selection

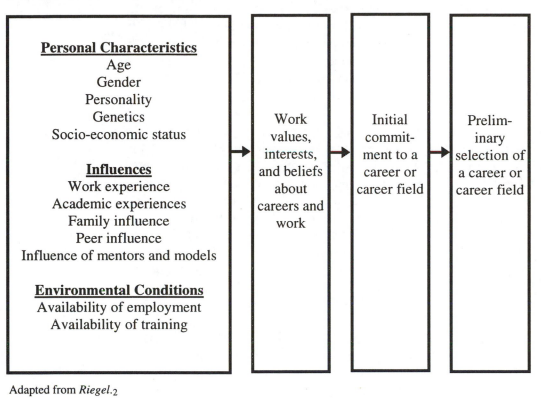

Personal Characteristics
Age
Gender
Personality
Genetics
Socio-economic status

Influences
Work experience
Academic experiences
Family influence
Peer influence
Influence of mentors and models

Environmental Conditions
Availability of employment
Availability of training

→ Work values, interests, and beliefs about careers and work

→ Initial commitment to a career or career field

→ Preliminary selection of a career or career field

Adapted from *Riegel*.[2]

While this model of career selection is straight-forward and relatively simple, it needs a bit of explanation. Basically, your life experiences and influences help to form your values, interests, and beliefs about careers and work. These, in turn, create beliefs that certain careers or career fields will fulfill your expectations.

[2] Carl D. Riegel, *Career Choice, Work Values, and Career Commitment of Food Service and Housing Administration Students at The Pennsylvania State University: A Social Learning Perspective* (Unpublished Doctoral Dissertation, The Pennsylvania State University, 1983), p. 34.

This is called your *initial commitment*. Your initial commitment is tested and refined by further experiences and influences, and leads to your initial choice of a career. If the field you chose fits your values and expectations, your commitment will be strengthened. If it doesn't, you will either change your career or be quite unhappy.

For example, Cyndi was raised in a family where both parents had successful careers. Her parents were outgoing and articulate, and this rubbed off on the young person. As you can see, early in her life, she was socialized by her family to be career-minded and to develop certain personality traits. Cyndi then attended high school, took college preparatory courses, and hung out with friends who also wanted to go to college and have careers. This reinforced the socialization already started by her parents.

After Cyndi turned sixteen, she got a job as a counter-person at a quick service restaurant. She worked hard, and was eventually promoted to a shift supervisor. She loved her work because it gave her an opportunity to serve customers, solve problems, and enjoy managerial status. Her manager, Melinda, an extremely competent fast-tracker, took a personal interest in Cyndi and coached and mentored her. In addition, Melinda often talked to Cyndi about the wide array of opportunities in the foodservice industry. As a result, Melinda served not only as a coach and mentor but, because of her success and high profile, she also became a role model for Cyndi. This experience, combined with her parents' influence, strengthened her desire to have a career and intensified her interest in the foodservice industry.

You can see how Cyndi started to develop a set of positive beliefs about work in the foodservice industry and the match between the industry and her interests. Chances are good that you may have experienced something very similar to Cyndi's experiences.

A few years later, Cyndi was accepted by a university and enrolled in the hospitality management program. She enjoyed her courses and was active in many student organizations on campus. In addition, she was hired by the campus foodservice contractor and eventually was promoted to a student manager. During her senior year, she actively interviewed with various hospitality recruiters and chose to begin her career with the same company she worked for while in college.

This example illustrates how *many* factors influence career choices and how commitment strengthens over time. Had Cyndi's work experience been negative, or had she had more positive work experience in another field, the story might have turned out differently. Cyndi could have chosen to ignore her parents, move to upstate New York, live in an isolated cabin, and write poetry. Similarly, she could have married immediately after high school, and started to raise children right away. Or, she could have entered an entirely different career!

Even though there are exceptions to the process of career development, our model seems to hold up most of the time. A study of 204 students enrolled in a hospitality management program strongly supports this model.[3] Actually, the study showed that the quantity and quality of work experience *as well as* on-the-job role models seemed to most influence the career choices of these students.

You are probably already thinking that the model does not end with career selection and you are right. As you go through life, your values and circumstances will change and new opportunities will become available. The cycle of career development is continuous and, according to many experts, most people will have four or five different careers during their lives.

Don't be tempted to think that careers are simply a matter of fate and circumstances. They are not! They come from *you* when you acquire new skills, re-evaluate and act on your interests, and identify opportunities as they come up. With this in mind, let's switch gears and take a look at some factors which are likely to affect the hospitality and tourism industry during the next century.

TOWARD THE 21st CENTURY

Although it's difficult to predict the number and types of factors that will influence the hospitality and tourism industry in the decades to come, the following are most likely to have an effect on your career:

- ◆ industry maturity
- ◆ technology
- ◆ demographics
- ◆ new products and product expansion
- ◆ international travel
- ◆ economic development
- ◆ social change

[3] Carl D. Riegel, *Ibid.*

Many of these are discussed in greater detail in Chapter 10, but let's take a brief look at them up front to see how they might affect your working future.

Industry Maturity

Most would agree that the hospitality industry has reached maturity. Looking at traditional components such as hotels and restaurants, there are more hotel rooms and restaurant seats available in proportion to the general population than ever before. This might seem to be a signal for doom and gloom, but it doesn't need to be – a number of indicators point to a very positive outlook for the industry's future. To begin with, travel for both business and pleasure is increasing. This translates into an increased demand for hotel rooms and, as a result, both rates and occupancy are up in many locations. Restaurant sales, according to Sandelman and Associates, are expected to reach $320 billion in 1997 – up from $313 billion in 1996. Average checks in leisure dining, for example, rose from $28.90 in 1995 to $39.51 in 1996. Looks pretty promising, right? If this weren't enough, the average adult dines out 4.1 times per week compared to 3.8 times per week five years ago.[4]

Furthermore, the definition of what constitutes the hospitality industry keeps expanding so that careers in areas such as convention management, meeting planning, and attractions management, to name a few, spell OPPORTUNITY. Not only that, but if you separate tourism from hospitality, most would agree that tourism is still a **growth industry**, particularly on the international front. This includes not only out-bound travel to other parts of the world, but in-bound travel to North America by tourists from other countries.

Now, another word of caution – even though the picture for hospitality and tourism is rosy for the short- and even intermediate-terms, it is subject to the laws of economics just like any other industry. For example, because of the 1992 recession, virtually no new hotels were built for a number of years because the demand for rooms was substantially less than the supply. This caused lodging firms to tighten their belts by reducing hiring levels, laying off people, and experimenting with more efficient organizational designs. Now that recovery has occurred, new hotels are being built, more staff members are being hired, and previously eliminated layers of middle management are beginning to reappear.

4   Sandelman and Associates, 1996.

For you, this is great news but, again, we have to add a word of caution. Many industry observers say that the boom and bust cycle is likely to repeat itself and that hotel companies should proceed with caution. Some of them say that business travel and social changes in the United States will contribute to growth in the middle and economy markets of the lodging industry so that no new luxury properties are needed. Only time will let us know the truth!

Technology

Many of us remember the times before computers, or at least remember when a good blast of wind could scramble a computer program in seconds – the one which we spent hours writing and laboriously keying onto punch cards. Of course, those times are long gone. Even those who do not own computers use them work. All of us are inundated by advertisements which give World Wide Web addresses and fax-on-demand numbers. There are predictions that computer-ready televisions which will fully link households and people will become common in homes within a few short years. This new wave of technology will make access more affordable and, as a result, will increase the use of computer technology. Furthermore, the variety of offerings as well as delivery speeds will increase, and individuals and companies will be able to communicate and share information like never before.

For you, the most important thing to keep in mind is that as access to information increases, it will be important for you not only to know **how to find information**, but to also know **how to use it** once you get it. You know how crowded the Internet is now? Well, imagine when even more people are using it! There will be more and more information available, and a search term that now gives you 500 "hits" could, in the future, give you 20 times that many! How will you sort through these 10,000 matches? Similarly, the amount of information shared in and between companies has to be used – and used effectively. This means that technology, information, and analysis will have to go hand in hand.

Obviously, the universal nature of technology will require that you continuously improve your skills in this area. But, while technology-related skills are important, your thought process is even more important. Effective use of technology requires good problem-solving skills – skills that are readily transferable between various types of technology. It's the logic that counts. After all, the most important question to ask when using any technology is not "How does it work?" but "How can I use it?"

You also have a professional responsibility to be aware of advances in technology and anticipate their effects on the workplace. Whether you get this information from seminars, newspapers, or your computer is up to *you* – but expect it to be part of your life, much like brushing your teeth or paying your bills.

True, advancements in technology can inspire fear in even the most daring and innovative people. You might be afraid of making mistakes that would cause a particular system to crash, or you might be afraid of losing your job to a machine. If it's any consolation, you're not alone because these feelings are probably still the norm rather than the exception.

Face It – Technology Is Here To Stay!

Once you can accept that technological advancement is **inevitable and necessary** for the continued growth and advancement of the hospitality and tourism industry, you can embrace this new age and learn all you can. Remember, though, that no learning comes without pain!

Demographics

Demographics are characteristics about people such as gender, age, ethnicity, or income, and they will most certainly play an important role in the future. They will affect the diversity of the workforce and customers, benefit packages offered to workers, products designed for different age groups, and product choices available to the consumer. The importance of this for you is that you will need to be able to anticipate demographic changes, adapt to them, and turn them in your favor – you need to think of them as opportunities rather than obstacles. For example, the leading edge of the post-World War II baby boom generation turned 50 in 1996. This generation is affluent, generally well educated, and healthy. What does this mean for the hospitality and tourism industry? **A LOT!**

The industry is going to have to come up with something better than "early-bird specials" to satisfy this bunch. In fact, as baby boomers retire, it is anticipated that they will be active travelers and require new products to satisfy their wants and needs. We'll discuss some of these products in the next section.

New Products and Product Expansion

Demographic shifts will undoubtedly create needs for new products and for the expansion of others. Some of these new and expanded products already exist. Take the case of leisure care communities. A far cry from the nursing homes of the past, these communities are designed to accommodate the housing, social, and recreational needs of retirees. Leisure care communities are a fast growing business and many major hospitality corporations are including these in their plans for the future. Many investment corporations are buying into them as a way to diversify their portfolios and to offer investors a safe haven for their money.

Leisure care communities often include a variety of restaurants, bars, club rooms, athletic facilities, and other amenities. As a result, they offer numerous job opportunities for you ranging from sales to foodservice management to recreation management. Since most of the baby boomers will not start to retire for another five years, there is little doubt that the demand for these facilities will accelerate at a rapid pace.

Product expansion is another force to be reckoned with in the future. Product expansion in the hospitality and tourism industry will likely occur as more and more companies view themselves as **total service organizations** rather than as hotel firms, travel agencies, or whatever. Already, many Japanese hospitality and tourism firms are said to be fully integrated. In other words, they provide a complete package of travel-related services including air transportation, hotel rooms, ground tours, retail shopping, and recreational activities. Perhaps this trend will catch on in North America, too.

Even now, many hotel and resort gift, souvenir, and sundry shops in the United States are operated by hotels when they used to be leased concessions. Why? For one, this arrangement enables the hotel to control the quality and variety of goods and services offered to its guests. Also, hotels and resorts are finding that these types of businesses are not really that far removed from their primary business. Finally, according to some hoteliers, self-operation of these facilities is more profitable than a lease arrangement.

ARAMARK, a major U.S. full-service hospitality firm, used to be primarily a contract foodservice company. However, it has recently taken on the view that it is a **total service company** and now provides everything from industrial cleaning and laundry services to management support of golf courses. Similarly, Taco Bell Corporation has expanded its business beyond individual units and now provides food for schools, family reunions, stadiums, and other non-traditional markets.

We predict that more and more hospitality and tourism firms will follow the lead of ARAMARK and Taco Bell in the next century.

International Travel

International travel is, in a word, exploding! This year, approximately 450 million people will travel to other countries and this number is expected to increase to 650 million by the turn of the century. These predictions include travel to and from North America as well as between other countries. In terms of employment, what does this mean? Well, that's difficult to say at this point because so many other variables will also influence the employment picture. For certain, it means growth in a variety of businesses including lodging, travel agencies, transportation, and personal services. It also means growth in a number of related industries such as retail and construction.

Where the jobs will be, however, is not clear. There is a trend at present toward the elimination of trade barriers and, as these barriers go by the wayside, perhaps immigration restrictions will ease as well. For example, the North American Free Trade Agreement (NAFTA) reduces immigration restrictions between Canada, the United States, and Mexico and allows employment across borders for certain types of jobs. Similarly, the European Union mandates the free movement of people throughout the region.

On the other hand, some countries such as Malaysia have severe restrictions on the number of non-nationals who are allowed to hold key positions in their travel industry. Since many of these restrictive countries have a shortage of skilled labor and trained managers, perhaps their immigration and employment policies will change in the near future.

Language and cultural preferences will also be of concern in decades to come. In Europe, it is not uncommon for people to speak three or four languages and this ability is a condition of employment in many cases. In both Asia and Latin America, English, the universal business language, is commonly spoken in addition to their regional languages. However, in the United States and, to a certain extent, Canada, even a second language is uncommon.

As more and more international visitors travel to North America, the expectation is going to be that travel-related businesses provide services in more than one language and that North Americans show sensitivity to cultural preferences in areas such as food and etiquette. So – to be competitive well into the future, you had better brush up on your Spanish, learn about the French, and know where Saipan is located. (Authors' note: As we write this, even the computer software doesn't know where Saipan is located – it automatically changed its spelling to "Sampan"!)

Economic Development

As we mentioned earlier, 75% of the countries in the world are considered to be undeveloped. As populations expand, business opportunities arise, and the desire of pleasure travelers to explore new destinations increases, some of these countries are likely to open up to tourism. As we will discuss in Chapter 10, tourism is most often the first step toward economic development because it provides the infrastructure such as airports, roads, hotels, and drinkable water for other industries to build upon. However, the type of tourism we are likely to see in these countries will probably be more planned than in the past. For example, the Peoples' Republic of China has plans that specifically designate which airports will be used for international or domestic travel as well as which cities will be developed for the primary purpose of business or recreation.

On another front, many developing countries have fragile eco-systems and social systems. This calls for a different type of travel to bring tourism to these locations. Mass market tourism, which presently dominates the tourism industry, would be destructive for many of these locations. It would pose serious threats to fragile cultures such as those which exist in certain parts of Africa and the Pacific Islands and to natural resources such as fishing stocks and coral reefs. Therefore, low-impact and high-value tourism, known as ecotourism, would more than likely be the most desirable type of tourism to develop in these countries.

But, this isn't as easy as it sounds because one of the first orders of business in tourism is to deliver people to locations. And, as we will discuss later, many airlines do not "fly the seats" to small market destinations such as Rwanda or Samoa.

Nevertheless, our take on this is that economic development is going to have a significant impact on hospitality and tourism businesses in many countries. You may even find yourself playing an important role in the progress of a small but developing country and, at the same time, trying to balance profits with the protection of the local culture and environment.

Things are changing and what is today is not likely to be tomorrow. As a result, your career is likely to take twists and turns you never thought possible – so, be ready!

Social Changes

Social changes are inevitable and while some are predictable, others are not. You know the old adage – "history repeats itself"? Well, people often have a funny way of making this saying untrue. Nevertheless, there are at least four social changes that are likely to affect the future of the hospitality and tourism industry – the break-down of traditional social class structures; the importance of education; increased sophistication of tastes; and the distribution of wealth.

Traditional social class structures are rapidly disappearing and this is even reflected in our language. For example, the term *worker* used to refer to someone who worked in a blue-collar job. Now, however, we are all referred to as *workers*. In our industry, there used to be a sharp delineation between *management* and *hourly* employees. Now, the term *associate* is frequently used to describe non-salaried employees and they play a much more important and independent role in making businesses successful.

The implication for you is that it is important to develop a healthy respect for **all** people and to recognize their contributions to the success of your organization. This should be evident by both your language and actions. Also, you need to be aware that the breakdown in class structures means that managers will have less power and decision-making autonomy. Teams are the future and you are a team member.

The importance of education is also changing. Early in the 20th century, college graduates were relatively rare, and many people did not even complete high school. Now, however, the number of young people who complete high school is higher than ever before, and more and more people are going on for post-secondary education of one sort or another. Combine this with the number of people who engage in professional or continuing education, whether on their own or through their company, and you have a better educated workforce – **and** a more informed and demanding consumer!

With the blurring of social class structures and a better educated population comes increasing sophistication of consumer tastes. This means that a steak, baked potato, salad bar, and a carafe of the house burgundy is no longer considered to be haute cuisine. Rather, customers are demanding variety in menus, preparation techniques, and ambiance. They are requesting exotic spices, non-traditional entrees such as ostrich, and unusual wines and coffees. They are seeking new dining experiences and are more anxious to try new foods than ever before!

In terms of travel, consumers are less willing to purchase traditional package tours and are looking for travel opportunities which will take them to new destinations and provide them with unique experiences. With respect to hotel services, at least at destination locations, travelers are expecting higher levels of service and more amenities than in the past.

While the first three changes we discussed were somewhat positive, the fourth is somewhat ominous. The middle class is shrinking and the number of people who earn incomes below the poverty line is increasing. One implication of this is that businesses, including travel-related businesses, are eroding their customer base because their own employees cannot even afford to buy their products and services. The meaning and outcome of this are uncertain. However, we would suggest that, more than likely, it will put pressure on companies to become more efficient so that wages can be increased.

As you can see, changes which will occur in the 21st century present challenges for the hospitality and tourism industry. This will require you to develop a set of skills which, while important today, will become even more important in the future. We will discuss these skills in the next section.

SKILLS AND QUALITIES OF THE MODERN MANAGER

Not so long ago, business was conducted on a rather formal basis – employees were employees and managers were managers. There were distinct differences between the two groups and employees primarily carried out their managers' instructions. Thus, the skills needed by managers were centered around planning, controlling, organizing, staffing, and directing. Unfortunately, these "managerial functions" are still included in many management texts.

However, as you probably noticed, times are changing. The responsibility for planning is placed throughout the organization. The resource control function, while still important, has more to do with technology and less to do with management. Organizing, like planning, is not solely a duty of management. Staffing has become "human resources management" and is more of a specialized staff role than a management one. And, the importance of directing has diminished and has been replaced with an emphasis on teams.

Managers in the modern workplace need a different set of skills and qualities if they are to be effective in their roles. Notice, we said skills *and* qualities! This is because many of the things we are about to discuss involve personal attributes as well as attainable skills. What are these things? We'll list them below and discuss each one in turn.

- ○ Problem-solving and decision-making
- ○ Communication
- ○ Flexibility
- ○ Leadership
- ○ Entrepreneurship
- ○ Personal qualities

Problem-Solving and Decision-Making

Problem-solving and decision-making are both conceptual activities. That is, they draw on understanding, analysis, logic, and other mental activities. They are important skills because problems surface and decisions must be made by every manager – and, given the nature of the hospitality and tourism industry, problems occur almost constantly and most decisions must be made on the spot.

All too often, hospitality and tourism managers shoot from the hip when it comes to making decisions. Most managers who try to work this way, however, frequently miss their targets and end up facing the consequences of a bad decision. The consequences of a poorly solved problem or a bad decision can be devastating. For starters, customers could take their business elsewhere or disgruntled workers could suffer decreased morale which would affect their performance and even cause them to go elsewhere as well. Beyond this, however, too many poor decisions will result in decreased revenues and profits. If you become one of these hit-and-miss type of managers, you could be unemployed!

Problem-solving and decision-making are both an art and a science. They require going through a process that includes accurately identifying the problems, investigating the facts, finding alternatives, evaluating these alternatives, and making a decision. This may sound academic and laborious, but that's just the way it is. Many managers object to this process because they say it takes too much time and, to them, we say, "Too bad," and "You're wrong." Like any other process, the more you use it, the faster you'll become.

Communication

Communication is a part of almost everything you do, so you had better do it well. Communication includes your tone of voice, verbal and written grammatical skills, competence in expressing yourself clearly, capacity for persuasion, ability to listen, style of conducting meetings, and quality of presentations. It even includes the way you present yourself to others. It might interest you to know that one of the most common complaints from seasoned professionals is that recent college graduates have woefully inadequate communication skills.

There's not much more we will say about this, except that you cannot discount this skill area and you need to take steps to ensure that you are a good communicator!

Flexibility

Flexibility means the ability to adapt to change, deal with different types of people, and, in general, roll with the punches. Today's business world is fast-paced and competitive, and when you combine this with advancing technology, you get change – lots of it! This requires you, as a manager, to not only be willing to adapt, but to be able to do so quickly. Resisting change and doing things the way they have always been done can be fatal to a manager's career. Being adaptive doesn't require any special skills or any special knowledge – it only requires an openness and willingness to recognize change and to do things differently when appropriate.

Another area that requires flexibility has to do with people. As hospitality and tourism managers, you will deal with people – employees *and* customers – from many different cultures and of many different mind-sets. Successful managers recognize and adapt to these differences, **and they respect them**. This, in turn, enriches their lives and improves their effectiveness. Similarly, respecting the individuality of your staff and co-workers will enable you to identify their unique talents and abilities and build a more effective and comprehensive team. Expecting our customers and employees to think and act like we think and act is short-sighted and can adversely affect both customer satisfaction and employee morale. Thankfully, everyone **is** different!

Leadership

The term *leadership* has almost become a cliché. What exactly does *leadership* mean? How can you become a leader if you aren't one already? Many studies in the 1970s and 1980s attempted to identify the traits, skills, or actions of a successful leader. Some found that physical stature was all-important, others found that charisma was the key, and still others found that setting examples made for effective leadership. Today's view on leadership is that the qualities that contribute to effectiveness vary from individual to individual and from situation to situation.

We offer this simple definition of leadership – leadership is the ability to gain the cooperation of others, including subordinates, peers, and superiors, to accomplish an agreed upon goal or task. Implicit in this definition is the notion of teamwork. This means that, depending upon the goal or task, leadership may shift according to the expertise of various team members.

The lesson for you here is fourfold. First, you need to develop a leadership style which stems from your personality and which is appropriate to the situation at hand. Second, even though you may be hierarchically superior in a given situation, you may need to give up a leadership role in situations where you lack expertise. Third, you need to trust the competence of your co-workers. And, fourth, you need to learn how to become a valued team member.

Entrepreneurship

No longer can managers rely on the tried and true methods, markets, and products of the past. Instead, they must be able to identify and act upon opportunities, both within their organization and in the world marketplace. This is called *entrepreneurship* and can be as simple as adding a chocolate shop to your collection of lobby stores or devising a plan to offer housekeeping services to private residences and smaller hotels. It could also be a large-scale venture such as identifying and fulfilling a new market niche. An example of this can be found in school foodservice. A few short years ago, school lunch was handled primarily by local school districts. Now, contract foodservice companies are vigorously pursuing this market as a worthwhile business opportunity and offering students more quality food choices than ever before.

Courtyard by Marriott offers another example. Recognizing the need for moderately priced, business-friendly accommodations outside of major destinations and in suburban locations, Marriott used the advice of frequent business travelers to design this product. Presently, the concept is growing rapidly and other hotel firms are imitating the Marriott product.

As you can see, entrepreneurship requires a number of things including vision, business savvy, and the willingness to take risks. It is an ability that combines both personality traits **and** skills. Fortunately for you, given the right environment and the willingness to let go of your fears, it can be learned.

Personal Qualities

The days when raw ambition and self-serving actions guaranteed success are long gone. In order to be a successful manager, you will need to develop and employ a broad range of personal qualities – qualities that do not always fit the conventional perception of the hard-driving manager.

These include qualities like:

- ➡ tolerance for others' mistakes
- ➡ a strong ethical base
- ➡ fairness in both decisions and actions
- ➡ a desire to serve others
- ➡ consistency and predictability

Do these sound like old-fashioned traditional values to you? Well, they are. The importance of these qualities really never went away but now societies and businesses demand them. If you think that good managers are head-strong, play games, and lack respect for others, you are very, very wrong.

CAREER OPPORTUNITIES

Regardless of your specialized area of study in your hospitality and tourism program, you will find that employment and career opportunities are excellent. Graduates start their careers in a variety of positions. We've listed some possibilities below just to give you an idea of the scope and breadth of the industry. In most cases, these are actual jobs taken by our graduating students.

- Chef on a professional fishing vessel in Alaska
- Corporate management trainee with a family-style restaurant in Vermont
- Tour guide working for the National Parks Service on Alcatraz Island
- Interpreter for concierge services in a large hotel in New York City
- Junior meeting planner for a high technology firm in Redmond, Washington (guess which firm??)
- Corporate management trainee for a large hotel in Buffalo, New York
- Outlet manager for a large theme park in Anaheim, California (again, guess which one??)
- Bowling alley manager in Toledo, Ohio
- Assistant convention services manager for a large hotel in Houston
- Operator of a small inn in Sitka, Alaska
- Junior consultant for a hospitality consulting firm in Chicago
- Private chef on a corporate yacht
- Sales manager of a specialty wine shop in upstate New York
- Assistant service manager for a food outlet at Busch Stadium in St. Louis
- Assistant controller for a full-service hotel on Hilton Head Island
- Junior marketing specialist for a convention and visitors bureau in Toronto
- Catering manager for a contract foodservice firm at a college in Chapel Hill, North Carolina
- Teacher in a technical college in Tacoma, Washington
- Airline flight attendant for an international airline
- Professional student (yes, we have had some of these!)

We hope that this list gives you some idea about the exciting and challenging positions this industry has to offer!

Salaries and Advancement

You may have heard that starting salaries in this industry are low. However, when you compare them to entry-level positions in other fields, they actually compare very favorably. (See Appendix 1.1 for examples of representative salaries.) Furthermore, the potential for advancement in the hospitality and tourism industry is excellent for capable individuals who are willing to work hard and pay their dues.

In some restaurant operations, for example, management trainees may assume full operating responsibilities for a million dollar + operation in as little as two years following graduation and command a salary which far exceeds the salaries of their college friends who specialized in other fields.

Advancement opportunities in hospitality and tourism are not limited to progression in individual restaurants, foodservice operations, hotels, or other travel-related facilities. There are also opportunities for advancement to multi-unit management or corporate staffs in major companies.

The industry also hires graduates in accounting, marketing, sales, finance, human resources management, and communications. Also, many vendors who supply products and services to the industry hire graduates of hospitality and tourism programs. After some seasoning and the acquisition of a little capital, you could even open your own business!

Now, let's turn our attention to the various industry segments and look at employment opportunities and salaries within each one.

Segments of the Hospitality and Tourism Industry

Because the industry is so large and broad, it is necessary to talk about it in terms of its segments. CHRIE, the Council on Hotel, Restaurant, and Institutional

Education, classifies the hospitality and tourism industry into four distinct segments based on the fact that each has its own set of unique features:[5]

➡ **Foodservice**
Quick service, specialty and fine dining restaurants, clubs, hotel dining, catering, educational foodservice, health care foodservice, nightclubs, casinos, airline catering, and just about anywhere else food is served.

➡ **Lodging**
Full-service, luxury, convention, all-suite, mid-scale and limited-service hotels; resorts; conference centers; inns; and bed and breakfast operations.

➡ **Recreation**
Theme parks, attractions, marinas, sports and leisure facilities, campgrounds, and parks.

➡ **Travel-related services**
Air travel, cruise lines, tour operations, travel agencies, meeting planning, convention center management, and event planning.

It should be obvious that a detailed discussion of specific job opportunities in each segment would make this book too thick and, therefore, too expensive, so we will limit our discussion to these four broad segments However, throughout the book, you will find many examples of both job possibilities and career opportunities in areas outside of these.

Because the foodservice segment is still growing, the need for entry level management is acute – *and* management positions in many foodservice organizations offer high starting salaries and a lot of advancement opportunities.

For the lodging industry, the short-term outlook is also excellent. Demand for entry-level management is currently high and, while starting salaries tend to be lower than those in the foodservice sector, advancement opportunities are moderate to good.

Employment in recreation services is stable. Although there is growth, particularly in attractions, theme parks, and sports and leisure, there are limited management

---

5 Carl D. Riegel, *A Guide to College Programs in Hospitality and Tourism* (New York: John Wiley & Sons, 1995), p. 3.

positions and turnover is relatively low. Still, for the creative and dedicated individual, opportunities for a rewarding career in recreation exist. One avenue into this segment is through the backdoor. Many theme parks and attractions operate foodservice and lodging facilities and it is entirely possible to advance to more general management positions through these routes – it may just be the best way to go.

Travel-related services are a mixed bag. Service positions with airlines and cruiselines are on the rise, but promotion to management is quite competitive. With regard to services such as tour operators and travel agencies, demand for employees is high. However, salaries tend to be lower than in other segments and advancement opportunities are limited.

Positions in meeting and event planning as well as in convention center management and exhibition management are often difficult to find. There are several reasons for this.

First, both meeting and event planning require extensive prior experience which is often difficult to get. Second, employment in these areas often comes about as a result of networking and it usually takes a few years to get to know the right people. Third, meeting and event planning positions are most often found *within* organizations whose main business is something other than travel. Finally, with respect to convention center management and exhibition management, there are a limited number of facilities and they maintain small permanent staffs. However, like in recreation services, it is also possible to gain entrance by going through the backdoor. For example, convention hotels frequently maintain large convention staffs and you can choose to pursue your career within a hotel **or** can transfer your experience to other venues.

We firmly believe that the hospitality and tourism industry offers varied, rewarding, and exciting career opportunities. We also strongly believe that the employment outlook is excellent.

We have been honest with you with respect to salary levels and employment opportunities. Although the more "glamorous" segments offer fewer management positions, if you are innovative and tenacious or are willing to take another route to get to the same destination, you will be successful in pursuing your career.

IS THIS INDUSTRY FOR YOU?

Like any other field of work, hospitality and tourism has both plusses and minuses. Sure, you get to meet all kinds of people including many famous ones, your work environment is quite attractive, and you receive a lot of perks such as discounted hotel stays and airline tickets. Also, the advancement potential is excellent in many segments, the work environment is often fast-paced and rarely boring, and mobility is easy because you can find a job almost anywhere!

However, the industry is *not* for everyone. We have found that a lot of people end up leaving this industry. It can be very stressful and can infringe upon your personal and family life. More than that, the pace of work is fast and often unpredictable, the hours can be long and you could have to work while others play, and, despite the fact that you get to deal with a lot of people, some of these people may not always be respectful, polite, or even civil.

Find Out if You Fit

By now, you are at least interested in hospitality and tourism or have made an initial commitment to a career in this field. However, you don't want to make a wrong career decision if possible. It's important that you realistically assess your values and personality to see if they fit the realities of this particular workplace.

Of course, the most obvious way to do this is to get as much pre-graduation work experience as possible. After all, it can be a lot easier to change your major than to change careers – especially at the beginning.

The lobby and guest rooms in a luxury hotel can be very glamorous and a trendy restaurant can be quite exciting. However, the back of the house is neither! It is often cramped, stark, and overrun with trash cans and other necessary but unglamorous things. Similarly, the thought of travel can be heady, but serving drinks and meals to 300 tired passengers is just plain hard work.

Other ways to find out if you fit include talking to other people in the industry about their jobs and careers, reading all you can, and observing what goes on in as many types of facilities as possible.

Figure 1.2 is a quiz designed to test your compatibility with the hospitality and tourism industry. Although this quiz is not scientifically validated, it should give you an idea of your suitability to the realities of this industry.

FIGURE 1.2
Is This Industry for You?

PART A

	Usually	Sometimes	Never
1. I like seeing a job through to completion even if it means working on my day off.	_____	_____	_____
2. I enjoy managing multiple tasks and projects.	_____	_____	_____
3. I communicate well with people who are different from me.	_____	_____	_____
4. I am willing to temporarily give up my leadership to someone who has more expertise.	_____	_____	_____
5. I see conflict as part of life and am not afraid to deal with it.	_____	_____	_____
6. Fast-paced work environments excite me.	_____	_____	_____
7. Serving people brings me pleasure.	_____	_____	_____
8. I prefer predictability to uncertainty when it comes to my work.	_____	_____	_____
9. I am able to separate my emotions from my work.	_____	_____	_____
10. I am willing to give up days off to get the job done.	_____	_____	_____
11. I like routine in my daily work.	_____	_____	_____
12. Other people see me as even-tempered.	_____	_____	_____
13. Other people respect my problem-solving abilities.	_____	_____	_____
14. I am good at finding different ways to do things.	_____	_____	_____
15. I get frustrated when I am not in control of my environment.	_____	_____	_____
16. When it comes to decision-making, I am thorough but fast.	_____	_____	_____
17. I prefer action over paperwork.	_____	_____	_____

PART B

	Yes	No
18. Other people say that I have a lot of energy.	_____	_____
19. Other people say that I have well developed social skills.	_____	_____
20. I consider myself to be a good communicator.	_____	_____
21. I am reluctant to relocate.	_____	_____
22. Having Saturdays and Sundays off is very important to me.	_____	_____
23. Remaining focused on the job is personally important to me.	_____	_____
24. My personal life always comes first.	_____	_____
25. I am comfortable using different types of technology.	_____	_____

Tally your responses as directed below and total your score.

➡ For each of statements 3, 4, 5, 9, 12, and 13, give yourself:
   ✓ 3 points if you checked *Usually*
   ✓ 2 points if you checked *Sometimes*
   ✓ 1 point if you checked *Never*

➡ For each of statements 8 and 11, give yourself:
- ✔ 1 point if you checked *Usually*
- ✔ 2 points if you checked *Sometimes*
- ✔ 3 points if you checked *Never*

➡ For each of statements 1, 2, 6, 7, 10, 14, 16, and 17, give yourself:
- ✔ 5 points if you checked *Usually*
- ✔ 3 points if you checked *Sometimes*
- ✔ 1 point if you checked *Never*

➡ For statement 15, give yourself:
- ✔ 1 point if you checked *Usually*
- ✔ 3 points if you checked *Sometimes*
- ✔ 5 points if you checked *Never*

➡ For each of statements 21, 23, and 24, give yourself:
- ✔ 1 point if you checked *Yes*
- ✔ 3 points if you checked *No*

➡ For statement 19, give yourself:
- ✔ 3 points if you checked *Yes*
- ✔ 1 point if you checked *No*

➡ For statement 22, give yourself:
- ✔ 1 point if you checked Yes
- ✔ 5 points if you checked *No*

➡ For each of statements 18, 20, and 25, give yourself:
- ✔ 5 points if you checked *Yes*
- ✔ 1 point if you checked *No*

What Your Score Means

❱ **70 - 83 points**
You are definitely well suited for the hospitality and tourism industry. Your work values are consistent with the realities of the industry and your personality traits fit well! While this doesn't guarantee success, it will certainly be easier for you to succeed. Jump in and go for it!

> **52 - 69 points**
>
> You possess a lot of the personality traits and work values that are necessary in this industry. Take a close look at the statements that gave you a lower score, and think about the reason you responded the way you did. If you don't like a fast-paced and constantly changing work environment, you can still fit. For example, you might not be as happy working in the front office of a hotel, but what about meeting planning? You fit the industry well, but you need to closely examine the segments and positions which appeal to you the most.

> **51 points or less**
>
> You really need to think about your fit with this industry, particularly in operations. Your work values and personality do not closely match some of the realities you will find in hospitality and tourism. We cannot say that you will **not** be happy and successful, but we ask you to take a close look at yourself and see if you might not be better suited for some other industry.

How Committed Are You?

Even if you found that you fit perfectly with the hospitality and tourism industry, you still need to figure out how committed you are to a career in this field. Commitment, as we use it here, is a term that was developed by a number of pointy-headed professors and its meaning is complex. However, for our purposes, commitment means the following:[6]

- ◆ the extent to which you are willing to act on behalf of your career field
- ◆ the extent to which you are willing to give your time and energy to improve you status within this field
- ◆ the extent to which you value this field over others you have considered
- ◆ how much you believe that your chosen career provides the satisfaction you want from work
- ◆ the strength of your desire to remain in this career field

Having said this, it's time for another quiz! This time, however, the quiz, Figure 1.3, has been validated and should give you a very good idea of how committed

---

[6] Carl D. Riegel, *Career Choice, Work Values, and Career Commitment of Food Service and Housing Administration Students at The Pennsylvania State University: A Social Learning Perspective* (Unpublished Doctoral Dissertation, The Pennsylvania State University, 1983), pp. 16 - 17.

you really are to a career in the hospitality and tourism industry.[7]

FIGURE 1.3
Hospitality and Tourism Commitment Scale

The following statements are ones that people might make about the hospitality and tourism industry. Some may represent your feelings and others may not. Indicate your feelings about each statement by circling the appropriate letter.

A = Strongly Disagree   *B = Disagree*   *C = Neutral*   *D = Agree*   *E = Strongly Agree*

1. I often talk about this industry to my friends.	A B C D E
2. I would not consider an offer to work in any other industry.	A B C D E
3. Sometimes, I am embarrassed to tell people that I plan to work in this industry.	A B C D E
4. I would just as soon work in another industry as long as the jobs available were appealing to me.	A B C D E
5. The nature of hospitality and tourism work inspires me to perform my best.	A B C D E
6. I have developed a sense of loyalty to this industry.	A B C D E
7. If another field of work offered similar advancement and compensation opportunities, I would be very interested.	A B C D E
8. I am happy that I chose a career in this industry over other industries I have considered.	A B C D E
9. There is little for me to gain by staying in this industry.	A B C D E
10. I see my future as being related to the future of this industry.	A B C D E
11. This career choice is the best choice I could have made.	A B C D E
12. Deciding to work in this industry was a mistake on my part.	A B C D E
13. I see myself advancing rapidly in this industry.	A B C D E
14. I regularly read trade publications about this industry.	A B C D E
15. I subscribe to one or more trade publications.	A B C D E
16. Work in this industry is challenging and interesting.	A B C D E
17. I will not be in this industry in ten years.	A B C D E

Scoring

➡ For questions 3, 4, 7, 9, 12, and 17, score yourself as follows:
   ✓ A=5   ✓ B=4   ✓ C=3   ✓ D=2   ✓ E=1

➡ For all other questions, score yourself as follows:
   ✓ A=1   ✓   B=2   ✓   C=3   ✓   D=4   ✓   E=5

---

7   Carl D. Riegel, *Ibid,* pp. 164 - 167.

What Your Score Means

) 70 - 85 points

You are highly committed to a career in the hospitality and tourism industry. Chances are excellent that you will strive to advance in your career and remain in this industry. However, since commitment grows over time, you need to examine whether or not your commitment comes from experience and first-hand knowledge or from misplaced excitement.

) 54 - 69 points

You are moderately committed to a career in this industry, but chances are 50/50 that you may not act to improve your industry-related status and, given a better opportunity, you would work in another field. However, you need to examine your personal circumstances to determine if you have enough work experience and information about the industry because these both affect your level of commitment.

) 53 points or less

At this time, you really are not committed to a career in the hospitality and tourism industry. This could stem from lack of experience or information on your part, or it could truly mean that you should consider another field.

IN CONCLUSION . . .

This chapter was designed to serve as an introduction to careers in an exciting and important industry. We had four major goals in writing this chapter. First, we wanted to acquaint you with the notion of careers and career development so that you could understand the difference between a career and a job, as well as how you came to choose your own career. Second, we wanted you to think about changes that are likely to affect this industry in the future and the skills that will be required of you if you are to be successful. Third, we gave you a brief and honest overview of career opportunities in the hospitality and tourism industry. Finally, we wanted you to be aware that it takes a unique person to be happy and successful in this industry and we wanted to give you an opportunity to examine yourself with this in mind.

APPENDIX 1.1
REPRESENTATIVE NATIONAL SALARIES
(Expressed in thousands)

Note of caution: These salaries are simply averages. They do not take into account the size of the facilities and they do not include bonuses and other forms of compensation which are common in the hospitality and tourism industry.

Hotel - Corporate	Low	Medium	High
Chief Financial Officer	75	95	136
Controller	44	58	74
Vice President of Operations	56	74	109
Vice President of Marketing	53	74	103
Food and Beverage Director	46	64	91
Corporate Chef	46	62	85
Director of Development	48	60	76
Director of Construction	44	60	77
Director of Human Resources	36	51	67
Director of Purchasing	32	43	61
Regional Manager	42	55	71

Hotel - Operations	Low	Medium	High
General Manager	40	57	81
Operations Manager	28	40	50
Controller	32	42	52
Director of Human Resources	27	35	43
Rooms Division Manager	27	37	47
Front Office Manager	22	30	36
Food and Beverage Director	31	44	61
Outlet Manager	23	31	38
Maitre d'	23	30	38
Beverage Manager	23	30	36
Banquet Manager	26	33	40
Director of Catering	25	34	48
Catering Sales	25	31	37
Executive Chef	30	45	58
Sous Chef	24	32	38
Pastry Chef	21	27	37
Banquet Chef	20	26	31
Director of Marketing	29	36	51
Sales Manager	24	31	37
Conference Manager	26	29	34
Housekeeping Manager	24	32	40
Asst. Housekeeping Manager	15	23	31

Restaurant - Corporate	Low	Medium	High
Chief Operating Officer	70	94	128
Division Manager	60	76	97
Regional Manager	54	69	84
Marketing Director	42	55	80
Controller	40	47	55
Director of Human Resources	34	43	58
Training Director	31	37	44
Purchasing Director	34	44	56
Real Estate Manager	39	49	63

Restaurant - Operations	Low	Medium	High
Director of Operations	48	60	72
District Manager	36	46	59
General Manager - Quick Service	26	32	39
Assistant Manager - Quick Service	20	24	29
General Manager - Non-Liquor	26	33	47
Assistant Manager - Non-Liquor	21	24	30
General Manager - Liquor	30	36	54
Assistant Manager - Liquor	24	28	35
Chef	27	33	43
Sous Chef	23	29	35
Kitchen Manager	24	29	35
Pastry Chef	22	27	33
Banquet Manager	23	28	34

Foodservice	Low	Medium	High
Regional Manager	41	49	61
District Manager	36	45	54
Foodservice Director	30	36	45
Cafeteria Manager	25	31	43
Unit Manager	24	33	45
Assistant Manager	20	25	30

Clubs	Low	Medium	High
Manager - Golf (500+ members)	42	54	70
Manager - Golf (250 - 500 members)	34	43	51
Clubhouse Manager	30	37	45
Athletic/City Club Manager	36	52	69

Adapted with permission from *Roth Young's 1995 Salary Survey.*

CHAPTER 2

CHARTING A CAREER PATH

"The man who goes alone can start today, but he who travels with another must wait until that other is ready."

Henry David Thoreau

After reading Chapter 1, you should have a good sense of what the hospitality and tourism industry is and what kinds of opportunities it offers. More than likely, you already have some idea about what you want from both your work life and your personal life and you have some notion of what type of position will meet these expectations. How you get from where you are now to where you want to be in your career is often called a career path.

This chapter discusses charting your career path. You should be that at this point in time − perhaps at any point in time − the best you can do is to plan for the short-term, say three to five years. Sure, you can have a long-term goal in mind, but, very often, as people progress in their careers, their final destination changes. Not only do career goals change, but outside forces such as economics, social change, and technology have a way of affecting the workplace. Furthermore, as you mature in your career, your interests will change. By enrolling in college and choosing to pursue a career in the hospitality and tourism industry, you have started a **general plan**, but you now need a **career plan** to give you direction.

Speaking of direction, you also need to bear in mind that *your* path will differ from the paths of others. There is **no best way** to get from point A to point B, and no one but you has sole responsibility for navigating your career path.

SAMPLE CAREER PATHS

Every professional you meet has a different story — a different way they got to where they are now. Some followed a career path laid out by the firm that hired them. For example, the management training program at Houston's, an Atlanta-based firm of 26 full-service restaurants, rotates trainees through the various areas of the restaurant during a six-month period. At the end of the six months, trainees are promoted to managers at stores where positions are available. From here, the next step is Senior Assistant to the General Manager, and then, finally, General Manager. Keep in mind that these are just steps available to you, but not necessarily **your** individual career path. A lot can happen in between.

At a Crossroads? There Are Lots of Opportunities!

Take the case of a worker in a hotel catering department who completes college and is then promoted to Catering Supervisor. After about two years, she becomes the manager of an outlet within the hotel, after which she is promoted to Assistant Director of Food and Beverage. After three years as the assistant director at two different hotels, she is promoted to Director of Food and Beverage. After this, assuming she performs well, she could move into a larger property in the same position, into a general manager's position, to the corporate offices, or to another related firm.

Following, in Figure 2.1, is a chart showing a traditional career path for a manager through the food and beverage division of a large hotel. The typical length of time for a person to move from Outlet Supervisor to Director of Operations is 10 to 15 years depending on ability, opportunity, geographic flexibility, and a number of additional variables.

FIGURE 2.1
Traditional Career Ladder for a Director of Operations Through a Food and Beverage Track in a Large Hotel

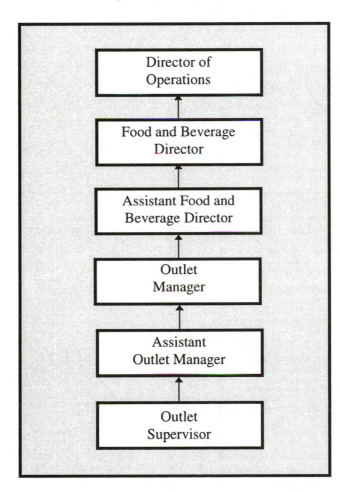

The next example, Figure 2.2, shows a less traditional path through a combination of both small and large hotels. The manager begins as a restaurant supervisor at a small hotel, then moves to Food and Beverage Manager at the same or at a similar hotel. From there, the manager moves to a larger hotel as Assistant Food and Beverage Director. The reason for the *Assistant* title at this point is that the food and beverage operations in a large hotel are more complex than in a small hotel, and the manager will need more experience managing various outlets, banquet and catering operations, and in-room dining services. The rest of this career path is the same as the traditional path and leads to a director of operations position at a large hotel. Typical number of years invested in a path such as this is the same as invested in the traditional path – 10 to 15 years.

FIGURE 2.2
Less Traditional Career Ladder for a Director of Operations Through a Food and Beverage Track in a Combination of Large and Small Hotels

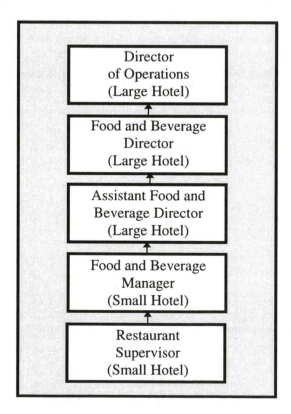

The final, less traditional career path we will mention, shown in Figure 2.3, is one that leads to Director of Operations through a rooms division track in a large hotel. Here, the manager begins as Floor Supervisor and is promoted to Assistant Director of Housekeeping. At this point, the manager moves from housekeeping to the front office as a supervisor, and is then promoted to Guest Services Manager which includes front desk operations, concierge and valet services, and reservations. The next step is as Rooms Division Manager in which the person would oversee both housekeeping and guest services. As before, the path leads to Director of Operations and, again, can take from 10 to 15 years depending on the person's abilities and geographic flexibility as well as the availability of positions.

FIGURE 2.3
Less Traditional Career Ladder for a Director of Operations Through a Rooms Division Track in a Large Hotel

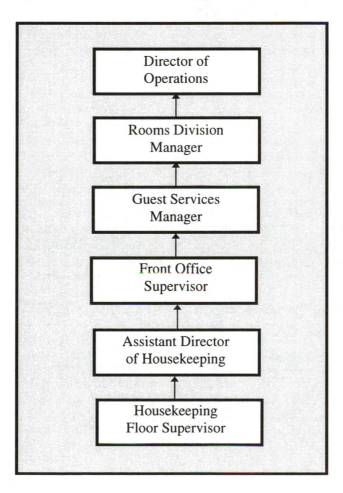

We have chosen career paths in the hotel segment because they present clear examples of different ways to achieve the same goal. However, as we write, organizational structures in hotels are changing rapidly. Many hotel companies, such as Ritz-Carlton, are experimenting with self-directed work teams. Others, such as Sheraton, are using a strategic business unit structure. Still others are eliminating multiple layers of middle managers. All of this is in an effort to reduce costs and, although the jury is still out as to their effectiveness, it is doubtful that any will return to traditional titles and structures. This means that the career path for many young managers will change as a result of forces outside of their control.

The *key* is to have reasonable expectations, use good planning, and be flexible. Combine these with dedication, continuing education, and a commitment to quality, and you, too, will enjoy a rewarding and challenging career.

REALISTIC EXPECTATIONS

We briefly mentioned the importance of having realistic expectations, but feel it deserves more attention. Unfortunately, some students graduate from college and expect to reach the pinnacle of their career within five years. Unless you are unbelievably talented and extremely lucky, this will **not** happen. Upper level managers did not get there by chance nor did they land there without paying their dues. Think about it – there is a large number of college graduates employed in the industry. If a college education was all it took to move into senior management, we wouldn't need very many college graduates. **A degree by itself is simply not enough**! However, **a college education combined with experience is**! A doctor cannot become Chief of Staff without years of experience; a professor cannot teach in the hospitality field without an advanced degree and/or managerial experience; nor can you become a senior manager without exposure to different departments and experience in planning, coaching, budgeting, and marketing.

Also, you need to understand that as you move upward in an organization, the number of positions available decreases. This, of course, means that not everyone will occupy a senior position! If you are realistic about your level of experience combined with your educational preparation, then you will not be disappointed and will most likely remain in the hospitality and tourism industry. Unrealistic expectations lead to frustration and disappointment, which ultimately lead to either separation (voluntary or involuntary) or personal problems.

Throughout this book, we offer you personal and professional assessment tools and these are just a few of the many that are available. Use them and pay attention to the results. If you realistically assess *you*, you will be more likely to excel. Multi-functioning is now the norm in the workplace and this means that you will have to be able to perform many functions within the operation. This takes time to learn! Concentrate on your development and the rest will follow naturally.

PLANNING A CAREER – THREE SCENARIOS

There are three basic ways to travel down a career path. The first – dumb luck with an occasional failure – is rare now that more skills are required for workplace success. The second – planned action – is still common in certain occupations such as higher education and the military. The last – a combination of the two – is by far the most common and requires planned action as well as the instinct and willingness to seize opportunities when they occur.

Dumb Luck

A few – a very few – are blessed enough to be extremely lucky. These are the ones who seem to be "golden" in all they do and to whom success in life and career comes easily. Without effort, they pass through college, get numerous job offers, and become the youngest-ever vice-president within three years after graduation. This was not their plan, yet it happened. Why? We have absolutely no idea, so we'll call it "dumb luck." Don't count on it.

Planned Action

At the other end of the spectrum is planned action. This type of methodical career planning is highly touted by employment specialists and involves an almost mechanical approach to career management. Planned action requires that you first identify your strengths and talents, then decide on a career that best matches them. Next, you target a specific firm, and develop yourself for *their* needs and wants. The interview process should be successful for you since you have spent all this time and effort preparing. You have in mind exactly where you will be in one year, in five years, and even in fifteen years and your career advances accordingly.

Do you see a problem with this? We certainly hope so. What if you miss a lucrative or challenging opportunity just because it did not fit into your well-developed plans? What if you don't meet your professional goals at all? In either case, you would be frustrated and angry and would feel defeated. Your plan is too confining and has actually been a detriment to your future. You have left no loopholes and have ignored contingencies.

Although we agree that career planning is desirable and necessary, we also warn of the dangers. The new workplace requires flexibility and this often means that you may not get the position you want with the company you want – at least not right away *and* maybe never.

The Middle Ground

We've all heard about the Horatio Alger stories in which young and penniless men came into great wealth through honesty and hard work. These stories were powerful motivators during the Great Depression in the U.S. and are still respected since they offer hope to *everyone*. These young men did not make it on luck, nor did well-planned and inflexible career paths lead to prosperity. Rather, success came from planning and flexibility combined with a lot of integrity and a strong work ethic. You, too, could be a part of the Horatio Alger story collection!

Although you might have a well-defined career plan in hand, you must realize the importance of flexibility and of seizing opportunities as they happen. Opportunities don't just happen. In order to seize opportunities, you have to be aware of them, so keep your eyes and ears open. Thus, networking by joining organizations and getting to know people in the industry is important, as is keeping up with company and industry news.

What if you have your mind set on being a district manager for an institutional food service operation, but one day you get a call about an opening in Chicago for a food and beverage director in a well-known yet small hotel? Would you turn down the job just because it wasn't "in the plan"? Or would you fully consider it? If you want to be a success in this industry, then you should give the offer full consideration. The hospitality and tourism industry has an extensive grapevine and once you have been around it a while, you will undoubtedly receive numerous employment offers from allied firms and even from competitors. Expect it, and use these offers as continual assessment tools. Maybe it's time for you to grow in a different direction and to seize an opportunity.

Always consider different routes and consider changing your destination. Often, different routes result in personal and professional growth opportunities that would not have happened otherwise. Inject a bit of entrepreneurial spirit into your career plan and think outside of the box. This industry gives plenty of chances for cross-industry movement, geographic relocation, and professional development. Through flexibility and awareness, you can resist burn-out and capitalize on your strengths and experiences.

IT'S NEVER TOO SOON TO START

If you are in college, you should start to plan your career path now. We know it sounds like a lot to do, especially with all the other demands on your time and attention, but it will be well worth it in the end. By now, you probably have experience in the hospitality and tourism industry. Don't stop here – **get as much experience as you can now** and you'll better know which path you want

You Can't Start Career Planning Early Enough!

to begin down when you graduate. Make the most of an educational opportunity, whatever and wherever that might be. It will help you to *define you, your goals, and your path*. Finally, get involved in volunteering and professional service and make the most of networking opportunities.

More, More Varied, and More Responsible Experience

The more experience you can get under your belt before graduation, the better. As we said before, the ability to multi-function is becoming the norm for successful hospitality and tourism managers. There is more emphasis on overall operational skills as well as on support activities such as sales, marketing, and human resources. The rigid career paths of the past no longer exist in our industry and the most successful managers of the future will undoubtedly be multi-disciplined. Therefore, if you are presently in school, your work experience plan should follow the maxim, *more, more varied, and more responsible*.

If you did an internship as a travel agent, do another as an assistant for a tour operator. You might also want to gain experience as a guest service representative at a hotel. These experiences will combine to enable you to see more of the travel and tourism picture and will make you more marketable. More importantly, this combination of work experiences could allow you to see career opportunities that you did not consider before and will introduce you to many different people within these intertwined fields. Similarly, if your area of interest is in restaurant management, get experience in both front-of-the-house and back-of-the-house operations. You might be quite surprised to find that you prefer to work in the front rather than in the back, or vice versa. If your career plans involve hotels, get experience in as many operational areas as possible including housekeeping, sales and marketing, food and beverage, and front office.

Very often, a graduate will accept a position in a food and beverage outlet just because that is where all of his experience has been. By limiting himself in this way, he has just ignored a huge part of any hotel – the rooms area. Again, an operationally well-rounded graduate is by far the most marketable, the most profitable, and the most valuable to any firm.

Also, if possible, make sure to explore different geographic areas while you are still in college and it is easy to do so. Even if you never thought you would like to live and work in Colorado, give it a try anyway. Even if you never cared for a big city, think about working or interning in New York or Toronto. Information on many work experiences and internship opportunities can be obtained through your program administrator, cooperative education office, or career placement center. You can also get leads by writing to the human resource director or owner of the firm on your own. (NOTE: If you do this, follow the exact same steps discussed in the next chapter and act as if you were applying for a "permanent" job upon graduation. This could indeed be your future employer!) Since many firms are decentralizing, students have found great success in this more direct method.

It is also helpful to gain increasingly responsible work experience. This may take the form of a supervisory position; leadership on a project; or a responsible position in purchasing, marketing, or human resources, for example. Of course, these positions won't be open to everyone and will probably require significant and broad previous work experience. However, having held a position in which you bore even minimal management responsibility prepares you for your career and increases your chance of obtaining a management position after graduation.

Your work experiences and internships are an essential part of your career preparation. Explore and be adventurous. There are many opportunities available, and while some (many, for that matter) may be comparatively low-paying and sometimes monotonous, the ultimate pay-off can be quite rewarding. Now is your time to act like a sponge and absorb all the experience you can!

Making the Most of an Educational Opportunity

You have, no doubt, attended many lectures, participated in endless discussions, and joined in numerous group projects since you began college. Although these experiences may seem mundane and stifling at times, they can greatly increase your career awareness and expand your horizons.

It is your chance to learn about *opportunity*. There are many lesser known career possibilities available and unless you take full advantage of your education, you may miss hearing about a career field that suits your abilities and desires better than the more well known ones. For example, maybe you never thought of a career in wine merchandising, ecotourism, association management, or retirement community management. If you knew something about these areas and rejected them, fine. But, if you never considered them because you didn't know much about them, you may be shooting yourself in the foot.

Jump at the chances to attend career fairs and professional meetings. Sign up for annual fund-raising events for your local, regional, or state professional associations. You can probably meet more people playing golf in your state restaurant association's annual golf outing than you could by attending two meetings of the same association. Ask questions of anyone who will answer you, listen to their advice, and learn from them.

Use technology to learn all that you can about different career paths and different firms. In the next chapter, we will discuss these technologies as they relate to specific job searches, but you can also use them to access more general career planning information. Find out the financial health and expansion plans of firms. See whether they are changing their corporate structure or if they are targeting a different market than before. This information should be used to help you to chart your career path. It could give you ideas for a career path you never thought of before and will put you in touch with the realities of takeovers and restructurings which can severely and immediately alter your plans. Sure, you could use trade journals and newspapers too, but technology makes the job easier and allows you to be more selective.

Finally, take advantage of student exchange programs if possible. Many academic exchange opportunities exist between hospitality and tourism programs. This experience will allow you to learn from different instructors and to study at an institution which offers courses your school doesn't. For example, let's say that you have always wondered about casino management, but are enrolled in a program that is more traditionally based regarding its academic offerings. You could apply for a student exchange program to attend a college which offers casino management courses and even get some work experience in a casino while you are studying – all without changing your student status, paying out-of-state tuition, or transferring schools. One such program is called National Student Exchange and you can find out about it from your program administrator, academic or career advisor, or cooperative education office.

Volunteering, Service, and Networking

Many other activities can contribute to good career planning and can open up opportunities which would otherwise be hidden from you – volunteering, professional service, and networking. Many peoples' careers unexpectedly soared because of these activities – yours could, too.

Volunteer Your Time and Talents

Working without pay can be an important tool for you as you begin to chart your career path. You can learn a great deal about yourself, specific jobs, and a variety of organizations by volunteering your time and talents. The experience itself can look great on a resumé. Fields such as human resources, sales and marketing, and convention and meetings management are so competitive that accepting an unpaid work assignment is often the *only* way to get experience while you are still in college. This is also true of some premier hotels and restaurants. The best time to do volunteer work in the industry is while you are still in college and are not facing the financial and professional challenges that will come soon enough.

A good way to land a volunteer position is to contact the firm directly in writing and then follow up with a telephone call. Describe the purpose of your request (to learn more about employee selection and retention, for example) as well as your availability to work. If the firm cannot accommodate you when you are available, ask them *when* and *if* they see a more convenient time for them. Give this volunteer request the same amount of professionalism and attention that you would any other job search – follow the same steps as outlined in the next chapter – but realize that some operations may be concerned about liability or may view your request as an imposition on their full-time staff and could deny your request.

Another excellent volunteer opportunity lies in community service activities. Food banks, soup kitchens, and Meals-On-Wheels programs can be found in most cities and are always searching for volunteers. Not only will you find this type of volunteer work personally rewarding; the experience itself could help you to refine your management and human relations skills. Volunteering has always been an integral part of the service industry and is guaranteed to increase in importance as long as economic hardships continue to exist.

Perhaps you will find that your volunteer work at a local recycling center honed your organizational skills and gave you ideas for instituting a recycling program in the restaurant in which you currently work. The time you spent working in the soup kitchen or preparing and delivering food to those unable to leave their homes or cook for themselves will help you to see the world a bit differently *and* will sharpen your basic culinary and interpersonal skills.

Wherever and however you choose to volunteer, make sure that you give it your best effort. And, remember, volunteering should continue to be a part of your life as you develop. There are opportunities **everywhere**!

Service and More Service

It should not be surprising that a service industry regards the ideal of service highly. Service to professional organizations should begin now – in college – and should continue and increase throughout your life. Whether you choose to run for an office in your college's hospitality student association or participate in the annual fund-raiser for the local hotel association, any service-related activity will improve your organizational and leadership skills and may even give you practice in public speaking. By offering your services to a hospitality-related professional association, you will get a better view of the industry as a whole and how it works under governmental and economic constraints. Best of all, you will gain knowledge of a variety of career fields and paths. You have little to lose, except for a few hours of your time each month, and have everything to gain.

Networking

Although networking is discussed at length in Chapter 3 as a job search technique, you can also network in order to explore different career paths. As we said before, everyone has a different career story – why not ask them *how* and *why* they are in their present position and *where* they see themselves going from here? What you hear will confirm that even the best planned career paths are seldom followed exactly. You will find that most well seasoned professionals have been with many companies and have worked in many different areas.

Ask others where they think the industry is heading and how you should best prepare yourself at this stage in your career. Ask them what they would do differently in their careers if they had the benefit of hindsight. Almost everyone is pleased to help someone else with career plans and will appreciate your curiosity and your request for advice and guidance. Most likely, these industry professionals will welcome the chance to help you. This is a mentoring industry – lucky for you – so take advantage of it.

Use every situation to learn more about this industry and various career possibilities. Ask questions of guest speakers, talk to instructors and peers, and seek guidance from industry professionals. They are there, they are willing to help, and their advice may prove invaluable as you begin your career.

REAL-LIFE EXAMPLES

The following examples illustrate just how unpredictable career progression can be. But, remember, you have to start **somewhere** and have to have a place to go. Although your destination will likely change, at least you will have some sense of direction. Be willing to change your path as Bryan Schira and Phil Belanger did. With a lot of flexibility and openness to new experiences, you will find your career to be richer and more rewarding each year.

"I began working in the restaurant industry when I was very young and it was always expected that I would make it my career. No one was surprised when I majored in hospitality management in college, nor when I completed almost all of my work experiences during school in both restaurants and hotel food and beverage.

Upon graduation, I was hired as a management trainee with Renaissance Hotels and Resorts and rotated through the various departments as required. I was really surprised to find out how much I liked working in the front office – my interpersonal and organizational skills I acquired in the food service segment were invaluable and the change of surroundings was very welcome!

At the end of my training period, I selected the rooms division as my preferred area in which to begin my management career. After moving up through several positions at two different hotels, I am extremely happy now as Director of Reservations and see my career advancing at a good pace. It's hard to believe that I am no longer in the food and beverage area, but I know the combined experience will be invaluable to me someday."

Bryan Schira
Director of Reservations
Renaissance Westchester Hotel
White Plains, New York

"In college, I double-majored in accounting and management which set me up well for an entry level position in Marriott's Assistant Controller Training Program. I worked in the accounting department at a Marriott hotel and, instead of 'doing numbers' for other managers, I showed them **where** the numbers came from and **what** they meant. Even though I was in the accounting department, I trained managers throughout the hotel to read budgets and profit and loss statements, interpret departmental reports, inventories, evaluate cost control measures, etc. My career goal, like that of most entry-level managers, was to be a general manager of a large property and I felt I was on the right track.

My plans at Marriott changed. By networking and helping a number of people throughout the corporation, I was offered a position at corporate headquarters as a recruiter in Marriott's College Relations area. It sounded like a great opportunity, albeit an unlikely one, and I accepted it almost immediately.

Then when Holiday Inns Worldwide re-instituted their College Relations Program, I applied for the position of Director and felt that my background in employment combined with my personality and experience would at least spark their interest. Well, I got the job! (It was my first upper-level experience with a human resource function – recruiting.) However, to continue to grow in human resources, I needed to broaden my exposure to include compensation and benefits, training, and employee relations which I was able to do – once again because of helping other managers.

My career goal of becoming a general manager had changed and changed drastically. Instead of looking for a bigger property to manage, I was looking for a more diverse position which could give me broader experience. With Arnold Palmer Golf, I am getting that experience. I **like** my job and although I fully intended to be a general manager (and still may be some day), I am extremely pleased that my career took an unusual turn."

Phil Belanger
Palmer Professional
Arnold Palmer Golf
Orlando, Florida

ADDITIONAL READINGS

Build Your Own Rainbow, Barrie Hopson & Mike Scally; Pfeiffer & Company (San Diego, California, 1993).

Power Networking, Donna Fisher & Sandy Vilas; Mountain Harbour Press (Austin, Texas, 1995).

Taking Care of Your Career, Nella Barkley & Eric Sandburg; Workman Publishing (New York, New York, 1996).

CHAPTER 3

STRATEGIES AND TECHNIQUES OF JOB HUNTING

"Doubt is not a pleasant condition, but certainly is absurd."

Voltaire

If you've read this far, you are probably very anxious to get on with your job search and that's what this chapter is about. However, as you know, the job market is changing – and changing dramatically. Right now, you are probably wrestling with questions such as: Will my resumé get me a job? What about cover letters? How do I tap into the job market? How can I find out about different companies? How can I be at my best during an interview? What should I wear and what should I say? What happens after the interview?

This chapter attempts to answer these questions and more. However, before we begin that discussion, let's talk briefly about what a job search really is. It is not a freewheeling, unfocused or haphazard process. Instead, it is a well planned and methodical marketing campaign and the product is YOU! The campaign begins with a careful assessment of your goals as well as your skills and abilities and ends with knowing and using the appropriate follow-up interview etiquette.

This self-marketing process is illustrated in Figure 3.1.

FIGURE 3.1
Self-Marketing
Process

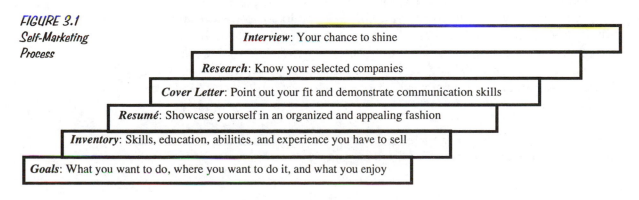

Interview: Your chance to shine

Research: Know your selected companies

Cover Letter: Point out your fit and demonstrate communication skills

Resumé: Showcase yourself in an organized and appealing fashion

Inventory: Skills, education, abilities, and experience you have to sell

Goals: What you want to do, where you want to do it, and what you enjoy

Like many important decisions you will make in life, how to proceed with your job search begins with reflection and analysis of yourself. Why? Because before you start the process, you need to know what you want and what you have to offer. You should also identify other important factors which might influence how you go about job hunting as well as what positions and organizations you might target and pursue.

Let's start with goals. Although your goals will likely change as you gain career and life experience, you probably have sufficient self-knowledge to chart a general course for at least the next five years. It is important to identify and analyze your personal and career goals for this intermediate period so that you can focus your search on companies and positions which are likely to help you achieve them.

Some questions you might want to answer are: What type of position would I like to hold in five years? In what segment of the industry? What types of experiences do I need to get there? What types of firms do I need to work for to achieve these goals? Where do I want to live? What lifestyle do I want to live? And so on. We'll cover this in depth in Chapters 5 and 8.

Not only will the answers to these questions help to start you out on the right career path for you, they will help you to discover potential conflicts between your goals. Say, for example, you plan to marry and want to stay close to your family in Carbondale, Illinois. But, you also want a fast track career which will get you an executive-committee level job in a large luxury hotel. These two sets of goals conflict because moving to several metropolitan areas (unlike Carbondale) would be necessary to achieve your stated career goal. Therefore, you either have to come to some sort of compromise to satisfy this conflict *or* set some new goals.

Similarly, you should also take some time to think about what you have to sell. Besides your education, what special skills and abilities have you gained by way of work, hobbies, and other life experiences? And how can these be of value to prospective employers? This inventory will help you to write your resumé and will give you direction in terms of what types of jobs you initially want to pursue. In line with this, you should also honestly examine your weaknesses. This will provide you with insight into a number of areas: your fit with particular organizations, entry level jobs in which you would perform the best, and areas which you should seek to improve.

Finally, it is a good idea to examine your career related preferences. Some areas you might choose to investigate are listed on page 51:

- The amount and quality of guest contact.
- The formality of the organizational climate.
- The degree of structure you want in a job.
- The number and variety of tasks you like to perform.
- The degree and quality of interaction you enjoy between yourself and co-workers.
- The amount of job security you prefer.
- Your comfort level with respect to the size of both organizations and operating units.
- The level and quality of guest service you would like to be associated with.
- The pace of work you prefer.
- Your choices with regard to hours of work.

While you probably won't find a job that satisfies *all* of your preferences, it is best not only to identify them, but to prioritize them as well. Once again, this exercise will help you to identify companies and positions with which you are compatible. It will also help you to clarify your goals and values and to assist you in evaluating job offers.

THE RESUMÉ – SELL YOURSELF!

Many students and new managers realize the importance of a resumé as a marketing tool, but do not really know how to go about developing the best resumé – one which will get noticed and will get them past the initial screening which, by the way, in today's job market, might be done by a computer. It's useful to think of your resumé as a **personal advertisement**. This may sound odd, but if you think about it, your investment in your resumé is considerable.

Of course, there is the direct investment in paper, printing, and postage. However, the more significant investment involves the work experience, the education, the community and college service, and the other skills and talents you have developed through the years. The years you have spent to get this far are represented on your resumé and sometimes it is your *only* chance to sell yourself. Consider this – if you owned a restaurant, you would spend considerable time constructing the most effective advertisement – one that would bring in the most customers and would result in a high level of revenues. Your resumé deserves *at least* the same amount of attention.

You are probably aware that many hospitality and tourism firms receive thousands of resumés each year. Each of these resumés is *lucky* if it gets even 30 seconds of attention from the human resources department. And to complicate matters even further, many organizations now use computers to scan resumés and look for key words. If your resumé does not contain these key words, it will fall into a black hole in cyberspace. This means that in this transitional period between reviewed and scanned resumés, you may have to develop two different types of resumés -one that can be read by a human and one that can be read by a machine.

In the remainder of this section, we will discuss resumés in general and then point out the differences between traditional and high-tech resumés.

Resumé Basics

To begin with, let's examine a few common sense rules about resumé writing. Of course, you want your resumé to be noticed. Of course, you want the person reading it to seriously consider you for an interview. However, there is a right and a wrong way to do this. Cute gimmicks designed to call attention to yourself are generally not acceptable in today's business environment and will probably hurt more than help you.

Although differentiation is an important marketing tool, don't send your resumé printed on hot pink paper to a conservative hotel or restaurant company. Don't fold your resumé in the shape of a boat when you send it to a travel agency. You can certainly add a unique touch to your resumé – in fact, a personal touch that is well thought out and appropriate for the firm you are targeting is often appreciated. However, the rule of thumb is to be conservative and business-like.

The best and most business-like way to go about the task of resumé writing is to present a well organized, logically displayed, and visually appealing document. This greatly increases the chances of its being read. Keep in mind that your resumé has two major goals:

1) to showcase your achievements, talents, skills, and experience to your best advantage; and
2) to overcome any gaps in experience, credentials, and even education.

Being cute does not achieve these goals.

Types of Resumés

Many resumé experts suggest one of three basic methods of presenting your background to a prospective employer. These are called **chronological, functional** and **combination chronological-functional**. The most common presentation is the chronological resumé which lists work and educational experiences in descending order; that is, starting with the most recent. This format is good for demonstrating your growth in a particular area or for highlighting your work experience. In fact, it is probably the best format for a recent college graduate to adopt. It is *not* suitable, however, for people who are changing career fields or for people who lack focused and substantial work experience.

The content of every resumé, of course, varies according to individual differences. However, a chronological resumé generally employs five basic parts:

1) *current* information about how to contact you;
2) education;
3) descriptions of work experiences;
4) special skills and abilities; and
5) other activities which may highlight or suggest additional skills.

By contrast, the functional resumé focuses on professional skills which you have developed over the years rather than the specific experiences that helped you acquire them. Although job titles and employers are part of a functional resumé, the major focus is on skills and abilities. The functional format is best used for people with the following personal circumstances:

- a mature professional who has significant expertise and abilities;

- recent graduates with limited work experience;

- people changing careers who want to focus on skills rather than experience; and

- people who are returning to the work force after a long absence.

Some words of caution about the functional format – recent graduates of hospitality and tourism programs who have managed their work experience along with their education should not use this format. Also, unless you have a very clearly defined employment objective in mind, your resumé will likely lose focus and it will appear as if you are looking for just any old job and not a career.

The combination chronological-functional resumé is best used by the upwardly mobile professional who has a strong track record. Many resumé experts agree that if you have a strong record of performance and are on a well-defined career track, that this is the strongest and most effective resumé style available.

In addition to the usual information about how to contact you and your career objective, the combination resumé includes the following features:

- a summary of your career that paints a personal portrait of success;

- a description of functional skills which highlight your achievements in different categories and are relevant to both the job and your career goals;

- a chronological job history which lists companies, dates, titles, and sometimes duties and responsibilities; and

- a list of your educational experiences and achievements which, again, are relevant to the job and to your career goals.

Following are examples of all three resumé types. Figures 3.2, 3.3, and 3.4 are examples of chronological resumés while Figure 3.5 is an example of a functional resumé and Figure 3.6 combines both approaches. Finally, Figure 3.7 presents an example of a scannable resumé.

We will discuss scannable resumés later in this chapter but, for now, suffice it to say that this resumé can be easily read by all types of computer software. As you can see, the focus of each resumé varies according to its presentation style and each is appropriate for different stages in one's career.

Special Circumstances

Recently, many people have decided to switch from a career in some other industry to one in the hospitality and tourism field. Often, they have extensive prior experience in their previous line of work and little experience in hospitality and tourism. Figure 3.8 shows how mature career-changers might handle their resumés.

FIGURE 3.2
Chronological Resumé

MAKIKO SEKI

Current Address
4019 19th Place West
Alderwood, Washington 98042-1855
(206) 555-7358

Permanent Address
9-3-9 Hashido
Seya-ku, Yokohama-shi
Kanagawa, 246 JAPAN
(045) 330-99-72

OBJECTIVE: To obtain an entry-level front office position with a large convention hotel.

EDUCATION:

Washington State University
Bachelor of Arts, Hotel and Restaurant Administration, August 1997.
Overall GPA: 3.5/4.0

Spokane Falls Community College
Associate of Arts, Liberal Arts major, August 1995.
Overall GPA: 3.6/4.0

CAREER-RELATED EXPERIENCE:

SALES CLERK – **Rotunda Dining Center**, Washington State University, Pullman, Washington, February, 1996 - May, 1996.
Responsible for display and service of baked food in the bakery area. Light cooking in the pizza area.

SALES CLERK – **Bellbe Bakery Shop**, Kanagawa, Japan, November, 1990 - April, 1993.
Worked as cashier and server in popular, high-volume shop. Also assisted store manager with scheduling and payroll.

OTHER WORK EXPERIENCE:

FRONT DESK ASSISTANT – **Fitness Center**, Spokane Falls Community College, Spokane, Washington, June, 1995 - August, 1995.
Assisted members in correct use of exercise equipment and performed reception and customer service duties.

JAPANESE TUTOR – **Foreign Language Department**, Spokane Falls Community College, Spokane, Washington, September, 1994 - June, 1995.
Assisted students with development of conversational skills in Japanese.

HONORS: President's Honor Roll, Spokane Falls Community College

ACTIVITIES: Sigma Iota, Hotel Management Club, September, 1995 - Present
International Club, September, 1994 - August, 1995

REFERENCES: Excellent references available upon request.

FIGURE 3.3
Chronological Resumé

CYNTHIA SCHULTZ

1109 1st Avenue NE #2
Seattle, Washington 98105
(206) 555-2398

OBJECTIVE
Hotel sales position utilizing my outside sales, marketing, and customer service experience.

SALES & CUSTOMER SERVICE EXPERIENCE

ACCOUNT MANAGER, Residence Inn by Marriott 1992 - Present   Seattle, WA
- Managed base of over 150 accounts.
- Developed 20 new accounts resulting in an additional $300,000 in revenue.
- Increased annual revenue by 21%.
- Met or exceeded goals of 20 outside calls and 50 contacts per week.
- Networked for leads/referrals through intense involvement in Chambers of Commerce.
- Completed quarterly and yearly strategic marketing plans which included forecasting and budgeting.
- Implemented successful sales promotions resulting in over 50 qualified leads.

SALES SECRETARY/RESERVATIONS AGENT, Red Lion Hotel 1992   Bellevue, WA
- Provided support to executive staff of five.
- Responsible for ten-line telephone system with over 240 extensions.
- Edited and proofed contracts, proposals, and memos.
- Handled guest complaints through creative problem-solving.

HOSTESS, Disneyland 1991   Anaheim, CA
- Trained new employees in Disney guest service, policies, and procedures.
- Prevented safety hazards through TQM practices.
- Coordinated efficient order-processing which provided services for up to 500 daily.
- Promoted to cashiering within six weeks.

SAVINGS SUPPORT CLERK, Cascade Savings Bank 1989 - 1990   Everett, WA
- Met quota of maintaining one million dollars through repeat sales and negotiating.
- Achieved goal of bringing in $500,000 monthly through prospecting.
- Turned over 50% of inquiry calls into sales appointments.
- Created marketing projects for finding high-income prospects.
- Promoted bank's image in community through involvement in Chamber of Commerce.

EDUCATION
B.A. Degree – Hotel and Restaurant Administration, Washington State University 1992

FIGURE 3.4
Chronological Resumé

MICHAEL PRICE
2312 Norfolk, Apartment 1
Houston, Texas 77098
(789) 555-3792

Objective   Management trainee or entry level rooms management position.

Education   **Conrad N. Hilton College of Hotel & Restaurant Management**
Bachelor of Science degree, May 1997, *University of Houston*

Ecole Hotelier Suisse
Completed five months of hotel studies in a hands-on European environment at this world-renowned hotel school, Summer and Fall, 1995

Experience

January-
August, 1996   **Front Desk Clerk**
THE MAGNOLIA HOTEL, New Orleans, Louisiana
(AAA Five-Diamond hotel, member of The Leading Hotels of the World)
Responsible for all rooms operations and credit reports in addition to daily registration and check-out procedures. Extremely knowledgeable in all aspects of Lodgistix System 1 and LANmark property management systems.

July-
October, 1995   **Management Training Program**
RITZ CARLTON HOTEL, Milan, Italy
(Five-Star hotel, a member of The Leading Hotels of the World)
Completed three-part training program split into three concentrations: Sales, Food and Beverage, and Front Desk. Learned management techniques from Hotel Director, a graduate of the Ecole Hotelier de Lausanne.

June-
December, 1994   **Concierge, Bellman**
THE MONTELIONE HOTEL, New Orleans, Louisiana
Full-time Concierge with added Bellman duties due to the small size of this luxury French Quarter hotel.

August, 1991-
May, 1994   **Bartender**
THE LOUIS XIV, New Orleans, Louisiana
Named one of "the hardest-working bartenders in New Orleans" (*Cajun* Magazine) at this high-volume college bar.

Personal   President, Hotel Management Society, 1995-96, Conrad N. Hilton College
Secretary, Eta Chapter, Pi Kappa Alpha National Fraternity, Fall 1991
Dual American and British citizenship, with both passports

REFERENCES FURNISHED UPON REQUEST

FIGURE 3.5
Functional Resumé

CYNTHIA SCHULTZ
23498 Corlis Avenue West
Seattle, Washington 98119
(206) 555-9932

OBJECTIVE
Outside Sales Representative position utilizing seven years experience in sales, marketing, and customer service.

SUMMARY OF MARKETING SKILLS

Outside/Inside Sales

Customer Service

Public Relations

Market Analysis and Trends

Key Account Management

Corporate Sales Presentations

Cold Calling and Telemarketing

Lead Follow-Up

SALES EXPERIENCE

<u>Outside Sales</u>

- ➢ Managed base of over 150 accounts.
- ➢ Developed over 20 new accounts resulting in $300,000 in revenue.
- ➢ Met quota of maintaining one million dollars through repeat sales and negotiating.
- ➢ Achieved goals of bringing in $500,000 monthly through prospecting.
- ➢ Increased annual revenue by 21%.
- ➢ Consistently met goals of 20 outside sales calls and 50 contacts per week.
- ➢ Networked for leads and referrals through involvement in Chambers of Commerce.

<u>Inside Sales</u>

- ➢ Completed quarterly and yearly strategic marketing plans.
- ➢ Supervised and trained new employees in product knowledge and customer service skills.
- ➢ Implemented successful sales promotions resulting in over 50 qualified leads.
- ➢ Nominated for Sales Manager of the Year (chosen runner-up out of 400 candidates).
- ➢ Received Marriott Annual Volunteerism Award in 1992.

EDUCATION
B.A. Degree – Washington State University 1992
A.A.S. Degree – Everett Community College 1990

WORK HISTORY
Account Manager, Residence Inn by Marriott 1992 - 1994
Sales Secretary/Reservation Agent, Red Lion Hotel 1992
Main Street Restaurant Hostess, Disneyland 1991
New Accounts Representative, Cascade Savings Bank 1989 - 1990
Sales Associate, Sears 1987 - 1989

FIGURE 3.6
Combination Resumé

CYNTHIA SCHULTZ
23498 Corlis Avenue West, Seattle, Washington 98119   November, 1995
(206) 555-9932

OBJECTIVE & QUALIFICATIONS

Seek a challenging hotel Director of Sales position utilizing:

- **Ability to pioneer Greater Seattle territory generating sales in excess of $500,000 annually.**
- **Proven history of meeting sales goals of $500,000 in new accounts.**
- **Ability to increase annual revenue 21% through customer contact and account penetration.**
- **Bachelor of Arts Degree from Washington State University.**

SALES ACHIEVEMENTS

**OUTSIDE
SALES**
- Managed base of over 150 accounts generating annual sales in excess of $1 million.
- Increased total annual revenue by 21% through ongoing customer contact.
- Met or exceeded weekly goals of 20 outside appointments and 50 contacts.
- Implemented successful sales promotions resulting in over 200 qualified leads.
- Networked for leads and referrals through involvement in Chambers of Commerce.
- Created proposals and promotional materials for sales correspondence.
- Sales Manager of the Year in 1994 for all Marriott Residence Inns.

**INSIDE
SALES**
- Managed over 200 key accounts while establishing 60 new accounts per month.
- Met quota of maintaining $1,000,000 through repeat sales and negotiation.
- Telemarketed over 200 accounts per month.
- Achieved goal of $500,000 in new accounts monthly through prospecting.
- Increased account base through add-on sales.
- Completed quarterly and yearly strategic marketing plans which included market analysis, forecasting, and budgeting.

EDUCATION

B.A. Degree – Washington State University 1992
A.A.S. Degree – Everett Community College 1990

WORK HISTORY
Account Manager, Residence Inn by Marriott 1992 - 1994
Sales Administration/Reservation Agent, Red Lion Hotel 1992
Sales/Customer Service, Disneyland 1991
New Accounts Representative, Cascade Savings Bank 1989 - 1990
Sales Associate, Sears 1987 - 1989

FIGURE 3.7
Scannable Resumé

Julia Hernandez
2599 Verona Lane, #96
Everett, Washington (206) 555-8203
Email: juliah@for.com

Work Experience:

The Wine Bar and Bistro
Kirkland, Washington, 1996
Cashier: Greet and seat guests at this 100-seat popular restaurant, cash out an average of 6 servers per shift, balance nightly receipts, and order various supplies for the bistro.

The New Moon Restaurant
Everett, Washington, 1993-1995
Cashier and Greeter: Welcomed guests, ran all cash and charge transactions for customers, and helped with employee scheduling at this 60-seat full-service restaurant.

Edmonds Community College, Career Center
Lynwood, Washington, 1993-1994
Office clerk: Assisted students in their career and educational searches, answered telephones, administered aptitude tests, and supervised a computerized data center for job-related information.

Education:

Seattle Central Community College
The Hospitality and Tourism Institute
Seattle, Washington
Degree: Associate of Arts, Hospitality Management
Graduation Date: May 1997
Areas of Interest: Banquets and Convention Services

Languages Spoken:

Bilingual - Fluent in both English and Spanish

Volunteer Experience:

Sales Blitz for the Ramada Inn in Seattle, 1996
Job Fair Worker at the Westin Hotel in Seattle, 1996
Teacher at Spanish Language School, 1994-1996

FIGURE 3.8
Resumé for a Career-Changer

SUSAN TUCKER

2300 Bellevue Avenue   Seattle, Washington 98122   (206) 555-4736

Career Objective

To improve Marriott's ability to provide consistently superior guest accommodations and services as a manager or in a regional quality management or training position.

Professional Activities and Attributes

- Highly effective in analyzing processes, developing and implementing improvements, and producing results
- Proven ability to use exceptional organization skills, attention to detail, and tenacity to achieve objectives
- Recognition by clients and peers for building rapport with people from diverse business, educational, and cultural backgrounds
- Strong presentation skills; delivered presentation on extensive computer graphic system to international user conference
- Experienced in training and information design; created material for corporate IS training program

Education

Washington State University, May 1997   **Certificate in Hotel and Restaurant Administration**
University of California Santa Cruz, May 1985   **Certificate in Graphic Production**
Bachelor of Arts in English Literature

Brief History of Professional Experience

Hyatt Regency Hotel   **Performed reservation services for 300-room, 4-star property**
Bellevue, Washington   ◆ Utilized yield management techniques toward achieving occupancy and
October 1996 - present   average rate goals
                             ◆ Sold rooms in four different categories, promoted many different guest packages

Museum Café   **Supervised front and back of the house operations at quick service café**
Seattle, Washington   ◆ Achieved improvements in customer service and procedures
May - October, 1996   ◆ Responsible for closing café, clearing all registers, and making deposits which
                                  averaged $2,500 per night

Automated Technology   **Responsible for graphics technology**
Santa Cruz, California   ◆ Supported over 200 clients on an on-going basis
1993 - 1996   ◆ Trained, managed, and promoted technology throughout the corporation

Roadway Trucking   **Provided client and systems support to diverse personnel**
San Diego, California   ◆ Trained various personnel to work with company-specific computer systems
1986 - 1992   ◆ Employed in both union and management positions

Membership: Eta Sigma Delta International Hospitality Honorary Society   References: Available by request

Once you have decided on the appropriate style for your resumé, you need to begin the rather serious task of writing it. In general, you should consider the following factors as you go about developing your resumé.

Presentation

Although the appearance of your resumé is not all it takes to land an interview, it definitely increases the chances of your resumé being read. It is the first impression of *you*, and while you might believe that content is more important (which it is), most resumé experts agree that the decision about whether to toss or read your resumé is made within three to five seconds and is based mainly on appearance. We are not talking about cute or gimmicky things here, but rather the layout, format, quality of printing, use of bolding, and other format considerations.

Substance

A quality resumé presents you and your qualifications in the most effective manner possible. The items you choose to include should highlight the strengths, qualifications and achievements which will promote you as a desirable candidate for the particular position you are targeting. You should avoid exaggeration or embellishing your qualifications with meaningless or frivolous adjectives. You can deal with unflattering information by simply leaving it out or by turning it into a positive when you interview.

Writing

Remember, a resumé is a marketing tool and its sole purpose is to get you to the next stage of the marketing process – the interview. Therefore, it not only has to have visual appeal and substance, but the writing style has to have **IMPACT**. Impact is achieved with concise writing which uses action words that accurately describe you and what you can do for the company. In Appendix 3.1, we list some action words which you can use or which might spur your thinking.

A good resumé provides essential information in an easy to read format. Unnecessary words and phrases, complicated sentence structures, and irrelevant information detract from this. As we said earlier, most people who review resumés are likely to devote less than 30 seconds to an initial screening. This means that it is important that you keep your reader in mind as you go about designing and writing your resumé.

On a final note, avoid typos, misspellings, grammatical errors, and punctuation errors *at all costs*. You might be the most qualified applicant out of a pool of 1,000 others, but poor writing will not only hide your outstanding qualifications, it will probably kill any chances for an interview. Look at it this way. Poor writing and grammatical or spelling errors say a lot about your communication skills, your attention to detail, your work habits, and your beliefs about quality. You can't write your resumé in one quick shot. It needs to be edited, and re-edited, and probably reviewed and edited by other people. This may sound like a real pain, but given the importance of this piece of paper, it's worth it!

Length

The rule of thumb for a recent college graduate is that your resumé should be limited to one page. There are a lot of reasons for this, including the sheer number of resumés companies receive for entry level positions; the comparative lack of experience many recent college grads have; and the fact that a great deal of conventional wisdom says that all pertinent information will fit on one page. The only exception to the one page rule of thumb, in our opinion, would be for people who have had substantial work experience which, if properly showcased, would give them a decided advantage in establishing credibility.

If your resumé exceeds one page, you should consider the following: First, your first page must be interesting enough to entice the reader to continue to the second. Therefore, you must pay special attention to the order of items you place on the first page and put the most interesting and enticing qualifications on page one. Second, we are aware of a number of recruiters who refuse to read more than one page and will make initial decisions only on information contained on that page – so make the majority of your case on the first page. Third, under no circumstances should your resumé exceed two pages unless you are applying for a highly specialized job in which a great deal of documentation is required. Also, we encourage you to take another look at Cynthia's resumé in Figure 3.6. Notice that she has had seven years of work experience, five jobs, and a large number of outstanding accomplishments. Yet her resumé is confined to one page!

Putting It Together

In this section, we will discuss the parts of a resumé, what data should be included, and how best to construct each component. However, before we begin this discussion, let's turn our attention to things that *don't* belong in your resumé, either because they are irrelevant or because they could hurt rather than advance your chances of being selected.

✖ **Reason for leaving previous employment**
Remember, you are trying to make an impact. Your reasons for leaving past jobs do nothing to contribute to this. In fact, they could be harmful to your cause. Besides, this is almost always covered in interviews anyway.

✖ **Names of supervisors or managers**
Again, this does nothing to establish impact. Furthermore, listing names wastes valuable space and your supervisors may be long gone from previous places you have worked. The same goes for phone numbers and addresses. The city and state will do just fine.

✖ **References**
Most organizations are not interested in checking your references before they decide if they are interested in you. This usually means that references will be contacted after the interview. Furthermore, under the 1972 Fair Credit and Reporting Act, employers are prohibited from checking your references until they have your written consent.

Although some people would argue that it is unnecessary, we encourage our students to put the old standby, "References Available Upon Request," at the bottom of their resumés. We believe that this is expected protocol and doesn't take up much room.

We also encourage you to have a separate list of references with up-to-date contact information to take with you to interviews. This need not be extensive – three to five contacts – and it should only include people who are in a position to vouch for you professionally, not your Aunt Sally, your drinking buddy Bubba, or your father's business associates. We recommend that you stick to recent instructors and employers (preferably a mix of both) and that you ask them first.

✖ **Previous salaries**
Do not put any reference to previous wages in your resumé, even if it demonstrates upward mobility. Salary negotiations occur much later on in

the job search process, and putting salaries in your resumé could disqualify you at an early stage.

✖ **Age, race, gender, religion, national origin**
It is against the law to consider these anyway. Furthermore, they do nothing to enhance the effectiveness of your resumé.

✖ **Health**
Who cares? But, more important, under the Americans with Disabilities Act (ADA), your health, or lack of it, cannot be a consideration for employment selection unless it specifically relates to job performance.

✖ **Weaknesses**
Don't be silly! But think about them anyway. You will probably be asked about them in your interview.

✖ **Marital status**
This is nobody's business but yours and doesn't relate to employment. Besides, employers are prohibited from considering marital status if it is used as a basis for gender discrimination.

Now let's turn our attention to what you *should* include in a resumé. We have chosen the chronological format because it is the most commonly used and is most appropriate for our targeted readers.

✔ **Date**
There are differences of opinion on this, but putting a date on your resumé gives prospective employers an idea as to how current it is. However, keep in mind that if you include a date, you need to make sure that you keep your resumé updated on a regular basis. We also suggest that you don't get too specific – November, 1996 is much better than November 12, 1996.

✔ **Contact information**
Although this would seem to be an obvious area for inclusion on a resumé, you would be surprised at how many resumés lack complete contact information. Interested employers *have* to be able to get in touch with you. If they are unable to do so or if you delay your response because a letter was sent to your school address while you were home over the summer, you could lose a golden opportunity.

So what *should* be included in contact information? Well, to begin with, your name. Many resumé advisors suggest that you use your first name, middle initial, and last name or just your first and last names. Avoid titles such as Mr. or Ms. and don't spell out your middle name unless you use your middle name as part of your last or are an accomplished professional such as John Stuart Mill, the distinguished British economist.

Next, include your address. Be sure to not abbreviate unless you absolutely have to, and don't take up more than three lines doing this. Also, if your present address (e.g., school) is different than your permanent address, be sure to include both addresses. Refer to Makiko's resumé in Figure 3.2 to see how this is typically handled.

With the wide variety of communication methods available today, it is also a very good idea to also include phone numbers *as well as* fax numbers and E-Mail addresses if these resources are available to you. In addition, *always* include the area code for your phone and fax numbers, because even if you submit your resumé to a local address, it might be scanned or read in some other city.

✓ **Summary**

Some resumé advisors recommend that job seekers include a short summary of qualifications or experiences early on in their resumé. We don't normally recommend this, but it can be helpful under two different sets of circumstances. First, if you have a strong track record in a specific area of expertise and you want to point out how this applies to a particular job, a qualifications summary can be very useful. Second, if you have limited work experience or you have worked in a number of positions for one or two operations and you need something to fill up the page, it can help. Cynthia's summary of marketing skills in Figure 3 .5 is one model of how to do this.

✓ **Objective**

This is a somewhat controversial area. Some people believe that it is important to write a career objective that includes your aspirations and type of environment you would like to work in. This might go something like:

> *Seeking a management position with a full service lodging firm which offers opportunities for growth and where I can use my sparkling personality and integrity to eventually become a senior level executive within six months, and then the lord of all existence the following day.*

Others, including ourselves, believe that this is wasted verbiage and acts as a turn-off to many resumé reviewers. We suggest that you use either an employment objective or simply an objective which tells the reader what type of job you are looking for, in what industry segment, and maybe in what type of facility. Here are some examples:

- Entry level management or management trainee in the full-service lodging industry.
- Front of the house management in an upscale or fine dining establishment.
- Sales and marketing position with a multi-national tour wholesaler.
- Customer Service Agent.
- Entry-level sales and marketing position in the lodging industry.
- Unit management in institutional food service.

These objectives tell employers exactly what you are looking for and in what industry. This enables them to quickly match your qualifications with the position you are seeking.

Now, as usual, come a few warnings. First, the more specific you are, the more you narrow your chances of being selected. For example, if you specify front office management in a hotel, you probably won't be considered for a housekeeping manager or for a food and beverage outlet manager. Second, you may be tempted to leave out any objective because you plan to include that in your cover letter. Don't. Quite often, cover letters and resumés are separated, and if your resumé is passed on to somebody else and they don't know what you are looking for, you invite a second chance for the trash can. Finally, many recruiters read the resumé first and the cover letter second, and would have to flip back and forth to search for a fit.

An objective just makes good sense!

✓ **Education**
Again, there is some debate about where to put education. Some say it should go before work experience, while others believe it should be placed somewhere at the end. Our take on this is that it depends. For most recent graduates of hospitality and tourism programs, the most marketable asset they have is their education. While most have had substantial work experience to prepare them for their career, they have not had a significant amount of professional or managerial work experience.

Furthermore, more and more hospitality and tourism companies are requiring degrees as a minimum hiring credential. Given this, we would recommend that you list your education immediately following your objective. After a few years of experience, you can move education down to the lower levels of your resumé. Notice the difference between Makiko's and Cynthia's resumés as an example of this.

Following are some *Dos, Don'ts,* and *Maybes* regarding your statement of educational attainment:

➡ *DO* list the degree or certificate, the institution granting it, and the date you received it or anticipate receiving it.

➡ *DO* list other degrees and certificates you have received from post-secondary institutions.

✖ *DO NOT* list major courses. These are very similar among institutions and, besides, they take up valuable space. If you have taken courses to create a sub-specialty in a particular area such as Human Resource Management, Conventions and Meetings Management, or Finance, for example, include these in another section of your resumé, such as *Special Skills.*

✖ *DO NOT* list schools you have attended but from which you did not receive a degree or certificate. This is irrelevant and might make you look like a "school hopper" and could translate, in some minds, to a potential "company hopper."

✖ *DO NOT* list your high school, junior high school, elementary school, and nursery school. If you have a degree or certificate, most employers can figure out that you have probably finished this part of your education as well.

? *MAYBE YOU SHOULD OR MAYBE YOU SHOULDN'T* list your grade point average. There are several reasons for this. One is that while it is obviously possible to have too low of a GPA, it is also possible to have too high of a GPA. There are still some employers who think that an exceptionally high GPA means that you are probably only good at being a student and probably would not be effective in what they like to call "the real world." This is an isolated belief, but, unfortunately, it still exists.

Also, higher education is in an era of grade inflation which varies from institution to institution. Some estimates of average GPAs range from 2.8 to 3.0. Many employers are aware of this. Therefore, it is probably not wise to list a grade point average below 3.0. If GPA is that important, it will be brought up in later stages of the hiring process.

? *MAYBE YOU SHOULD OR MAYBE YOU SHOULDN'T* list the city and state of your institution. This is only necessary if you are concerned that your college or university might not be immediately recognized – maybe it is a new program, small in size, or located in an area which might not be familiar to someone reading your resumé. For example, if you were a graduate of an Australian university applying for work in the U.S., you might consider providing the location of the institution.

✓ **Work Experience**

This is the most critical area of your resumé. It is your opportunity to call attention to a large number of factors which might directly influence a hiring decision. Just to show you how important this is, we have listed a few of these factors below:

- skills you have acquired
- the variety of your experience
- the amount of responsibility you have held
- the types of establishments and service levels with which you are familiar
- the amount of work experience you have
- upward mobility
- how well you have prepared for your career
- customer service skills
- dedication to quality

Depending on how you word your descriptions in this area, you can call attention to these and a host of other factors that you might want a prospective company to know. Remember that you don't want to bury this information in wordy descriptions, so be careful to use concise and tight phrases – perhaps even bulletted phrases such as Susan uses in Figure 3.8.

Let's start our discussion of how to present your work experience with a few simple rules which we'll explain in detail later.

1) Use job titles that are recognizable.
2) Put your job title first.
3) Make use of formatting options to call attention to important aspects of your work experience.
4) Include the city and state of places where you have worked.
5) Indicate the dates of your employment.
6) Keep your descriptions brief, but make them effective.
7) Always include descriptive information about your place of employment.

How you express your job title is a very important consideration. It should always be listed in terms that can generally be understood by most people reading your resumé. For example, if you have worked as a senior reservation agent in a hotel where your specific job title was Reservation Agent 1, you should probably use the title Lead Reservations Agent or Senior Reservations Agent because people outside of that particular organization are not likely to know what a Reservation Agent 1 is and would miss the fact that you held a leadership role. In fact, they might interpret the "1" to mean that you were at the lower level. This is not fabrication, but rather an act of simplification to make your resumé more understandable.

We also strongly suggest putting the job title first because, after all, what you are selling is your experience. Some resumé advisors recommend putting the place of employment first, but we advise against this because doing so hides your experience. Sure, it's great that you worked for Disneyworld – this would interest many prospective employers – but what is of more concern is what you did there. The rationale for this becomes even more pronounced if you worked as a travel consultant at Banana Boat Travel. Your job is important but nobody outside of your immediate locale has probably ever heard of Banana Boat Travel.

This brings us to some formatting advice. We suggest that you highlight both what you have done and where you have done it *if* you have recognized brand name experience. In order to get your message across, make use of bold-face and upper and lower case options. When we advise people on how best to call attention to their work experience, we tell them to bold-face and use only upper case letters when listing their job titles and to use bold-face and upper and lower case when indicating their place of employment. This puts a spotlight on both what you did and where you did it. See how effectively Michael handles this in Figure 3.4.

Following your statement of position and the company or place you worked, you should always be sure to put the city and state or country. People outside of your immediate area may not have heard of the establishment or firm. Moreover, to leave it out simply looks dumb. This is true even if you are confining your search to the area in which you already live.

You should also always include the dates of your employment. Prospective employers want to know how long you have been employed and how recent your experience was. True, they are also looking for gaps in employment, but this is not much of an issue for people who are just finishing their education and does not signal much of an alarm for applicants with otherwise acceptable credentials. However, in the latter case, they should be prepared to answer questions concerning periods of unemployment in an interview.

The next step is a description of your responsibilities and duties. Your goal here is to tell your targeted company as much about yourself as possible in two to three lines. Some of the information you can get across here includes skills, leadership roles, level of responsibility, description of the property, and customer service orientation. Sounds like a lot for two or three lines, doesn't it? It is, but you can use this space effectively and make your critical abilities stand out. The keys are using tight language and describing the key elements of jobs. You should also use action verbs in the case of resumés read by humans or key words in the case of those scanned by computers – or a combination of both. Again, see Appendix 3.1 for a list of key and action words.

Be very careful here! Too much description can bury your best attributes – too little can sell you short. You don't have to use complete sentences and, in some cases, a bulletted format is very effective if you have the space. Consider the examples below:

Example 1

> **GUEST SERVICE AGENT**, **The Barclay Hotel**, ST. LOUIS, MISSOURI
> *February 1994 to February 1995*
> Responsible for checking guests in and out, cashiering, and occasionally acting as a van driver.

This description may accurately describe what this person did, but for all intents and purposes, she could have just skipped the description because, except for driving the van, her narrative describes what any GSR or front office clerk might do.

Example 2

> **GUEST SERVICE AGENT**, **The Barclay Hotel**, ST. LOUIS, MISSOURI
> *February 1994 to February 1995*
> Provided excellent customer service in this 75-room luxury boutique hotel. Duties included handling $5,000 cash bank, using LANmark property management system, and serving as relief supervisor.

Much better! Here she uses a small amount of space to get across a great deal of information about herself including:

✓ positive customer service attitude and recognition of its importance;
✓ experience in a small luxury hotel;

✓ substantial cash handling responsibilities;
✓ familiarity with a commonly used property management system; and
✓ supervisory experience.

She has also included a number of key word nouns which would show up on a computer scan. Now, if she wanted to provide even more information, she might try a bulletted format:

Example 3

GUEST SERVICE AGENT, The Barclay Hotel, ST. LOUIS, MISSOURI
February 1994 to February 1995
Provided excellent customer service in this 75-room luxury boutique hotel.

◆ Managed $5,000 cash bank	◆ Substituted for night audit
◆ Served as relief supervisor	◆ Prepared management information reports
◆ Used LANmark property management system	◆ Employee of the Month - November, 1995

Although she expanded the number of lines by one, she used two different type sizes to condense the space and to capture the reader's attention. She also added three important pieces of information: her selection as employee of the month, her familiarity with the night audit, and her preparation of reports.

On a final note, as in Examples 2 and 3, it is important to include a description of the type of facility or operation. The Barclay is, of course, fictional, but without the description of the hotel, a resumé reader would have no idea about what type of facility it is. It could be a flop house, a small motel, or a large, full service property. Therefore, we cannot stress enough the importance of providing descriptive information such as:

* high volume, quick service restaurant;
* 120-room extended stay lodging facility;
* 15,000-student school district;
* luxury liner;
* 150-seat fine-dining restaurant; or
* full-line tour operator.

✓ **Honors and Awards**
These are important because they display your achievements both inside and outside of school. For example, if your GPA was high enough to earn you *Cum Laude* status, you might consider listing it here rather than by your degree, because Honors and Awards is a category all to itself. Other items

you might want to consider listing here are scholarships, service awards, athletic awards, membership in honorary societies, and employer recognitions.

Stay away from awards received from religious or political organizations as they do not relate to your employment qualifications and they may have the opposite effect you wanted them to have. Besides, in the case of religion, employers are prohibited from considering it anyway. By the way, if you don't have awards or recognitions, don't worry – you are in good company. Simply leave the category out.

✓ **Activities and Interests**
This, like Honors and Awards, is an optional area. Including it can show that you have a number of desirable qualities such as being a team player, having leadership qualities, and having a variety of interests. However, not inserting this section in your resumé will not hurt you. This is particularly true in the case of many hospitality and tourism students who must juggle work responsibilities with their school work.

Nevertheless, it is an important section for those who have something to put here. Items that you might want to consider for inclusion are team sports, organizational memberships (particularly those in which you exercised a leadership role), volunteer work, and other special activities such as marketing blitzes in which you have participated. Things that you should probably consider avoiding are individual sports interests and hobbies. Unlike team sports, individual sports don't point to your ability to be a team member, and hobbies, while they might be interesting, are not particularly strong selling points.

✓ **Special Skills**
Here you want to list or reinforce skills which might be of value to a future employer or which help you to stand out from the crowd – skills such as knowledge of software packages, languages, property management systems, or reservation systems to name a few. Avoid skills that are irrelevant or are best left to observation, such as *excellent human relations skills* or *customer skills*. Figure 3.9 provides a handy summary of this section.

FIGURE 3.9
Resumé Components

✓ **Date** (optional)
✓ **Contact Information**
  - Name
  - Address (both permanent and school)
  - Phone/Fax/E-Mail
✓ **Objective** (short, specific, to the point)
✓ **Education** (degrees received only)
✓ **Experience** (most recent first)
  - Dates
  - Job title
  - Company
  - Location
  - Description of duties
  - Location description (e.g., 250-room 5-star hotel)
✓ **Other information**
  - Activities that highlight additional skills
  - Honors that call attention to special abilities
  - Other skills that distinguish you from competitors (e.g., languages, special training)

Resumés and the Computer Reader

We are in an age of transition when it comes to resumés. About half of mid-size companies and almost all large companies now use computers to scan resumés and store them for future needs. This means some substantial changes in the way resumés are worded and formatted.

As we have said earlier, key words (nouns) more often than action verbs are the ticket because they describe *you*. Words like sales, front office, tour agent, and food and beverage are words that define experience, skills, and job requirements. Using a sufficient number of key words will increase the chances that your

entire resumé will be read because a search will be more likely to reveal a match between your name and the key word. This doesn't mean that you should avoid action words, however. You should include these because they still remain important if your resumé is eventually read by a human.

The other area of concern is in formatting. According to Joyce Lain Kennedy, a nationally syndicated career columnist, the key word is **simplicity**. She and other experts suggest the following:[8]

✔ Use non-decorative fonts. Helvetica or Times Roman are best.
✔ Make sure that the resumé is free of typographical errors.
✔ Use key words in your objective.
✔ Use white, standard sized paper, printed on one side.
✔ Avoid italics, script, and underlining because scanners often translate these into hieroglyphics. Capital and bold letters are okay.
✔ Don't use graphics, shading, horizontal or vertical lines.
✔ Avoid staples and folds. If you must fold, make sure that the fold is not on a line of text.
✔ Make sure that your name is the first readable item on *each* page.

By following these simple rules, you can develop a resumé which is fit for both machines and humans. Refer back to Figure 3.7 for a good example of a scannable resumé.

Putting Your Resumé On-Line

In this age of cyberspace, you can use the Internet to find both job search information as well as to post your resumé for review by prospective employers. There is an ever-growing number of employer information databases. Some are simply databases of job listings, while others will take your resumé and make it available to prospective employers. Some charge an access fee, others don't. Many companies maintain home pages as well, to provide information about employment opportunities.

Like other methods of submitting your resumé, you should be selective when using the World Wide Web to submit your resumé to a database. Be aware that databases are likely to contain thousands of resumés and that the more selectively you target databases, the better your chances of having yours read.

[8] Joyce Lain Kennedy, *Computer-Friendly Resumé Tips,* **Planning Job Choices: 1996**, p. 35.

We briefly visited the World Wide Web and, using the Alta Vista search engine, found 70,000 sites containing the words *resumé* and *hospitality* or *tourism*! As you well know, even if a site does not offer exactly what you are looking for, you can easily and quickly jump from one site to another by clicking on a highlighted link. A glance at a few of the sites proved this to be the case and led us to areas in the web where resumés can be easily posted.

In addition, many institutions require that your resumé be on-line. The National Association of Colleges and Employers operates JobWeb which provides both career planning and employment information. The JobWeb URL (uniform resource locator) is <http://www.jobweb.org>. It can also be accessed through a number of commercial services.

While this has not been an exhaustive discussion about resumés, we hope that you have picked up some good pointers about how to construct a resumé which will help you to effectively market yourself. Remember, it is very similar to an advertisement and good ads require work, attention to detail, and a great deal of thought. Do it! It will pay off.

WRITING A COVER LETTER

A resumé without a cover letter will not be read and will immediately halt your movement through the hiring cycle. A cover letter is not only a means of introducing yourself and citing your interest; it demonstrates your written communication skills. As you know, both written and spoken communication skills are essential in today's customer-oriented service industries. Many recruiters read your resumé first and then review your cover letter solely for the purpose of evaluating your written communication skills. Writing a cover letter should not be an afterthought because, in conjunction with your resumé, it is what will get you noticed and land you an interview.

A cover letter is not meant to recap your entire resumé. Rather, it is meant to express your interest in a position or corporation. It is yet another piece which is used to promote you! As with your resumé, a cover letter will rarely receive more than 30 seconds of actual read time, so you must write it carefully and succinctly.

Certain things work better than others when putting together a cover letter. First, each letter must be customized – the old all-purpose cover letter is no longer acceptable. Next, it must be kept to one page since second pages often get detached and even ignored. Your letter should include key phrases and catchy words which will get the attention of the reader and make her want to speak with you in person. Finally, your cover letter must be straightforward regarding your skills and abilities.

In this section, we will first go through some cover letter basics and will then suggest a basic format. We will also include two examples of effective cover letters, ones which successfully landed interviews, as well as a checklist for writing an effective cover letter.

Customize Your Letter

At all costs, avoid a cover letter which resembles a mass mailing. Instead, you should customize each letter to a particular person, firm, and position. Later on, we will talk about researching a company – incorporate this research into your cover letter to make the reader aware of your genuine interest in the firm.

Most companies want to hire someone who **wants** to work for them, and not someone who just wants a job. Include some facts specific to the corporation such as "The recent restructuring of the Alpha Hotel Corporation is a direct reflection of its increased importance of service and enables all employees to take more responsibility for customer relations. I strongly agree with this philosophy and know that my excellent communication skills and attention to service quality will make me a valuable front-of-the-house employee."

Let your prospective employer know that you know about the company, are aware of current industry trends, and, in short, have done your homework.

Keep It Short and Lively

Remember – you are not attempting to write a best-selling novel, but instead you are attempting to get the attention and interest of the reader. Accordingly, your cover letter should be no more than one page long!

Most people find that thinking too much about length hampers their creativity, so you might find it easiest to begin with a two-page letter and then shorten it. If you choose this route, after you write the long version, ask yourself the following questions:

- Where have I repeated myself?
- Where can I substitute a word for an entire phrase?
- Can I delete any paragraphs?
- Can I delete any sentences?
- Would I want to interview this person after reading this letter?

As a rule of thumb, your cover letter should contain facts and action words -- nothing else. For example, instead of writing "My two internships in college allowed me to develop good communication and computer skills which led to two promotions during my six month experience with T.G.I.Friday's," write "My communication and computer skills resulted in two promotions during my six month internship at T.G.I.Friday's." See how the second sentence more directly relates your skills to your promotions? Also, it has 10 fewer words than the first sentence! If you have difficult writing in the direct mode, try incorporating action verbs into your sentences such as are listed in the Appendix 3.1.

Vary your sentence structure and keep all sentences under 20 words – a good rule of thumb is to average 15 words per sentence. You can combine sentences with connectors such as *and*, *therefore*, and *since*, or you can use a semi-colon. You can shorten sentences by either restructuring them or cutting a longer sentence into two. Remember, your goal is to capture and keep the reader's attention!

Always test your cover letter by trying to read it yourself within thirty seconds. Ask yourself what sticks out in this brief period and what should be changed in order to make you more likely to get an interview. Make sure that the things you feel are most important are highlighted in short paragraphs or by using bullets.

Straightforward Is Best

Your cover letter should not read as if you held sole responsibility for the start-up of a multi-million dollar enterprise. There is a vast difference between confidence and blatant arrogance! Employers do not expect someone who is just starting his career to have the experience of someone who has been in the industry for twenty years. Instead, employers at this stage will hire you based on your potential. Honesty and integrity are highly valued, and an honest and realistic cover letter will show that you have these attributes.

A Basic Format and Style

Regardless of the style of your letter, it should generally follow this five-paragraph format:

1) The first paragraph should get the reader's attention and generate her interest in you. If you are applying for a specific position, don't forget to state the position! Also, include any referrals here – they almost always buy instant credibility.

2) The second paragraph should highlight your strengths and explain what you have to offer.

3) The third paragraph should briefly summarize your accomplishments, whether in college or at work.

4) The fourth paragraph should stress why you are uniquely qualified; that is, it should tie your strengths and accomplishments to the specific position or firm.

5) The last paragraph should be brief – one sentence is fine – and should state a follow-up action. This is your last chance to make an impression, so make it strong and obvious that you are serious about the position and the firm. Don't be afraid to state that you will follow up with a phone call within two weeks or that you would like to meet when you are in the area next month.

Sample Cover Letters – Two Examples

Following are two examples of cover letters which resulted in interviews. Feel free to use them as a guide to customize yours.

Example 1

Dylan Smith
100 Central Park Lane
 Anytown, USA 00000
(555)555-1212

(Date)

Karen Williams, Title
ABC Hotel
123 Corporate Plaza
City, State   Zip Code

Dear Ms. Williams:

I recently spoke with Peter Jones from the ABC Hotel at Corporate Plaza and he told me about the vacant Assistant Guest Relations Manager position. Knowing the requirements for the job, he felt that I would be an ideal candidate and encouraged me to send you my resumé.

My hospitality degree combined with over 1,500 hours of experience at the XYZ Hotel Corporation required dedication and hard work. I also learned excellent communication and organizational skills. In my internship, I capitalized on my ability to learn quickly, work as a team member, and deliver quality service. In turn, I was promoted to Front Desk Assistant Supervisor within four months.

I have also worked hard to develop leadership skills while in college and also in the workplace. I organized the development of our hospitality program's Internet Homepage and coordinated a spring fund-raiser which raised over $5,000 in student scholarships. At the XYZ hotel, I was recognized by the Operations Manager for my outstanding performance during my internship.

My education, experience, and dedication to quality service will enable me to succeed with ABC Hotel Corporation. I offer a high energy level and strong interpersonal and organizational skills and would very much like to be part of your team.

I look forward to hearing from you, Ms. Williams, and will give you a call within two weeks to follow up on this letter.

Sincerely,

Dylan Smith

Example 2

Dylan Smith
100 Central Park Lane
Anytown, USA 00000
(555) 555-1212

(Date)

Karen Williams, Title
ABC Hotel
123 Corporate Plaza
City, State Zip Code

Dear Ms. Williams:

In response to your advertisement for a Front Desk Guest Relations Manager which appeared in the *City Times*, I enclose my resumé for your consideration.

My educational and professional experience includes:

- ❍ a (name of degree) degree from (institution);
- ❍ over 1,500 hours of internship experience; and
- ❍ management experience as a Front Desk Assistant Supervisor.

My personal and professional strengths include:

- ❍ excellent communication and organizational skills;
- ❍ proven leadership skills at both college and work;
- ❍ the ability to learn quickly and to work as an effective team member; and
- ❍ attention and dedication to quality service.

I believe my education, experience, and dedication to quality service will enable me to succeed with ABC Hotel Corporation. I offer a high energy level and strong interpersonal and organizational skills and would very much like to be part of your team.

I look forward to discussing my qualifications with you, Ms. Williams, and will give you a call within two weeks to follow up on this letter.

Sincerely,

Dylan Smith

One Last Check

Before you send your cover letter to prospective employers, you should complete the checklist in Figure 3.10. Believe us, it will make your cover letter more effective and will better your chances of getting an interview.

FIGURE 3.10
Cover Letter Checklist

____	1.	I stated my purpose for writing.
____	2.	The letter is customized for the firm and position.
____	3.	I included relevant strengths and accomplishments.
____	4.	I eliminated all extraneous information.
____	5.	The letter is long enough to whet the reader's appetite, yet short enough to keep the reader's attention.
____	6.	My sentences average fifteen words each.
____	7.	Every paragraph is five lines or less.
____	8.	I varied the length of the sentences.
____	9.	The letter has a professional appearance.
____	10.	I used action words and phrases.
____	11.	The letter is free from typographical and grammatical errors.
____	12.	My education, experience, and skills are presented honestly.
____	13.	My closing is gracious, yet points toward follow-up action.

If your cover letter passes the previous check sheet test, you are ready to go. Type the envelope and affix a stamp – and don't forget to include your resumé (on matching paper, of course) as the second page!

BE A SNOOP – KNOW THE COMPANY OR ORGANIZATION

Knowledge of your targeted company or organization is absolutely critical to the success of your self-marketing campaign. Without it, you can't customize cover letters and you can't ask intelligent questions should you be fortunate enough to land an interview. Also, many employers expect that you research their organization and use this as a critical evaluation factor in the selection process. Anyway, why would you want to pursue employment with a firm about which you know nothing? This doesn't mean that you have to be an expert on any particular organization, but it does mean that you should know, at a minimum, the following:

- the various lines of business operated by the company (for example, Marriott Corporation has various brands of hotels and also operates business in a number of other areas including food service)
- the geographical markets in which the company operates
- their service philosophy
- their reputation
- major competitors
- something about the corporate culture

In addition to these essentials, it would also be impressive if you were familiar with information such as annual sales, future plans, number of employees, and, if appropriate, the number of operating units.

Snooping Around Works!

This may sound like a lot of work, but there are virtually hundreds of resources available to you. Finding them and using them is neither difficult nor all that time consuming. Let's examine a few of these resources.

Recruiting Literature

The hospitality and tourism industry is labor intensive. Many organizations are quite large and, as a result, their need for new employees is great. Because of this, many companies develop and distribute an impressive array of recruiting literature. Recruiters visiting colleges and universities frequently make this literature available at placement or career centers and at hospitality and tourism program offices. If this material isn't available or if you are not in school, it wouldn't hurt to write the company and request it. Chances are fairly good that you will get something mailed back to you.

Trade Journals

If you are a hospitality and tourism student or professional, these should be readily available to you. Trade journals and magazines provide invaluable information on corporate strategy, restructuring, key players, and new concepts. As a pre- professional or practicing professional, you should be reading these anyway.

Directories and Reference Books

There are a large number of directories available in both school and public libraries. These range from being very general to very specific and provide information regarding corporate descriptions, key executives, sales, and number of employees. In addition, hospitality and tourism students can make use of a number of directories which provide information on firms in a variety of industry segments. Following are some of the directories available:

- *Million Dollar Directory*
  Provides information on U.S. businesses, each with a net worth of over $500,000. Over 160,000 listings.

- *Ward 's Business Directory*
  Offers thumbnail sketches of both publicly and large privately held companies.

- *Standard & Poor's Register of Corporations, Directors, and Executives*
  Lists information on over 45,000 firms.

- *Everybody's Business*
  Descriptions of a large number of U.S. companies, including histories.

- ***Reference Book of Corporate Managers***
  Brief biographies of executives in major U.S. firms.

- ***Who's Who in Finance and Industry***
  Biographical information on leading North American executives.

- ***World Business Directory***
  Profiles on firms around the world engaged in international trade.

Corporate Annual Reports

All publicly held firms produce these for their stockholders, and many libraries keep these on hand. Annual reports provide a wealth of information, including performance in the past year, financial data, and future plans. If you can't find the report you need in the library, you can often obtain one by writing to the public information office at the company in which you are interested.

Professional and Trade Organizations

There are numerous professional and trade organizations which can provide you with information about firms in specific segments of our industry. The names and addresses of some of these organizations are listed in Chapter 6, Table 6.2.

Informational Interviews

An informational interview is one in which a job seeker makes an appointment with a department head, human resource manager, or other manager at a firm or operation in which they may have an interest. The purpose of this interview is for you to gather information, so make sure that you have prepared a comprehensive list of questions in advance – not too comprehensive, however, because you need to be mindful of the person's time.

The average informational interview should not take more than 30 minutes, and you should not expect it to lead to a job offer. However, you should realize that by asking for and participating in this type of interview, you are making a contact which could potentially harm or hurt you. Therefore, it is important to present yourself in a professional way which includes proper dress, etiquette, and well-planned questions. Also, keep in mind that you may not always be successful in securing an appointment. If you don't already know it, managers in this industry are very busy people, and while most genuinely want to help others get started, operational and other concerns are at the top of their priority list.

Electronic Sources

There are basically two sources of electronic information about businesses and industry – CD-ROM products and on-line databases. CD-ROMs contain databases, information on specific companies and industries, and many of the directories listed earlier. You will find that many libraries offer access to these. On-line information services are also often quite useful. Many professional groups and industries maintain databases and other information. Some offer free access; others do not. Therefore, you should be selective. Also, as we said earlier, many companies now have home pages, and the number is growing daily.

Other Sources

As final sources, we suggest two other fact-finding alternatives: 1) go visit an establishment, and 2) talk with employees. These methods won't necessarily get you the corporate information you need, but they will provide you with information such as level of service, employee satisfaction, and operational procedures. This can help you evaluate your desire to work for the organization, provide you with points of discussion should you interview with this company, and give an interviewer a sense that you have done your homework.

DOWN TO BASICS – JOB SEARCHING AND INTERVIEWING

Now that you have some tools – a resumé, a cover letter, and company and industry information – it's time to get down to the basics of looking for a job and securing an interview. First, we'll take a look at where to find jobs and then we'll explore ways to land those jobs.

Jobs – Where to Find Them

There are, of course, numerous ways to look for a job and we suggest that you use more than one. In this way, you will find the job and company that's right for you and the organization will find someone that wants to work there and is not just merely looking for a job! What a match! Let's take a look at a few sources you can use in your search.

On-Campus Placement Services

If you are presently a student, you should definitely make use of on-campus recruiting services. Most colleges and universities offer extensive placement services and many hospitality and tourism programs solicit firms to interview on campus. Generally, firms that come to campus to interview are familiar with the program and past successes of graduates, and know many of the faculty members. This means they *want* to be there and this puts you at a decided advantage.

The rules for on-campus recruiting are becoming stricter. Students are frequently required to submit resumés on disk, sign up early, and show up when they sign up. Make sure you find out what the rules are and follow them to the letter. Also make it a point to visit your campus placement center from time to time so that you are aware of who is coming to campus *when* and *what* the sign-up times are.

Of course, on-campus recruiting is not the only source of jobs. Companies that recruit on campus do so for a variety of reasons including their ability to pay for recruiters to travel, preference for particular schools, and previous experience with interviews on that particular campus. Therefore, it makes no sense to confine your search solely to on-campus sources unless you are one of the few who finds their dream job with the company of their choice and needs to look no further.

Job Fairs

Job or career fairs are often sponsored by institutions, professional organizations, and trade associations. Usually, these fairs involve a number of companies maintaining booths to provide information, to collect initial candidate information, and sometimes to conduct initial screening. Depending upon how you use job fairs, they can be very valuable tools in your job search. To begin with, don't expect to get hired on the spot. Job fairs aren't designed for that.

Rather, they are designed for companies to provide information about their firm and the career opportunities they offer and allow their representatives to make contact with prospective applicants. Use these opportunities to find out as much as you can about various companies, their employment needs, and their training programs.

You may even fill out an application blank or drop off your resumé. It is important to remember that the number of attendees can range from the hundreds to the thousands. Obtain a business card from the representative and follow-up with a letter re-stating your interest. Don't forget to enclose another copy of your resumé!

Networking

Networking is concerned with making contacts with people who can help you in your job search both today and in the future. It is not, however, concerned with insincerity and using people. Done right, networking can help you know about present and future positions and can help you get referrals. However, always keep in mind that networking is a two-way street. You not only receive leads and referrals, but you will eventually give them as well, so you need to employ proper follow-up etiquette such as thank you notes to keep your network going and growing.

So, how do you network? The goal of networking is to expand your base of contacts. We have already discussed several ways to do this including informational interviews, job and career fairs, and talking to employees. There are several other ways, and we will discuss a few of these below.

- **On the Job Contacts**
  Many of you are already working in positions in the hospitality and tourism industry. This may be a front-line job, an internship, or a managerial position. While you may or may not be in the most senior position, your present job can serve as a launching pad for making mutually rewarding contacts which can help you in the future. It's a pretty safe bet that at least some of your co-workers are as career minded as you are, and developing business relationships with them can be a real help! Also, your organizational superiors who serve as role models and mentors can also be a valuable source of future referrals.

- **Alumni Associations**
  Both institutions and hospitality and tourism programs have alumni associations. Some of these are more active than others but if your school or

program has an active alumni association, use it. Those who have gone before you make excellent contacts and they have an interest in promoting their alma mater.

- *Student Organizations*
  Frequently, student organizations in hospitality and tourism units sponsor guest speakers, tours, and the like. These are excellent opportunities to meet people and to collect business cards for future reference.

- *Professional Associations*
  Many professional associations such as Meeting Planners International (MPI) offer student memberships. Still others such as Club Managers Association of America (CMAA) sponsor student chapters on campus. For students, these provide an excellent opportunity to learn more about a given field and to meet practicing professionals. If you are not a student, joining professional organizations and being active in them keeps you in touch with your field and provides excellent networking opportunities.

We have listed a few of the many ways in which you can make contacts and use networking to obtain leads, meet others, and expand your professional knowledge. Like a lot of things, however, networking is not a passive or a one-shot process. You have to make it work for you and you need to continue to build your network throughout your career. Showing up late and leaving early at a professional gathering is a waste of time. So is not introducing yourself to guest speakers after class. By the same token, beginning to network when you need a job is not likely to be fruitful because it takes time to build the relationships necessary to make this activity pay off. As we said earlier, networking may have a payoff, but if that's your only reason for doing it, you probably won't be successful. So no matter where you are in your career, start building your network now.

Advertisements

Trade journals and newspapers are filled with ads for various positions. It would seem that this would be an excellent source for getting hired. It isn't. Experts believe that only about one in ten job seekers land a job this way. The reason for this has to do with timing and the fact that many ads are designed to attract resumés for future use. Still, 10% does not exactly constitute bad odds, so keeping in touch with the job market in this way could be useful.

Human Resources vs. Department Heads

Many writers suggest bypassing the human resource department and contacting a department or division head who has the authority to hire. This can work for you and it can work against you. True, the human resource department sometimes simply recruits and screens candidates for future needs, but often, particularly in the case of hotels, they also recruit for immediate needs as well. Probably, the best rule of thumb is this: If you know who to contact in an operating department or division, send your resumé to them *and* to the human resources department. This covers you from both ends and makes sure that you don't offend anyone.

The Interview – Your Chance To Shine

Although the opportunity to interview on campus may be more or less automatic, landing an interview through other types of job searches is no small feat. It means that somebody has read your resumé, is interested in your qualifications, and believes that you might be a viable hiring candidate.

In either case, the employment interview has a number of purposes. First, of course, is to learn more about you, particularly about those things that cannot be determined from your resumé – your social interaction skills and the way you dress, for example. The second purpose is to question you to determine how well you would mesh with the firm and the position. Third, believe it or not, is to sort you out – to find out what's **wrong** with you!

Keep in mind that once you have reached the interview stage, all candidates look pretty much like you on paper. One goal of interviewing is to eliminate people from the pool of qualified job seekers. As a result, one *faux pas* – one mistake – can remove you from the list of candidates. This means that you have to prepare yourself intellectually, psychologically, and even physically for your interview. It's your chance to shine, but it's also your chance to fail, so don't try to wing it.

Types of Interviews

Interviews differ widely according to their purpose and the techniques employed to interview you. Generally, there are three types of interviews: 1) the screening interview; 2) the selection interview; and 3) the hiring interview.

The screening interview is just that – a short and structured interview designed primarily to determine if you are a viable candidate, sort of an enhancement to your resumé. Some hospitality and tourism firms use on-campus interviews as screening devices. If you make the cut, you are invited back for a longer, more intensive and probing interview. This can either be an intermediate step leading to a final interview or it can be the interview at which a hiring decision is made.

The selection interview, as we just said, can either be an intermediate or final step. Its purpose is to take a second look at you to probe deeper into your suitability and to allow you to ask more informed questions. Frequently, this interview is conducted by a different person than interviewed you initially and often it is less formal and more relaxed. Sometimes, too, you will be asked to visit an outlet operated by this organization and to talk with the manager before your second interview. Make sure you do. If this second interview is the final interview, it is the time to bring up issues such as salary and benefits.

Sometimes, there is a third interview which is frequently called a hiring interview. Unlike the screening and selection interviews, the primary purpose of this third interview is to finalize matters. The decision to hire you has pretty much been made and if your interviewing process goes this far, this is the time to bring up matters such as salary, conditions of employment, and fringe benefits.

Interview Techniques

Interview techniques also vary widely. In the first interview, however, many employers use a technique called focused interviewing. This method is based on the idea that past behavior is the best predictor of future behavior. The interviewer takes great care to ensure that the interview is objective and assesses your job related capabilities by focusing on specific examples of your past performance. Interviewing follows a rather predictable pattern.

First, the interviewer attempts to put you at ease, explains the procedure, and asks questions to clarify background information. Most interviewers then ask questions to gather the information they need. Several basic types of questions are used. (A list of typical questions appears in Appendix 3.2.) Open-ended questions such as, "Tell me what you liked best about being a tour guide," are designed to allow you to elaborate and to gather information about your motivations, likes, dislikes, communication ability, and so forth. Pretty sneaky, huh?

Another type of open-ended question is sometimes called a behavioral question. It might be phrased like this: "Tell me about a leadership role you held. What was your greatest challenge? How did you meet it?" Obviously, this type of question is designed to test how you have handled things in the past. Since more and more interviewers are using these types of questions, you had better be prepared for them with specific examples. Typical areas for behavioral based questions include:

- integrity
- time management
- customer service orientation
- leadership
- ability to be a team player
- how you handle conflict
- how you solve problems
- how you make decisions
- how you deal with stress

Closed-ended questions requiring a short answer or a *yes* or *no* answer are used to gather information or clarify points. It is important to be sensitive to the difference between open-ended questions and questions requiring only a brief answer. If you respond briefly to an open-ended question and don't provide examples, the interviewer will not get the needed information. On the other hand, by elaborating when the question simply calls for a brief response, you can turn off the interviewer and you can waste valuable time destroying the plan for the interview.

Finally, many interviewers make use of encouragement and silence. Encouragement terms like *that sounds difficult* are designed to get you to open up – to tell more. Don't waste the opportunity by saying, "Yeah, it was." Go further. Say why the situation was difficult and how you handled it. Also, interviewers will often ask a question and then remain silent. This doesn't mean they are trying to put you on the hot seat or to make you feel awkward. More often, all they are trying to do is to give you time to think and to respond fully.

Preparing for an Interview

Since each interview will be different and since, in a certain sense, each interview will be the same, careful preparation is necessary for each and every interview you have. You can prepare for interviews by following the steps below:

1) Review your research on the company or organization. Jot down notes and make sure that you are familiar with the company.

2) Anticipate questions based on what you say in your resumé and prepare and practice answers to them. Also, anticipate questions based on what you know about the company. For example, "Where would you consider relocating?" or "Where do you see yourself in five years?"

3) Consider your strong points as well as your weaknesses. Be prepared to sell your strengths and to respond to probes designed to uncover your weaknesses.

4) Practice answering the sample questions listed in Appendix 3.2. Make sure you are able to include specific examples for open-ended questions.

5) Develop a list of three to five questions which you might like to ask the interviewer. They should relate to the company and demonstrate your knowledge. You may not use them all but you should be prepared. Examples of these are also included in Appendix 3.2.

6) Decide what you will wear to the interview and make sure that this clothing is in good condition – clothes are clean and pressed and shoes are shined.

What To Wear

First impressions are lasting, so what you wear and how you present yourself can actually make or break the interview from the start. As recently as the 1980s, dark, conservative suits and white shirts or blouses were standard interview attire. In fact, most of our students back then owned what they called *interview suits*. Today's standards are a bit less stuffy, but still tend to be conservative. The following guidelines are designed to help.

Women

✓ Wear conservative clothing. This doesn't necessarily have to be a suit – blazers and skirts or tailored professional dresses are fine; but when in doubt, wear a suit.

✓ Avoid navy blue or gray suits – they are drastically overused. Choose colors that are conservative and which flatter you.

✓ Keep hem lines no higher than one inch above the knee.

✓ Wear the best quality clothing you can afford.

✓ Make sure your nails are well manicured.

✓ Avoid fragrance.

✓ Keep jewelry to a minimum and make sure it is not flashy or distracting.

✓ Wear dark, well-polished shoes.

✓ Wear a neutral shade of hosiery and make sure that they have no runs.

Men
✓ Wear a professional suit – dark, solid colors are the best.
✓ Wear a solid color shirt – white or pastel only.
✓ Keep ties conservative.
✓ Make sure your belt color matches your shoe color.
✓ Avoid fragrance.
✓ Make sure your hair is neat and trimmed.
✓ Facial hair? This is a conservative industry.
✓ Wear dark, well-polished shoes.
✓ Wear dark, over-the-calf socks.
✓ Keep jewelry to a minimum.

The Big Day

If you have prepared properly for your interview, this day should be no big deal. The following can help you be at your best and make the most effective presentation of yourself. In other words, these suggestions can help you to shine.

➡ **Be on Time**
This may sound obvious, but it is a rule that is frequently broken and which some people feel is okay to break because they have a good excuse. Sure, traffic can be bad or parking places tough to find, but these are not acceptable excuses. You should plan to arrive at least 15 minutes early and if you run into problems, instead of being early, you will be on time.

➡ **Present a Positive Attitude**
Be friendly, straightforward, and at ease. If you have done your homework and have the proper qualifications, this should be easy to accomplish. Also, keep in mind that the interviewer doesn't want you to be subservient, timid, or uncomfortable. These are turn-offs. You really have nothing to lose because you don't have the job yet anyway, so be positive. If you are not selected, there will always be other opportunities.

➡ **Shake Hands Firmly and Warmly**
This speaks for itself. If the interviewer doesn't offer his hand offer yours anyway.

➡ *Smile!*
Friendliness is a desired attitude. A smile conveys an attitude of liking people. After all, this is an interview, not an interrogation!

Be Prepared for the Big Day!

➡ *Project A Professional Image*
Use good posture, clear speech, and maintain eye contact. Also, answer questions in a straightforward and positive fashion.

➡ *Emphasize Your Strengths with Examples*
Don't just say you are a good leader but say *why* and give an example of *how* you have been one in the past. Don't be afraid to get specific here.

➡ *Think Before You Speak*
Take a couple of seconds to make sure you understand the question and to phrase the most positive and clear response. If you don't understand the question, ask the interviewer to rephrase it. Here, you can ask something like, "Would you mind rephrasing that because I'm not clear on the question?" or "Do you mean my job at ABC Company or at XYZ Company?" Incorporate the information you found in your company

research into your responses. There will be opportunities to do this throughout the interview. Take advantage of them, but remember not to overdo it!

✖ ***Don't Take Control of the Interview***
As a rule, the interviewer will spend 75 - 80% of the time asking you questions and leave 20 - 25% of the time for your questions. Answer questions completely, but do not stray from the subject and do not give excessive detail.

✖ ***Don't Talk about Salary and Benefits***
These usually are brought up in subsequent interviews. If the interviewer brings them up, that's a different matter.

✖ ***Don't Bad-Mouth Previous Employers***
Whatever you do, avoid discussing personality conflicts, impossible work situations, incompetence of previous supervisors, etc. If you are asked why you left a job, turn it into a positive such as "I had an opportunity to gain experience in a full-service facility."

Your interview should be a positive experience – the final stage of your job search. But, win or lose, if you have prepared properly and have performed your homework, you have done a good job!

FOLLOW-UP ETIQUETTE

Your follow-up to the interview is actually the end of the job search process. A personalized thank-you note should be sent within 24 hours of the interview – whether by snail-mail or overnight delivery. A good thank-you note has three parts: 1) express your thanks for the interview; 2) restate why the firm should hire you; and 3) offer to provide additional information if needed.

In the *thank you* line, thank the interviewer for his time and for the company's interest in your skills and potential. Then repeat the *thank you* at the end of the letter.

The second section needs to personalize you to the interviewer and should recap your strengths and your match with the firm. No longer is it enough to write "Thank you for the interview. I look forward to hearing from you soon." Rather, you must make it clear that ***you*** are the one they want. Restate the job requirements and suggest that your background and career plans match perfectly.

If the interviewer had any qualms about hiring you, address these directly in the letter. For example, if the interviewer was concerned about your lack of experience with their specific property management system, why not include a line such as "Although I have not used the XX property management system, my mastery of Microsoft Word 6.0 and Excel prepare me well for other applications." Be direct, be honest, and, most of all, act confident (even if you aren't)!

The third and last section of the note should offer additional information for the interviewer. A succinct "If I can provide you with any additional information regarding my education or experience, please let me know" will suffice. It leaves the lines of communication between you and the interviewer open and lets the interviewer know that you are willing to help in the hiring process if necessary.

It is entirely appropriate to call the interviewer after one or two weeks to check on the status of your employment. Remember, they have already invested time and interest in you and it is expected that you will follow up. If you have to leave a voice mail or a message, clearly state who you are, the nature of your inquiry, and leave your telephone number and a good time to contact you.

Good etiquette shows prospective employers that you will also be respectful on the job and its importance cannot be overstated. It takes just a few minutes to write a thank-you note and the omission of one could cost you the job!

SUMMING IT UP

Although the steps required to market yourself and get a job – assessing goals; inventorying your strengths and weaknesses; writing a resumé; composing a cover letter; researching companies; interviewing; and following up – may seem overwhelming right now, there is really no other way. If it's any consolation, all career professionals have been through the same process and they survived! If you start your job search early, are diligent, and use every opportunity available to showcase you, you will be pleased with the offers that could come your way.

But, remember, successful job searching is an on-going process. Periodically revisit your goals – are they still important to you? Continually assess your strengths and weaknesses – are there areas in which you should improve? Keep your resumé current – you never know when you might need or want it. Always keep up on industry trends and **network, network, then network some more**! No job is forever and you need to be ready for the next step.

ACTION WORDS

Adjectives

Capable	Courteous	Determined	Effective
Efficient	Ethical	Exceptional	Friendly
Goal-Oriented	Helpful	Important	Lasting
Loyal	Mutual	Permanent	Pleasing
Polite	Practical	Proficient	Reliable
Responsible	Satisfied	Simplified	Skilled
Substantial	Superior	Useful	Vital

Verbs

Accomplished	Advanced	Assisted	Balanced
Built	Coached	Conducted	Developed
Evaluated	Focused	Generated	Improved
Initiated	Integrated	Launched	Manages
Marketed	Negotiated	Organized	Planned
Prepared	Presented	Produced	Purchased
Reduced	Researched	Restructured	Reviewed
Shaped	Streamlined	Strengthened	Supervised
Supported	Trained	Transformed	Upgraded

KEY WORDS

Airline	Banquets	Bartender	Catering
Controller	Conventions	Culinary	Food and Beverage
Food Service	Front Desk	Front Office	Guest Interaction
Guest Service Agent	Hospitality Degree	Hotel	Hotel Degree
Housekeeping	Human Resources	Leadership	Lodging
Management	Manager	Marketing	Meeting Management
Motel	Production	Reservations	Restaurant
Restaurant Degree	Sales	Service	Supervisor
Team Player	Tourism	Travel	Travel Agent

APPENDIX 3.2
QUESTIONS MOST OFTEN ASKED DURING INTERVIEWS

Most Often Asked by Interviewers

- What goals have you set for yourself? How are you planning to achieve them?
- Who or what has had the greatest influence on the development of your career interests?
- What two or three things are most important to you in a position?
- Tell me about a project you initiated.
- How do you solve conflicts? Tell me about a time when you solved one.
- What work experience has been the most valuable to you and why?
- Describe the project or situation that best demonstrated your analytical skills.
- What are your team-player qualities? Give an example.
- In a particular leadership role you had, what was the greatest challenge?
- How have your educational and work experiences prepared you for this position?

Most Often Asked by Person Being Interviewed

- How many individuals complete your training program each year?
- What career paths have others generally followed after completing the training program?
- How does the position and the department contribute to the overall company mission and philosophy?
- Does the position offer exposure to other facets of your organization?
- How much decision-making authority and autonomy is given to new employees?
- Are employees ever transferred between functional areas?
- What is the greatest challenge your organization faces during the next year?
- How often is it necessary to relocate?

Compiled from the *Northwestern Lindquist-Endicott Report* (The Placement Center, Northwestern University, 1991).

ADDITIONAL READINGS

50 Ways To Get Hired, Max Messmer; John Boswell Associates (1994).

The Job Search Handbook, John Noble; Bob Adams, Inc. (Holbrook, Massachusetts, 1988).

Make Your Job Interview A Success, J.I. Biegeleisen; Macmillan General Reference (New York, 1994).

The On-Line Job Search Companion, James C. Gonyea; McGraw-Hill, Inc. (New York, 1995).

The Perfect Cover Letter, Richard H. Beatty; John Wiley & Sons (New York, 1989).

Resumés That Knock 'Em Dead, Martin John Yale; Bob Adams, Inc. (Holbrook, Massachusetts, 1988).

FROM SCHOOL TO CAREER

In the first section, we stressed preparation for a career in the hospitality and tourism industry. We shared information on the industry, its realities, and where it is likely to be heading. We talked about the concept of career paths and how you could plan one for yourself. Finally, we dispensed advice (whether you wanted it or not) on the ways to track down and land jobs.

In the second section, we get "up close and personal." Why? Because getting prepared for a career, while not easy, involves making a personal transition. Regardless of your age and experience with life and work, transitions are not easy. Section Two deals with both the professional and personal realities of making the switch from school to the work you have been preparing for.

PROFESSIONAL REALITIES

If you are like most hospitality and tourism students, you accumulated quite a bit of work experience both before you started school and while you attended school. More than likely, you picked up some skills and, through observation, you might have noticed some organizational peculiarities. You had some good experiences and many of you may also have had some bad ones.

Experience is a great teacher and you probably learned a great deal. However, you are now embarking on your first professional job and the realities of that are, well, just different. You are no longer "just a student" gaining experience, you are a professional worker starting a career. Everything you do from now on counts even though it isn't on the exam.

If you choose, for example, a management path, you will be tested by both those you supervise as well as by those who supervise you. You will be assigned both routine tasks and non-routine projects and high quality results will be expected. You won't be told how to proceed by a step-by-step instruction book, either! You will be expected to be part of a team and, more often than not, *you* will have to find a way to fit into that team and not the other way around. Yes, you will have to deal with organizational politics on a level you probably haven't been exposed to before, and you will become aware of the fact that ours is a dues-paying business – in fact, it is quite rare to find an individual who can escape paying dues.

On another front, you will discover that even though you have finished school, you will need to continue to develop if you are to have a career. You will need to find out what success means *for you* and design a professional development plan accordingly. Also, you will become aware of the fact that no one is going to plan your career for you. Not only is professional development your responsibility, but the quality of your plan and the extent to which you carry it out will have a profound influence on the quality of both your professional and personal lives.

CONCERNING THIS SECTION

Professional transitions also mean changes in your personal life. You may experience a substantial pay increase but, in reality, it may put you just above the poverty line. How do you select a place to live and sustain yourself on your new salary? You may also find yourself relocating to a new city. How do you make friends and find happiness in a different location? Do you stay put or do you relocate? Anther personal challenge you may face is striking a balance between your personal life and your work life.

The goal of this section is to address some universal concerns about making the transition from school to your first professional job in the hospitality and tourism industry. Some topics may be very important to you, whereas others may not apply because you have "been there and done that." Still, there is something of value for everyone faced with a school-to-work transition in this section, and we encourage you to take full advantage of the information provided.

Chapter 4 is designed to give you insight as to what professional realities to expect on a new job. It covers topics like establishing yourself, attitude, organizational politics, and paying your dues. Chapter 5 will help you overcome some common personal obstacles – pay, budgeting, relocation, avoiding pitfalls, and achieving balance are among the topics discussed. Chapter 6 introduces you to professional development and to the fact that this is a career-long process. We discuss definitions of success, determining development needs, and designing and using a professional development plan.

CHAPTER
4

THE FIRST JOB AFTER GRADUATION: PROFESSIONAL REALITIES

"I find that the harder I work, the more luck I seem to have."

Thomas Jefferson

By now, you probably think that you are well prepared for your first job after graduation. You have more or less mastered the theory and practice required to earn a certificate or diploma; you probably have performed at least a couple of jobs within the hospitality and tourism industry; and you have already targeted your *preferred* companies.

The problem with all this preparation is that **it is never enough**! Although a formal education is important, most colleges and universities do not teach the nuts and bolts of day to day practice – nor should they. In classroom situations, you do a specified amount of work or learn a certain amount of material in order to earn a grade. The traditional grading system often rewards students who participate in class and excel in test-taking.

You have the opportunity to prepare to participate and, possibly, you have planned the exact day on which you will gain extra points and prepared for that moment well in advance. And, *hopefully*, you have never taken a test without studying beforehand, or at least reviewing your notes or text book in advance. Some of your teachers or professors require you to analyze cases in class. You usually have a lot of time to prepare your analysis, and then present it to a captive audience – your peers and your instructor. Throughout college or university, you have almost always had time to prepare. You are never expected to answer each question perfectly, complete a final exam within fifteen minutes, or propose a detailed strategic solution to an operational problem within an hour.

The tide is rising and rising quickly! Although the theoretical and practical bases you learned will be invaluable to you in your career, you still need to *do it*. Remember the adage that experience is the best teacher? Well, it is true. Your education will supplement your career, but there is no substitute for actual experience. Until you have had to make critical decisions such as those which pit the revenue of your operations against the morale of your employees, you have not yet "been there." No amount of education can prepare you for the harsh realities of the workplace, but at least there are tools that can lessen the struggles and, hopefully, minimize the chances for and the severity of mistakes.

First, you must realize that you are the new kid on the block and will be treated as such – at least for a while. This requires some expertise in dealing with supervisors, subordinates, and co-workers. Next, it is important that you adopt an attitude of *I want to learn*, not *I already know*. Also, you must realize the importance of organizational politics to your career. Although it is tempting to ignore them or discount their importance – **don't**. Finally, it is *really* true that you need to pay your dues. Rarely does a recent college graduate with only two years of industry experience get promoted to regional manager of a restaurant chain. You need to learn how to perform your job as well as the jobs of others and you need to understand financial statements and strategic plans.

In short, you need to be seasoned. And for now, **you need to be patient**.

THE NEW KID ON THE BLOCK

One of the most difficult parts of a new job is to experience the *new kid on the block* effect. Many of your co-workers will have been at your new place of employment for years – some for two and others for twenty. They already know their jobs well and have established a circle of colleagues. They have survived down-sizing, management turnover, financial difficulties, and possibly corporate takeovers or restructuring.

How can you fit in when they have all this shared history? Don't worry, it is *not* hopeless. Fitting in can be difficult at first, but with a little bit of effort on your part, you can quickly establish your dedication and commitment to the operation. In your new job, you must deal with your supervisors, subordinates, and co-workers, and each calls for a unique strategy in order to become a full-fledged team member. You have a distinct hierarchical relationship with each one of these groups and must approach each one differently.

Dealing with Supervisors

Your supervisors in your new position undoubtedly have more experience than you, especially in the managerial ranks. If they survived the first few months in their first job after graduation, so can you!

You were hired for your potential to succeed, as well as for your education and experience, so you already know you are valued by the firm – otherwise, you would not be there. You will probably be cautious, a bit scared, and extremely excited. Be careful, though, not to seem too eager at first. By this, we mean that you should not attempt to benefit your new bosses by sharing all the knowledge you gained through college within the first few hours on the job. Although you might not agree with certain rules or procedures, there is probably a logical reason for them. Rarely are rules made without some basis, and rarely are procedures developed and adhered to without some relationship to efficiency or quality goals.

There will be plenty of time for you to present your idea for improved efficiency at the front desk, better procurement procedures for the restaurant, or a higher quality employee recruitment program for the convention center. When you begin a job is the best time for you to view the operation without blinders. You probably can see problem areas more clearly since you are new to the operation. However, it is best to keep these observations to yourself until you have the complete picture and are an accepted team member.

Keep a weekly journal of your observations. After a few months, if you still agree that something should be reviewed or changed, then take charge. This will give you time to assess *why* something is being done, *if* it needs to be changed, and *how* to change it. Your ideas will be taken much more seriously if they are well thought out and accompanied by an implementation plan rather than if they are off the cuff and given with no workable solutions. By presenting your ideas at the appropriate time and in the appropriate manner, you will be more respected by your supervisors. This can pay off in terms of recognition and trust in the short term and in terms of more tangible rewards in the longer term.

You also need to show your supervisors that you are a member of the team. The culture in most operations encourages management to work together and to be empathetic to each other. Some companies achieve this by rotating management through departments, so that knowledge and experience of managers is more broad based and they can better understand the importance of *each* department to the entire operation. At the very least, most firms hold weekly or bi-weekly meetings in which management members can voice concerns and develop ideas.

To show that you are a team player, be helpful and ***not harmful***. Stay out of the grapevine – also known as the gossip mill. In fact, stay as far away from it as possible. Gossip is unbelievably destructive to any firm – it can tear apart the team, pollute the corporate culture, and devastate professional and even personal lives. Instead, cooperate with other managers. If you see that a big event is running behind schedule, ask the manager in charge if she needs some extra help. If you see a manager staying late every day for a week, ask him if you can help him on a project. Sometimes, just a few hours of your time can make all the difference.

Finally, when you are assigned a task, do it professionally. When you begin any job, you will probably be assigned some tedious tasks that can be downright boring. Do them thoroughly and **without complaining**. You cannot expect to do only the things that you want to do. Drudgery is part of every job at every level and this is even more true for new kids on the block. Calculating inventory on hand is not anyone's favorite job, but it is necessary in order to determine this month's profit or production efficiency. Scheduling employees is often tedious, but how else will they know when to report to work? As we have already said, no job is all glamour, and most jobs are even less glamorous at the beginning.

You can successfully deal with your supervisors if you follow three simple rules:

1) You do not have to change the workplace within thirty days, so save your ideas until it is proper to discuss them with the appropriate person.

2) Unless you are hired as a turn-around manager, showing dedication to the *team* is everything.

3) Show professionalism in every task you are assigned, regardless of its perceived importance to you or to others.

Dealing with Subordinates

Many new managers find it relatively easy to work with their new supervisors, but have no idea how to motivate people to work for them. You probably took at least one class in human resources management or supervision which gave you a theoretical base. Now, get ready for the practical challenges!

Many non-management employees take great pride in their performance. They have found short-cuts through the years and have developed their own methods to serve the customer. They have developed many habits – some good and possibly some not so good. But, one thing you can count on is they will test you during your first few days on the job. Some will want to become your buddy, while others will view you as just another one of *them*.

Being New Doesn't Need To Be Scary

This is the time to begin establishing your managerial personality. You need to be firm and demonstrate strength, but also need to recognize the skills and talents of the workforce and realize that, sometimes, longevity and tenure has something to offer you. That is, the *we have always done it this way* statement frequently has merit. Chances are good that if something has always been done a particular way, it will continue to be done that way until you are seasoned enough to create change through leadership or until you are in a position to restructure the workplace.

The best advice is to *observe first and not react*. Be wary of subordinates who want to be your pal – friendship at work between those at different levels can be dangerous. Also, be wary of those who treat you like an adversary – the *them* and *us* attitude can be fatal to an operation. Instead, treat every employee equally. You have no preconceived ideas about any of them anyway, so this is the perfect time to begin to practice fairness. Assume that all are excellent workers until they prove differently. Trust their abilities. The operation has been in existence long before you got there, and probably has been quite successful. Something *has* to have been going right in the past!

If you are young, you might find that the age difference between you and your subordinates makes you a bit uncomfortable. After all, you might be the manager of someone who is older than your grandfather. What gives you the right to praise or reprimand him? **Remember, you are now a manager**. Act like one. Just because you reprimand an employee does not mean that you hate him. The best managers can separate their personal selves from their professional selves in this regard. Let the people know that it is their *work* that needs improvement, not them.

If you follow the Three BFs, you will find your transition from college student to manager easier, especially with regard to management/employee relations:

- ✔ **Be Friendly.**
- ✔ **Be Firm.**
- ✔ **Be Fair.**

This may sound trite but it is a tried and tested way of effective leadership, and despite the simple wording, it takes practice and patience to perfect.

Many of us have worked for managers who make us nervous the minute they walk into the room. We have also worked for managers whose moods affected the entire department or operation. Learn from your past experiences and from others' mistakes. Be friendly to *all* employees. This does not mean that you have to invite them over for a weekly barbecue, but it *does* mean that you should smile and *greet each one by name*. Take the time. You will find that you will get a great deal of personal satisfaction as well as positive reactions from this!

Be firm in your decisions. If subordinates question your decision *and* you have the time, explain the logic behind it and let them know that your decision is well thought out and fair. Few people can successfully argue with logic and equity, and most feel more satisfied with a decision if they know the policy behind it.

Finally, be fair. If you get a reputation as a fair manager who never shows favoritism, you will have more satisfied subordinates. Everyone likes to be treated equally and, most of all, **the law requires it**. The days of the "good old boy network" are dying fast. Consistency and fair play are the new names of the game.

The best time to develop a professional reputation is when you first start out. If your employees see you as a team member, a fair manager, and a dedicated and ethical person, they will probably reflect these qualities in *their* work.

Dealing with Co-Workers

When you begin your new job, you will quickly find other new or recent hires on the same hierarchical level as you. Their apprehension and excitement will be similar to yours and they are probably testing the waters, too. As hard as it might be, do not look at your co-workers as competitors. True, they may have similar backgrounds to yours and, in some sense, are your competitors for promotions, raises, and recognitions. However, first and foremost, they are your co-workers and part of the same team. The so-called game of success takes years to play out and it will not serve you well to view your peers as competitors at this early stage in your career. After all, their long-term aspirations are probably quite different from yours!

Again, be part of the team. If co-workers have a stellar idea, let them take the credit for it. Be professional and supportive of their success. After all, you have your own strengths. Trust in them and do your best. There are many opportunities for promotions, and you can all succeed.

Keep in mind that there are many different operational and support areas within your profession. Remain open to new opportunities for growth. Even if all your recent experience was in food and beverage, don't rule out the rooms division of a hotel. If your previous experience was in convention services management, also consider sales and marketing positions or a career in visitors' bureaus. If you have always had your eyes on a career in travel agency management, don't ignore the possibility of opening your own office. Again, there are many opportunities out there in the hospitality and tourism industry. Both your co-workers *and* you can succeed as long as you work as a team and do not limit yourself.

IT'S ALL IN YOUR ATTITUDE

Service is a big business. In fact, the United States Department of Travel & Tourism expects hospitality and tourism to be the world's largest combined industry by the year 2000. You are beginning your career at the right time!

Hospitality and tourism offers myriad opportunities. You can live almost anywhere, travel if you want to, work in a pleasing and even exotic environment, and every day is different. The industry is all about pleasing people through the delivery of quality service. Only through quality service can your operations be profitable and can you achieve your professional potential. However, it requires a **special attitude** to be able to deliver high quality service consistently. This attitude requires you to develop a reliable work ethic, to value the philosophy behind **service**, and to get your hands dirty. This attitude *will* lead to success. Count on it.

What Is a Work Ethic Anyway?

You have probably heard about the Protestant work ethic, but perhaps never understood its roots. The Protestant work ethic came from the belief that hard work would pave one's way to heaven. The truth of the claim is open for debate, but the importance of adhering to a work ethic is not. The hospitality and tourism industry is labor intensive, and that means that you, as a manager, must develop a work ethic that is conducive to hard work, quality performance, and consistent results.

A work ethic means that you value work. You refuse to look for the easy way out and take pride in the results of your work. You look for ways to make the workplace more efficient and stay at work later than scheduled if necessary. Of course, this does not mean that you sacrifice your personal life for your professional life. Later, in Chapter 8, we will talk about the potential dangers of workaholism. Instead, **work hard and work smart**. The payoffs will come.

We ARE in the Service Industry, Aren't We?

Developing a service attitude does not mean that you have to develop a subservient attitude. These are two very different things. You are entering an industry that drives the world economy. Professionalism, politeness, and a smile are *job requirements*. Unfortunately, the service industry has traditionally suffered from lack of understanding and recognition as a *legitimate* profession. Many people worked their way through college by waiting tables or cleaning hotel rooms, but they disregard it as a profession.

Don't fret. As other, more traditional professions including law and accounting become increasingly competitive as jobs become more scarce, you will find that your profession will probably be envied by your friends. After all, you will have a secure career and a constant paycheck. Can they expect the same? As more and more production facilities are closing their doors and as technological advances replace workers in other arenas, the hospitality and tourism industry continues to grow.

In the past, the industry has not kept pace with the sophistication of some other fields, but are now doing so at an accelerated rate. You are a part of this exciting change. Develop the right tools and you will realize both professional and personal fulfillment. **Live it, love it, and believe in it!**

Do I Really Have To Get My Hands Dirty?

Your success also depends on your willingness to work, and that involves getting your hands dirty. After all, if you have never worked as a dishwasher, how can expect to manage in the stewarding area? You need to help out when and where it is needed, and in this field, that often requires you to break down a dish machine, answer some telephones, stuff some envelopes, tear some lettuce, or clean a room.

The service industry is unique in that there is no chance for a repeat performance and no opportunity for you to replace a customer's service experience as you would replace a defective product. In the service industry, production and consumption occur simultaneously. You know quite well by now how hectic and pressured certain events can be, and without everyone chipping in to make it happen, the team is destroyed and the service experience will suffer.

Chances are that you worked hard during your internship as a college student and that you did everything from answering telephones to working in the dish room. The purpose of this experience was so you could see if you truly wanted a career in the service industry. Another purpose of the work experience requirement was so you could do the jobs your future subordinates would do. You don't need to be an expert in pastries or computer programming to be respected by your co-workers, but you *do* need to know how to do it – at least a little bit. There is no better way to become part of the team then to get your hands dirty when needed.

If you move into senior management, you will find that your attention will shift to profit and loss statements and strategic thinking and you might lose touch with the daily operations. Don't let this happen! You do not need to work the line every day, but you need to remember what it's like for people who are paid lower wages to work at sometimes tedious jobs. If you can empathize, you can develop appropriate recruitment, retention, and motivational plans. If you are blind to their work-related frustrations, however, your plans will be unrealistic and ineffective. Keep in touch. Keep your hands in the operations, if only a little bit.

Competent, Hard-Working, Nice People Do Not Finish Last!

Remember your early days in school when children were labeled as "Teacher's Pets"? It connoted something wrong with being a responsible and hard-working student. If you had this label, you probably tried to shake it by adopting certain behaviors that were not quite so perfect. Luckily, your early school days are over, and so are the childish labels that accompany them.

In the real world, competence is rewarded in a variety of ways – by recognition, promotion, pay increases, or transfers. Successful hospitality and tourism managers are the ones who are competent in most things they do, from hiring employees to interpreting the monthly income statements from each department or unit. Of course, they will make mistakes. But they will also minimize the effect of these mistakes by circumventing their potential harm if possible, or by developing a plan to counteract any undesirable effects. They know that they can reduce the frequency of their mistakes if they get complete information *before* making decisions by talking with employees, supervisors, managers, and owners.

Competence drives quality operations. If the manager is competent, chances are she expects the same from her employees and co-workers. Competency is contagious. All you need is a work ethic and some tools, and the rest should follow naturally. Pay attention to any professional development you might require to remain competent in your job and, if necessary, search out continuing education classes or professional seminars to develop yourself in that area. Expect competency from those around you. If you find that an employee cannot perform his job as required by the job description, you should consider training, coaching, and counseling. Disciplinary action should only be a last resort.

Be known as a hard-worker. Your work ethic should be evident to those around you within a few months after you begin your new job. Be known as someone who can be trusted to deliver what they say they will. Do not leave promises unfilled and be direct in your communications.

Hard work *is* rewarded, especially in our semi-capitalistic society. In fact, the entire basis of capitalism is hard work, survival of the fittest, and economies of scale through the most efficient use of limited resources. You are already a limited resource in that you are educated, experienced, and determined. Your hard work will ensure that you will be rewarded in time, and rewarded richly in a variety of ways – such as increased self satisfaction, expanded job responsibilities, and even wage increases.

Finally, don't think that you have to be unapproachable, unyielding, and overly demanding to be effective. You do not have to be invincible and build a wall between you and your co-workers. To show a little compassion is to be human. Machines and technology are great – they can make our personal and professional lives more productive and more fulfilling. BUT, a machine or computer can *never* replace a human being. The concern and understanding one human shows to another, whether at the workplace or at home, separates us from machines.

The most effective managers are those who are not afraid to open part of themselves to their employees and co-workers and who recognize their ability to show emotion as a strength, not a personality flaw. Although you should separate *your* personal life from your professional life as often as possible, you cannot always expect others to do the same.

You will find that many people tend to bring their personal problems to work, either directly or indirectly. A divorce, the death of a family member or friend, or profound financial problems will probably affect their job performance, and you must be patient as the person begins to heal. This does not mean that you should give the person time off with pay while he mends his personal life. Rather, you should try to act as a coach, supporting him in the areas which adversely affect his job performance. Although you never want to assume the role of a professional counselor, you *should* assume the role of a caring and concerned manager.

Do not pry, though. If people have problems, they will come to you if it is appropriate. If it is affecting their job performance, you have every right to speak with the person regarding the problem, but be ready to listen, listen, and then listen some more. Work with troubled employees, try to help them separate their personal and professional lives as much as possible during the crisis, and point them in the right direction to get counseling if they need it. You will most often find that your compassion will be respected and, in turn, employee turnover will decrease and productivity will increase.

Many situations will require you to be firm. It takes time to be able to recognize these situations, but as you progress in your professional career, you should find that this comes naturally. Be cautious at first, though. Do not try to be everyone's friend. Intercede only when appropriate. And again, leave *your* personal life at home. You will be viewed as strong, compassionate, and effective.

ORGANIZATIONAL POLITICS ARE REAL AND YES, THEY DO COUNT!

Organizational politics are as much a part of your daily life at work as your computer, absent employees, and last minute event changes. Some will try to tell you that politics don't matter – wishful thinking. Although we all know that hard work pays off, you will also need to play the political game, whether you want to or not. The trick is to play it in accordance with your *own* rules whenever possible.

No two political cultures are the same. So, size it up *first*, and *then* determine how you are going to act and react. Next, you should choose a mentor to help you through the political maze. A mentor should help your career progress more smoothly and eliminate some of the awkwardness you will invariably experience as you try to be a team member, and be recognized by upper level management at the same time. Finally, learn to avoid the bull in the china shop syndrome. Move through your career with foresight, logic, and without unexpected "breakage" or surprises whenever possible.

Sizing Up the Culture

Politics necessarily imply some interdependence and, logically, the more interdependence within an operation, the more politics contribute to the distribution of power and resources. Your first few weeks in your new job are the time to observe the internal political situation. Don't act, just watch. If you view your new work environment with open eyes, you will be astonished at how quickly you can learn some tools to help you in your career development. Politics and power do not have to be ugly; in fact, they can be useful!

There are different levels of political strength within an operation including individual strength, departmental strength, and unit strength. Each calls for a different role for you to play. The more people are viewed as being irreplaceable, the more power they wield. The better a department performs in respect to other departments, the more likely it is that it will receive a larger increase in the allocation of operating resources. And, more recognition is afforded to its operating and leadership team. The trick is *how* to develop and maintain this power within the confines of individual differences and organizational structures.

Feel Too Small or Too Big for Your Job? Play Attention To Politics!

When you first begin your job, you will quickly notice which department or unit manager is the most respected and the most powerful. Power comes from many sources – position within the firm, performance, access to full information, and timing. These can combine to position you firmly in your career, or can work to negatively affect your promotional opportunities.

Part of playing politics well requires that you attain the necessary skills to succeed. Look at the most successful manager within your operation. Make a list of the activities and skills that you believe sets her apart from other managers. Your list will probably look something like this:

- ✓ Motivates employees to consistently perform at their peak levels
- ✓ Reads a profit and loss statement quickly and thoroughly
- ✓ Spends more time on the floor than in her office
- ✓ Completes reports in a thorough and timely manner
- ✓ Conducts employee performance reviews in a way that motivates
- ✓ Encourages empowerment and recognizes good decisions made from lower levels
- ✓ Praises employees openly and often
- ✓ Disciplines employees privately
- ✓ Performs under pressure without losing concentration or control

Most of these actions **can be learned**. Once you notice them, try them out yourself. Practice reading financial statements. Commend an employee who has done a good job. Count to ten rather than lose your temper on the job. You will find that these activities and skills can become good habits after a few months.

Language, Actions, Timing, and Positioning of Leaders

A few successful political behaviors stand out regardless of one's profession within the industry: using the right language, acting like a manager, and remembering that both timing and positioning is important.

Learn to use the right language – language is important in exercising influence. Effective language skills can be used to present proposals in a clear and concise manner, to explain job expectations to a confused employee, and to calm an angry customer. They can also be used to take the pain out of corporate transitions. You probably know about the down-sizing within hotel industry during the late 1980s and early 1990s. Did you ever hear it referred to as "mass lay-offs"? Probably not, since down-sizing is a much more civil and palatable term.

Learn to articulate your thoughts clearly. Practice positive word choices – coined phrases are entirely appropriate if they help take out the sting. Use the word *we* instead of *I* and the word *us* instead of **them**. Change the tone of your language, and you will find that your political reputation of power changes with it.

You can begin to develop your language skills by joining a nearby chapter of Toastmasters, International. Toastmasters provides an outlet for people to learn how to influence people through language and can provide you with plenty of practice and feedback. Dale Carnegie courses can also help you improve your speaking skills and self confidence.

Your actions, even at the beginning of your job, will also influence the power you have within the organization. You need to be a manager who can recognize the need for change and constructively promote it when necessary. Your actions should reflect your ability to adapt, to lead, and to be fair. Act like a leader and you will become one.

Timing is also important to success. Good timing is not solely a product of luck. Rather, it comes from a combination of *a little bit* of luck and *a lot* of observation, insight, and action. Actions that are well-timed have an infinitely better chance of succeeding than actions that are undertaken at a less opportune moment.

Sometimes, you will have to delay your actions in order to succeed. For example, if you developed a proposal for the introduction of a new vegetarian item which can bring a high margin throughout all 100 units in your firm, do not introduce it when produce costs are extremely high. Other times, you will have to act quickly. If you have an idea for implementing a new follow-up procedure for the tour operators who use your agency, and if your agency has been experiencing a lot of complaints regarding your firm's services, introduce the proposal immediately as a way of improving services and increasing the bottom line. Be aware of the changing environment around you and think before you act. With some practice, you will begin to learn when the time is right and when it's not.

Finally, positioning can help you excel within your operation and your profession. If you have a choice, do not choose your first employment location near the South Pole if your firm's regional or national offices are near the North Pole. Chances are that visits from upper level management will be rare and you may not be noticed as quickly. If you can, start out at a location that already employs some superstar managers. You can not only learn from them, but you can increase your own visibility since you will be a part of the proven *Dream Team*.

An opposite, but equally effective, strategy is to start out at a troubled operation. If you can help to turn the operation around and make it profitable, you will undoubtedly get recognized and promoted. In short, be where the action is *or* where you can make the action occur!

Choosing a Mentor

Don't think that you can go it alone. Organizations are often large, interdependent, and complex. They can be overwhelming at times since they take on their own personalities and make their own written and unwritten rules. Choosing a mentor with experience and some organizational power can be a very easy way for you to learn the secrets of success and avoid potential pitfalls. A mentor is not necessarily a friend, but is a professional confidant. A mentor is there to answer your questions, give you advice, and help you plan your career. Now, how do you choose the best mentor for you?

Sometimes, mentorship relationships are developed by accident. You might be placed in a distressed unit with a seasoned turn-around manager. The stress of turning the operation from a loser to a winner might just be the catalyst which helps you to develop a mentorship relationship with the manager.

Many larger firms have formal mentorship programs that are quite effective. Some mentorship relationships are promoted by professional associations which match someone new to the profession with someone who is more seasoned. Still other mentors are developed intentionally by either party.

You might identify someone within your operation or organization with whom you want to be identified and from whom you want to learn. Take the initiative and make an appointment with this person or invite him to lunch at your expense. Conversely, you might be chosen to be mentored by an upper level manager or executive. Perhaps this is due to your personal similarities or her opinion of your potential success. If this happens, let *her* take the lead in the professional relationship and then let it take its natural course.

There are a few important and lasting rules that govern all mentorship relationships. Respect your mentor's time, ask questions, listen carefully to the answers, and thank your mentor for the advice. Realize that your mentor also has a job to perform and is probably quite busy. Respect your mentor's schedule and work demands and suggest a meeting only when it is convenient for *both* of you. Ask any questions (you might want to keep an on-going list as you think of them), and listen to the answers. Don't interrupt and, if you disagree, keep quiet.

Your mentor is giving you advice – *not* demanding that you follow it. Finally, remember to thank your mentor for the advice **every time you meet**. Graciousness and manners are just part of a successful professional – show that you have them!

Avoiding the Bull in the China Shop Syndrome

You know the bull in the china shop syndrome – the case in which the customer enters the china shop where everything is displayed in an organized and attractive manner. Well, the customer ends up knocking down china every time he turns a corner, running into display units and breaking valuable pieces. The same thing can happen to you when you begin your career. Be careful of the corners, watch out for the display units, and stay away from breakable things! In other words, keep your eyes open, perform your job carefully and with pride, and don't try to change what already works well.

Keep Your Eyes Open and Be Informed

Always watch what happens around you at work and not just in your immediate work area, but in the *entire* operation or corporation. Read all memos that come across your desk and listen to the lunch room talk. Although the grapevine can be vicious and potentially destructive, it can also be a valuable source of information to you as a manager. Of course, don't believe everything you hear, because much of it is exaggerated and untrue. However, at least it can let you know the feelings of the employees. Most often you will hear the fears and concerns that they are afraid to voice to management directly.

Also, read any information you can regarding other departments, areas, or units within your firm. You can find out who is the best performer and the worst performer, and learn from their successes and failures. You should also use the information as a team-building and career-boosting device.

If you read about a successful retention plan another department implemented, arrange a meeting with the department head and see if your department can implement a similar plan. If you read about a new product another area successfully introduced, why not consider the product in your own area if it's appropriate for your market? If you read about a recent accomplishment of a manager at another unit, give him a congratulatory call or write him a quick e-mail or note.

It is also important that you keep abreast of corporate policy changes and current industry trends. Success is most often a result of action and this information can provide you with reasons to act. Whether you are the first to inform your co-workers of a corporate-wide policy change, or you are proactive in the development of a marketing campaign based on industry-wide information, you will shine. **Subscribe to trade journals and read them**!

Keeping informed makes good business sense. Make it part of every day. It will help you to move throughout your career with grace and success.

Perform Your Job Carefully

Be careful and thorough in your job performance so you do not look like the corporate klutz. Know your job assignments and, if you have any questions, ask your supervisor *before* you begin your work. Ask if there are protocols you should follow to complete the job or project and **follow them**! If you begin every day with the most complete information you can get, you will make fewer mistakes and will have less potential to "run into things."

Give your memos and reports an extra proofread, check the schedule you just developed one more time, and double check any details regarding an event which you are coordinating. Know your potential clients and market as well as you can. Don't be afraid to ask another manager to glance at your work – she could see something you missed. Do your research, check your work, and perform your job carefully.

Don't Break What's Not Already Broken

When you first start out, it is easy to get side-tracked by what *you* think are obvious flaws in the operation. Remember, just like in the china shop where the pieces are displayed in a particular manner for a certain reason, things are organized in your operation for a certain reason. Maybe the reason that the breakfast crew is continually over-staffed is that the operation experiences high absenteeism during that shift. Perhaps the glasses are stored in the overhead storage area rather than at ground level because very little breakage occurs in the unit and the flow space can be better utilized. Perhaps the reason your firm does *not* market to a certain group is that they have been traditionally slow-paying and difficult to please.

This is not to suggest that there isn't always a better way to do something, but it *does* suggest that there are reasons for policies and procedures. Over time, you will learn to prioritize problems and to assess them within the limitations of your available resources.

Some problems are virtually impossible to solve. For example, even if the location of your operation is less than optimal, the major expenses involved in relocation would probably make a move impossible. If your firm is located in a city that experiences a high crime rate, you might feel helpless. Maybe the only thing you can do is to do your best to protect your customers from robberies and assaults while in your establishment and parking lot.

Other problems are solvable, but require expenditures that far surpass the projected increase in revenue. For example, although it might be more efficient to install a new delivery ramp in the back of your store so purveyors could unload your orders quicker, would the installation *really* help your bottom line? Perhaps you discovered a newer and slightly faster computer system, but would the required expense *really* justify the slight time savings for your employees and guests?

Only with experience can you learn to balance your operational wants and needs with your available resources. You will find that some changes can be made immediately and have a quick pay-back period. Other changes are just too expensive and may not really be necessary for organizational efficiency.

The skill of prioritizing does not come easily to most people. However, in time, you will be able to recognize the difference between *important* and *solvable* problems and *unimportant* and *unsovable* problems. You will also be able to research potential solutions and implement them with maximum pay-off to your operation. As with everything in life, it just takes some time and a lot of patience.

A WORD ABOUT PAYING YOUR DUES

Paying your dues is a hard pill to swallow. You have gone to school for at least fifteen years, have worked in hospitality or tourism for at least two years, and now you have to start all over. Know that paying your dues is not just a hazing process – it is a necessary part of your learning and professional development process. Perhaps it would be more appropriately called ***building your career***!

The bright side is that this is the time in your professional life in which you can learn the most. You can grow both professionally and personally in ways that might be hard to imagine right now. The bad side, of course, is that the initiation period is inevitable.

Regardless, view the next period in your life with excitement and learn all you can. If it's any consolation, every other employed person in the world made it through. In no time at all, your adjustment period will be over and you, too, will be a seasoned manager or someone's mentor. When that time comes, remember *your* apprehension and try to help another make it through as easily and successfully as possible!

ADDITIONAL READINGS

Managing with Power, Jeffrey Pfeffer; Harvard Business School Press (Boston, Massachusetts, 1994).

The New Rules, John P. Kotter; The Free Press (New York, 1995).

Reflections for Managers, Bruce Hyland & Merle Yost; McGraw-Hill (New York, 1993).

Service Within, Karl Albrecht; Business One Irwin (Homewood, Illinois 1990).

What They Still Don't Teach You at Harvard, Mark H. McCormack; Bantam Books (New York, 1989).

MAKING IT AFTER GRADUATION: PERSONAL REALITIES

"If you have built castles in the air, your work need not be lost; that is where they should be. Now put foundations under them."

Henry David Thoreau

When you accept your first job offer after graduation, you will undoubtedly experience a sense of both relief and elation. You can finally begin to reap the rewards from the many years you have spent in school. Your sense of achievement at this point is strong and the anticipation of the future will be exhilarating. Your friends and family are quite proud and supportive of you and no doubt share in your excitement. However, this sense of excitement must be tempered with the new realities you will face.

It is very important that you are prepared to meet these challenges realistically, or you may "crash and burn." The major challenges confronting the new hospitality or tourism manager are: realistically assessing your pay; managing your home or apartment; establishing and sticking to a personal budget; minimizing professional and personal pitfalls; balancing the demands of your new career with your personal needs and/or those of your family; and, in general, adjusting to your new professional life.

YOUR PAY AND REALITY

Earlier, in Appendix 1.1, we listed some examples of starting salaries for various segments of the hospitality and tourism industry. You may have noticed that, on average, those salaries range from $20,000 to $22,000. Assuming a *mythical* forty hour work week (pay attention to the word *mythical*), this works out to about $10 or $11 per hour. If you are used to earning $6 or $7 per hour, this is like receiving a 40% raise – even more if you worked only part-time before graduation. However, if you think you are going to be well off, forget it!

First, a professional job is going to *cost* you. Depending on the circumstances, you will be faced with acquiring and maintaining a more expensive and expansive wardrobe, transportation costs might increase, or you might find that increased claims on your time require you to eat out more often. Also, if you have children, you may find that your new job requires increased childcare expenses. Second, the old adage, "The more you make, the more you spend," has at least a little bit of truth to it. Even if you are now part of a dual-income family, an increase in total family income might make what were previously considered luxuries look more and more like necessities.

Furthermore, $22,000 in not always $22,000. Obviously, $22,000 earned in New York City will not stretch as far as it would in Little Rock, Arkansas. If you were offered two jobs with identical titles, responsibilities, and salaries in St. Louis, Missouri, and Pittsburgh, Pennsylvania, a major factor in your decision might involve comparing the purchasing power of your paycheck between the two cities.

Table 5.1 comes from *National Employment Weekly* and is updated frequently. You can use it to compare the cost of living between two or more locations. To compare offers, you would look up the index number for the cities you want to consider as listed in Table 5.1, and then insert the index number and your salary offer into the formula listed below:

$$\frac{City \#1}{City \#2} \quad \frac{(\text{Index \#}) (\text{Starting Salary})}{\text{Index \#}} = \$ \underline{\qquad}$$

Example

What is the Pittsburgh equivalent of a $25,000 salary in St. Louis? In other words, what would you have to make in Pittsburgh to provide the same purchasing power that $25,000 would give you in St. Louis?

$$\frac{Pittsburgh}{St.\ Louis} \quad \frac{(111.2) (\$25,000)}{96.7} = \$ 28,749$$

Put another way, you would need to earn an additional $3,749 per year to have the same life style in Pittsburgh that you could have in St. Louis for $25,000.

TABLE 5.1
Cost of Living Comparisons

STATE/CITY	INDEX	STATE/CITY	INDEX	STATE/CITY	INDEX
Alabama		**Kansas**		**North Carolina**	
Birmingham	100.9	Wichita	96.7	Charlotte	101.6
Montgomery	97.0	**Kentucky**		Raleigh/Durham	98.3
Arizona		Lexington	100.3	Winston-Salem	95.8
Phoenix	102.3	Louisville	91.5	**North Dakota**	
Arkansas		**Louisiana**		Fargo	97.1
Little Rock	90.0	Baton Rouge	101.3	**Ohio**	
California		New Orleans	94.4	Cincinnati	105.8
Los Angeles	126.7	**Maryland**		Cleveland	109.1
Palm Springs	114.8	Baltimore	105.9	Columbus	110.9
San Diego	129.1	**Massachusetts**		**Oklahoma**	
Colorado		Boston	142.1	Oklahoma City	93.3
Colorado Springs	99.6	Framingham	135.3	**Oregon**	
Denver	105.9	**Michigan**		Portland	108.8
Connecticut		Ann Arbor	121.0	**Pennsylvania**	
Hartford	129.1	Detroit	116.6	Philadelphia	127.5
Delaware		**Minnesota**		Pittsburgh	111.2
Dover	107.7	Minneapolis	102.5	**South Carolina**	
District of Columbia		St. Paul	100.2	Charleston	99.8
Washington	135.1	**Missouri**		Columbia	95.2
Florida		Columbia	94.5	**South Dakota**	
Jacksonville	96.4	St. Louis	96.7	Sioux Falls	96.6
Miami	111.8	**Montana**		**Tennessee**	
Orlando	99.0	Billings	103.4	Memphis	98.3
Tampa	98.9	**Nebraska**		Nashville	90.8
Georgia		Lincoln	89.7	**Texas**	
Atlanta	98.4	Omaha	92.4	Dallas	104.4
Augusta	98.4	**Nevada**		Houston	96.7
Idaho		Las Vegas	109.9	San Antonio	94.0
Boise	104.2	**New Hampshire**		**Utah**	
Illinois		Manchester	111.4	Salt Lake City	98.0
Chicago	108.6	**New Mexico**		**Virginia**	
Schaumburg	119.9	Albuquerque	103.9	Richmond	107.5
Indiana		Santa Fe	110.8	**Washington**	
Indianapolis	97.3	**New York**		Seattle	116.2
South Bend	94.0	Buffalo	114.8	Spokane	104.3
Iowa		New York City	208.7	**West Virginia**	
Des Moines	104.2	Rochester	110.6	Charleston	99.6

Adapted with permission from *National Employment Weekly*, 1995.

Finally, $10 or $11 per hour, even if it *is* 40% more than you make now, isn't a lot of money in today's economy. It is still a relatively low salary!

The reality is that unless you are extremely lucky, connected, gifted, **and** blessed, you will not begin your career at a salary which will enable you to purchase a new Lexus, buy ten new suits for work, rent a three-bedroom condominium with a view and security, and vacation in Aruba on your free weekends. Instead, you will be shoved into upper-lower or lower-middle class status, which is not too bad at all as long as you are aware of your financial limitations.

How Can Your Income Meet or Exceed Your Expenses?

The healthiest attitude toward a low salary is to view it as a challenge. A low starting salary is certainly no indication of your earning potential in the hospitality or tourism industry. Instead, it is a realistic estimation of your actual value to your employing firm at this stage of your career. For $20,000, you will not be expected to make strategic decisions, nor will you be permitted to. Instead, the corporation that hires you realizes that first two or three years of your career is an adjustment phase for both of you. You will probably undergo extensive training, which is expensive for your company. You will also make a variety of mistakes, which carries a cost for your employer. However, the company will continue to benefit from your advanced experience and training throughout the years. Logically, as your value to the operation and industry increases, so will your rate of pay.

Let's assume that you just hired a lawyer fresh out of law school to represent you in a landlord-tenant suit. Would you expect to pay this lawyer the same hourly rate you would pay a lawyer who has had twenty years of success in federal district court cases? Of course not. Would you hire an eighteen-year-old cook with no experience at the same rate that you would hire a cook with over ten years of experience? We would hope not!

The differences between the previous examples and *you* at this stage of your professional career are slight. Although you know that the lawyer might someday command at least $200 per hour, she is not worth that now due to her lack of experience. Along the same lines, although you know that the prep cook is going to enter culinary school in the fall in order to become a chef, you also know that he has not yet acquired the skills to justify a high rate of pay.

Even though *you know you are worth it*, depend on your abilities, skills, dedication, ethics, and effort to eventually lead you to the salary level you know you deserve. In two small but powerful phrases: **Be patient! It will happen!**

RELOCATION: FINDING A PLACE TO LIVE

If you relocate upon graduation, finding a suitable place to live in your new city will be one of your first priorities. Unless you have been prudent throughout the years and are prepared to purchase a house, chances are that you will live in a rental unit relatively close to the hospitality or tourism operation that hired you. Sometimes, organizations may offer temporary housing until you find housing of your own. But more often than not, you will be responsible for acquiring your own housing, often in a very short period of time, and sometimes a great distance away from the city to which you are going to relocate.

There are a lot of resources available to assist you in finding an apartment, condominium, duplex, or rental house within your salary range and all should be explored. If you are single, you must make the additional decision of whether or not to have a roommate in order to defray your living expenses. Finally, once you find a place to live, you must set up some semblance of order – a household in which you or you and your partner or family can feel comfortable and safe.

Where To Search for Housing Leads

First, you should inquire at your new place of employment if it is appropriate. Often, the Human Resources Department is a good place to begin. Someone might know of a fellow employee who needs a roommate or of the impending transfer of an employee which will leave a rental unit vacant. If you want to purchase a home, perhaps you can get a referral to a top-notch realtor. Sometimes, the grapevine is a great way of finding a bargain on a home! You might also ask colleagues in your department for leads.

Another valuable resource for apartment hunting is the local newspaper or bulletin boards in grocery stores. Often, you will find good values on apartments, condominiums, and even houses from these advertisements. Most advertisements for rental units are up-front regarding security deposits, permission to have a pet, responsibility for the payment of utilities, and the amenities of the apartment. If you call and the apartment you thought was ideal is already rented, do not be afraid to ask the owners or management company representatives if they know of any comparable places around the area.

The same holds true if you are considering purchasing a home. Often, leads can be found at work, in the local newspaper, or on area bulletin boards. Sometimes, you can even avoid paying real estate commissions if you can purchase the home directly from the owner. Most of all, you now know how small the hospitality and tourism world is – the real estate world is no different. Take advantage of any opportunity to find the best buy.

Another way to find a place to live is seldom used, but is quite logical when you think about it. Go to a few local haunts and just ask! Chances are that if the coffee house has been in existence for two decades or if the diner has been around since World War II, the patrons of these establishments will probably be locals who might just know of the perfect place. Sometimes real estate owners are reluctant to advertise and would rather rent via word-of-mouth and personal referrals. Often, these rental situations are the best since the apartment, condominium, or house has been selectively rented in the past and is probably in excellent condition.

Potential home buyers can also find prospects through local leads. Be wary, though, and have the house thoroughly inspected, since houses that are not sold in the primary real estate market have usually not been inspected by real estate professionals. You should have the electricity, plumbing, foundation, and roof checked as well as the septic system if there is one. Do not take the current owners' word that the house is functionally sound – get it checked out yourself! To make it easier, in all major cities, there are home inspection firms which, for a modest fee, will perform this service. Not only will this small investment buy you peace of mind, it might provide you with bargaining ammunition. Let's say a house you are interested in has a faulty roof which would cost $4,000 to replace. In some soft real estate markets, you might be able to negotiate as much as a $6,000 price reduction from motivated sellers who do not have the time or money to take care of the repair themselves.

Some renters who are located in towns with a university will find that housing listings at the campus housing office are helpful. Be aware, though, that you might end up in the same living environment which you just left – the noisy neighbors, the loud bass on the CD player, and the late night parties on Thursday nights. That might be acceptable while you are in college, but when you have Friday morning staff meetings at 8:00 a.m., the loud party which ends at 5:00 a.m. is no longer tolerable.

It might also be beneficial to inquire about where your predecessor lived, if in fact you had a predecessor. If she was transferred, the apartment is probably vacant and it might be possible to take over the lease and avoid the security deposit. If you can contact this person via telephone, you could also learn about the living conditions in the rental unit. This information might either sell you on the rental or turn you off, but it will most certainly give you an idea of what to look out for when selecting your living arrangements.

To Have a Roommate or Not?

If you are a single professional, the question of whether or not to have a roommate can only be answered after you realistically weigh a number of factors. Some are personal and some are professional, but all are equally important since you will find that both your personal and professional selves markedly affect each other, particularly in the beginning of your career. The variables to consider are the demands and hours of your new job, your need for solitude or companionship, the cost of housing in the area, and the compatibility of your lifestyle with that of others.

You may find that your new job will demand that you work various shifts throughout each month or period in order to learn all aspects of the job. If your initial training period requires you to work 6:00 a.m. - 4:00 p.m. for the first month, 11:00 a.m. - 8:00 p.m. for the second, and 10:00 p.m. - 7:00 a.m. for the third, could you comfortably live with someone who consistently works from 8:00 a.m. - 5:00 p.m.? Varying work schedules of roommates require respect for each other's sleeping, eating, and leisure times. If you must come and go in the wee hours of the morning, be aware that your roommate might not enjoy the refrigerator door opening at 3:00 am, the shower running at 4:00 am, or the door slamming at 5:00 am if her workday runs a normal 9:00 am - 5:00 pm.

Everyone's need for solitude differs from time to time, but you probably know whether you are the type who needs time alone when you feel stress, or if you are the type who would rather share your feelings with a friend. If you get irritated easily when someone interrupts your solitude or when someone demands your ear when you are tired, then perhaps you should consider living alone. On the other hand, if you are good about getting out of bed before the second extra-loud snooze alarm wakes up your roommate and enjoy the company of others outside of work, perhaps you should consider sharing your living environment.

The cost of housing in the area in which you will relocate is a definite factor when deciding whether or not to have a roommate. In the next section, we will discuss personal budgeting and you should read that section carefully before you even consider living alone! If housing costs are high, it may behoove you to have a roommate, at least at first. On the other hand, if housing costs are relatively low, your consumer debt and student loan payments are reasonable, AND you enjoy living alone, you might want to consider going it on your own.

The final factor to examine when you are deciding to share the rent or not is how compatible your lifestyle is with that of others. You might be rather cavalier regarding the cleanliness of your living space in college or in your parents' home. Conversely, you might be a neat-nik, in which case, your tendencies could irritate a roommate who is unlike you in your cleaning habits. You might become very angry when you come home to find the milk still on the counter from your roommate's breakfast and the dishes still on the kitchen table. If you decide to have a roommate, make certain that your lifestyles and living habits are compatible. Yes, we all have habits, regardless of our ages and, yes, those habits are difficult to change, particularly for a temporary roommate with whom you will probably not establish a lasting and deep personal relationship.

The questionnaire below is to be used as a tool to help you decide whether to live alone or whether to have a roommate. It is not all inclusive, but should provide you with a starting point in your decision. Respond to each statement by putting a check mark underneath the response that best describes your work and living habits.

FIGURE 5.1
Roommate or Not?

PART A			
	Usually	**Sometimes**	**Never**
1. My job will require that I work various shifts throughout the week or month.	_____	_____	_____
2. I like to spend my free hours alone.	_____	_____	_____
3. I need someone else in my house to feel safe.	_____	_____	_____
4. I will have to go to work before 7:00 am.	_____	_____	_____
5. I will have to work past 11:00 pm.	_____	_____	_____
6. My living space is disorganized and dirty.	_____	_____	_____
7. I tend to be possessive about my possessions.	_____	_____	_____
8. I like to invite friends over or entertain.	_____	_____	_____
9. I listen to only one kind of music.	_____	_____	_____
10. I like to be alone when I am upset.	_____	_____	_____
11. I prefer to eat meals with someone.	_____	_____	_____

PART B		
	Yes	**No**
12. My utility bills are relatively low or are included in my rent.	_____	_____
13. I will probably be transferred within a year.	_____	_____
14. I own an animal or intend to buy or adopt one within a year.	_____	_____
15. My rent is reasonable.	_____	_____

Tally your responses as directed below and total your score.

➡ For each of statements 1, 4, 5, 6, 8, 9, and 10, give yourself:
   ✓ 1 point if you checked *Usually*
   ✓ 2 points if you checked *Sometimes*
   ✓ 3 points if you checked *Never*

➡ For each of statements 2 and 7, give yourself:
   ✓ 1 point if you checked *Usually*
   ✓ 3 points if you checked *Sometimes*
   ✓ 5 points if you checked *Never*

➡ For each of statements 3 and 11, give yourself:
  ✔ 5 points if you checked *Usually*
  ✔ 3 points if you checked *Sometimes*
  ✔ 1 point if you checked *Never*
➡ For each of statements 12, 13, and 14, give yourself:
  ✔ 1 point if you checked *Yes*
  ✔ 5 points if you checked *No*

➡ For statement 15, give yourself:
  ✔ 1 point if you checked *Yes*
  ✔ 5 points if you checked *No*

What Your Score Means

❱ 52-66 points

You should strongly consider having a roommate and should begin the search early. Your living habits are quite adaptable and you value companionship in your free hours. The search for a compatible roommate can be difficult, but if you follow the same steps as listed in the previous section, you should be successful in a relatively short period of time. Remember, though, it is appropriate and even recommended to ask for personal references! Your new job will be tough enough – you do not need trouble at home, too!

❱ 30 - 51 points:

You will probably be happy with or without a roommate and the choice is all yours! You might want to reexamine your needs and values, particularly those which relate to your financial situation and companionship. If you decide to have a roommate, be wary of sharing an apartment with an employee who is at a different level in the corporation than you are. Difficulties may occur at work which would make it quite uncomfortable at home. Power differences are challenging enough to deal with, so don't put yourself in this potentially difficult position.

❱ 15 - 29 points:

You value your time alone and your lifestyle is not always compatible to that of others. You should probably not have a roommate unless your rent is so high that you have no choice, in which case, you had better be ready to practice a little give-and-take! If you must have a roommate, be certain you are extra careful in screening and you are totally honest about your living habits, work schedule, and future plans!

PERSONAL AND FAMILY BUDGETING

The importance of realistic personal and family budgeting cannot be stressed enough. Many people have different methods for sticking to a budget, but the initial stage of formulating a budget seldom varies. You already know your monthly rent or house payments. Your utility bills can be determined from other renters in your building, your landlord, area utility companies, or the previous home owners. Other expenses are difficult to estimate, particularly at first, but the budgets below should provide you with basic budgets and guidelines.

In Figure 5.2, the beginning salary is $20,000 in Anytown, U.S.A. It also assumes that you are single, you lease or are buying a car, and that you will make at least two long distance phone calls each week, during the evening hours or on weekends, of course.

FIGURE 5.2
Personal Budgeting Guide for a Single Professional

Total Monthly Take-Home After Taxes		**$ 1330**
Monthly Expenses		
Rent	$ 350	
Car payment	150	
Car and apartment insurance	50	
Utilities	60	
Television cable	30	
Gasoline	30	
Telephone	50	
Groceries	150	
Personal items/sundries	40	
Clothing allowance	50	
Savings	50	
Total Monthly Expenses		**$ 1010**

Disposable Monthly Income (amount left for student loans, gifts, medical, charity, entertainment, consumer credit payments, etc.) $ 320

In Figure 5.3, your beginning salary is $20,000 in Anytown, U.S.A, and your combined household income is $40,000. It also assumes that you lease or are buying two cars and that you have childcare expenses.

FIGURE 5.3
Budgeting Guide for a Dual-Income Family

Total Monthly Take-Home After Taxes		$ 2600
Monthly Expenses		
Rent or mortgage payment	$ 650	
Car payments	300	
Utilities	90	
Television cable	30	
Gasoline	70	
Telephone	50	
Childcare	450	
Medical	50	
Groceries	300	
Personal items for household members/sundries	60	
Clothing allowance	100	
Savings	100	
Total Monthly Expenses		$ 2250
Disposable Monthly Income (amount left for student loans, gifts, charity, entertainment, consumer credit payments, etc.)		$ 350

The above budgets are just guidelines, but are quite realistic in most areas. Now, how do you stick to the budget? Some people find that they are just naturally disciplined and have no problem adhering to pre-set dollar amounts. Others, however, find that their paycheck always seems to be gone before it is received and they use credit cards to supplement a lack of cash – this leads to something we like to call credit card hell and once you get there, it can take years to get out.

If this sounds like you, perhaps you should consider cashing most of your paycheck, except for the rent or mortgage payment, car payment, utilities, and savings, and putting the budgeted amount into separately marked envelopes. When the envelope is empty, you cannot spend any more in that category. In other words, you are all "spent out" for the month! If necessary, you may transfer from envelope to envelope, but under no circumstances should you withdraw more cash from the bank. And, by the way, Automatic Teller Machines count as cash, so **don't do it if you have a tendency to live beyond your means!**

Most important is for you to realize the need for budgeting a monthly amount for savings, even at this first major stage in your new career. If your place of employment has a plan in which you can have a fixed amount automatically withdrawn from your paycheck every month, do it! Also, consider putting half of your monthly savings into an accessible account and one-half into long-term savings. The $25 or $50 per month you put into an account that is easily accessible could be used for that annual vacation, for at the end of twelve months, you should have approximately $310 or $620, respectively, assuming you invested in a savings account which generates 5% per annum, compounded quarterly.

Saving for the Long Term

Now, for the amazing fact. If you save $50 per month, you will have $9,060 in ten years. If you do not touch the money then and continue to squirrel away $50 per month, you will have $29,060 in twenty years. And, if you still decide to leave the money untouched and continue your savings plan, you will have approximately $112,470 in savings in thirty-five years. All this at an estimated interest rate of 8% per annum, compounded quarterly.

Although it might sound unrealistic and even silly to begin saving for your retirement already, it could certainly make your later years in this world a bit more carefree. Do you dream of traveling some day with few worries? Would you like to own a winter house in a warmer climate or a summer house in a cooler climate? It is certainly possible *if* you begin to save early. If you are interested in long-term savings, perhaps you should open a retirement account since every dollar you put into a retirement account is exempt from current taxes. If you put $1,200 per year into an Individual Retirement Account or your company's 401(k) retirement plan, your taxes could be reduced by as much as $380 per year, and your disposable income would immediately increase by around $30 per month!

A common drawback of retirement plans is that they are only tax deferrals. You should know by now that you always have to pay the government eventually, one way or the other. Most retirement plans require that you wait to withdraw funds until you are 59 1/2 years old and you are taxed on the amount of the annual withdrawal at your applicable rate of taxation at that time. However, remember that chances are you will not be in as high of a tax bracket when you are 59 1/2 as you are when you are 40, so don't fret.

Granted, tax deferral is a calculated risk, but you must have faith in the political and economic system to ensure that tax rates do not go so high as to make your initial investment fruitless. Americans have an extreme dislike for high taxes, and that is unlikely to change within the next century. And, even if tax rates are higher than they are now, you have still realized an immediate tax saving as well as the compounded interest of your tax savings over a period of years. This is *in addition* to the direct benefits you will receive from your retirement plan.

Final Words on Budgeting

A final note – do not be afraid to put the amount left over from your envelope or checking account at the end of the month into your short-term savings account. By shaving off just $30 a month from the hypothetical budget, you could have at least $380 extra to spend in any way you desire at the end of twelve months! And wouldn't it be fun to splurge without guilt, knowing you saved for it and earned it?

The importance of the adherence to a personal budget cannot be overstated. Financial burdens can cause many problems for you, both personally and professionally. Personally, financial burdens cause undue stress which can lead to health disorders, problems in relationships, family discord, psychological disturbances, and even compulsive behaviors. Professionally, financial struggles can lead to missed workdays, marginal or poor productivity, unpredictable behavior toward other employees, and, ultimately, in warnings or dismissal based upon poor job performance.

If you find that you are having financial difficulties that are becoming overwhelming, do not hesitate to consult the employee assistance program (EAP) if your firm has one. An EAP is a service designed to help employees deal with personal issues which might affect their work performance. Most large corporations, and some smaller ones, offer this service for free or at a very modest cost. An EAP can offer financial counseling which may include suggestions for loan consolidations or re-budgeting. If you truly are a compulsive spender, which is not all that uncommon, you might consider seeking counseling or psychological assistance. Always know that there are many ways to get help if you need it. Although you are ultimately responsible for the debts you incur, you will find that most creditors are cooperative and understanding if you have a realistic repayment plan and stick to it!

Most of all, remember that you must balance a good credit rating, your situational needs and wants, and your future welfare. None should be sacrificed, even in this stage of your career. Plan carefully, spend wisely, and save aggressively!

STAYING PUT OR RELOCATING: THE GOOD AND THE BAD

The decision is often difficult: Should you remain in your current city, return to your hometown, or relocate? If you have the promise of a promotion in your current firm or have family ties, you might want to stay put. If you miss your family and want to return to your hometown, you can do that, too. If you are flexible and open to new adventures, you might want to relocate. All decisions have consequences – some good and some not so good.

Remaining in Your Current City

If you choose to accept a position or a promotion in the city in which you currently live, you will undoubtedly reduce many uncertainties after graduation. You already have a place to live and supportive friends or family. You are quite familiar with the area and are already known in industry circles. If you are in a city which boasts a large number of hospitality and tourism operations, you can probably change jobs over time, and your career may not be jeopardized if these job changes involve promotions and pay increases. If you are remaining at your current workplace, you already know the ropes and have proven your abilities.

Be aware, though, of the realities. There are trade-offs if you choose to remain in one city. Even though your employer might be a national firm, some companies make a distinction between *local hires* and *national or regional hires*. In some cases, this might mean a lower salary, placement at a lower position, and less consideration for promotions as vacancies become available. Also, if you live in an area that is particularly attractive, there will be more competition for existing and future jobs because people will want to relocate to that area. You will be competing with both the national and local labor markets. You might also find that opportunities for advancement are limited because hospitality and tourism markets are stagnant or declining in your area and this decrease in demand results in fewer opportunities for career-advancing job changes. Finally, if you obtain a position with a regional or local company, you may find that starting salaries compare unfavorably with national corporations and that your advancement will be limited because there are fewer opportunities.

Be sure that you can accept the professional limitations you will face if you choose not to relocate. Your reasons for making this choice are probably personal and might offer you greater personal rewards than frequent promotions and high salary levels. Just be aware of the trade-offs involved!

Returning To Your Home Town

If you accept a job in your home town, you may still find the adjustment difficult. Like anything else, working in your home town has both advantages and disadvantages.

If your starting salary is low and you are single, you can probably live with your family or friends for a year or two until you get on your feet. If you have a partner and/or children, you can probably count on support from your family regarding domestic responsibilities or childcare. Furthermore, you already know the immediate environment which might be beneficial to you if you have to hire employees or if you have to develop an area-wide marketing campaign. If, for example, you have to make area sales calls, the familiarity you have with the city and its people might help you close the deal more easily than if you were new to the area.

As easy and natural as it may seem to move back to your hometown, you also need to consider the disadvantages, and they are many! The professional pitfalls include those mentioned in the previous section – lower salaries, initial placement at a lower position, and less consideration for promotions as they become available. Remember that promotions and salary increases come faster and easier if you are willing to move away.

Furthermore, living with your family may be cost effective, but it could cause you an unbelievable amount of stress if your family's values and living habits clash with yours. If you are married, you might find that unexpected drop-ins by family members infringe on your family time. And if you have children, you might find that your household rules do not mesh with those of your parents, grandparents, or friends who watch your children while you work.

If you are from a small- or medium-size town and part of your job is recruiting and hiring employees, you might find that your prejudices against certain "locals" affect your ability to realistically assess their strengths and weaknesses as potential employees. If you are charged with developing a new marketing or sales plan, you might *assume* certain local characteristics and thus overlook a potentially valuable target market.

It is perfectly acceptable to return to your home town as long as you are willing to forego certain opportunities and know the risks involved.

Relocating

Choosing to accept a position elsewhere also requires preparation. You might be placed in a new location by the corporation that hired you or you might intentionally select the location. Regardless, it will now be your home.

Moving is a harrowing experience in its own right, and unfamiliarity with your new surroundings will prove challenging. You need to find a place to purchase groceries, a doctor and dentist, a trusted automobile mechanic, reliable childcare for your children, and so on and so forth. Most of all, you need to find new friends!

The grocery store, doctor, dentist, mechanic, and childcare dilemmas can often be solved by making workplace inquiries. It is extremely proper and even expected that you ask your coworkers for these types of referrals. However, as we previously discussed, finding new friends is another ball game. As you have noticed by now, good friends are difficult to find and even more difficult to keep. Interests, experiences, and priorities change over time and these all ultimately affect friendships. However, keep in mind that people move to new cities by the thousands and they, too, have to make new friends. You are not alone. You may have to *work* at developing social and relational outlets, but it can be done.

Probably the best way to find a friend is *not* by actively searching for one, but by making yourself amenable and available to a friendship. You could very likely find a new friend totally by accident. That is, you shop at the same time every week and continue to bump into the same person at the store. A friendship may ensue. You might develop a friendship with the person who cuts your hair or the teller at your new bank, just because it feels right. Most often, however, deep friendships require a certain level of common interests, whether personally or professionally based.

Later, in Chapter 7, you will have the opportunity to evaluate your interests, values, and skills. Most likely, you will find it easiest to make friends with persons who are similar to you in these areas. A word to the wise, though. Most of your coworkers will share your same interests, values, and skills. Do you want to be best friends with someone whose work performance you may have to evaluate? Do you want to be best friends with someone who may have to evaluate *your* work performance? And do you want to be best friends with someone who is on the same management track as you and with whom your performance may be compared before the end of the year?

Friendships in the workplace are normal and expected. The stress is such that frankness is common, emotional work-related highs are part of the job, and a genuine feeling of cooperation and teamwork is necessary. But the friendships you will develop at work should remain that way – **at work**! Occasionally, the two can be separated, that is, the personal and professional, but this is difficult to do. You or your friend may be accused of favoritism or, conversely, you or your friend may try so hard to minimize the importance of the friendship that the trust in the friendship is eventually destroyed. The pitfalls here can easily outweigh the benefits.

Now that you know that you should probably *not* develop close friendships at work, where should you look? One of the best places to begin is at a place that supports your values and interests. For example, if you value religion and want to have friends with similar beliefs, then begin to go to church or explore religious groups within the city. If you are a closet artist, attend art show openings at galleries or universities. If you like conversation and intellectual challenge, peruse your local paper for groups with similar interests, visit your local library, or take a course in a special interest area. If you like sports, consider joining a softball, volleyball, or soccer league. Also, special interest groups center around such diverse activities as hiking, animal rights, or photography. The key is to begin your search in places where you will find people with similar interests. You can take it from there. Just be open to new ideas and new cultures.

Those of you with children will find that this common bond will bring you into contact with other parents in your neighborhood, apartment complex, day-care facility, or your child's school. Similarly, partners or couples will find that each others' contacts will be a source of new friends.

Since you will remain relatively unknown in your new city for some time, this may be the ideal opportunity for you to experiment and to reach out to people whose interests are similar to yours in some ways, but vastly different in others. You might find that your deepest friendships develop with people whose differences infuriate you, but at the same time demand your respect and pique your curiosity. Most often, a certain level of sameness has to be present for a friendship to develop, but sameness can be stifling! Subtle or even drastic philosophical differences in friends often spur deep personal growth and acceptance in both parties. It is not wrong or even dangerous to look beyond the provincial and expected.

THE PITFALLS OF A PROFESSIONAL LIFE

The pitfalls of a professional life are many and varied. Loneliness, financial difficulties, workaholism, lack of organization, strains on your marriage or relationship, eating disorders, sleep deprivation, lack of physical exercise, substance abuse, and a general feeling of being overwhelmed are more common than most want to admit.

If you are single, it may initially sound great to be able to eat popcorn for dinner or to change your bed sheets every other month, but is that a healthy lifestyle? If you are married or in a relationship, it may sound great to be able to assume fewer responsibilities at home in exchange for your new work-related responsibilities, but is that fair to your partner? If you are a single parent, it may sound great to be able to truly afford childcare or to bring home take-out every other night rather than slave over a hot stove, but is that a fulfilling lifestyle?

Loneliness

If you are single, you might find the new job exhilarating and rewarding, but find your social life less than acceptable. The demands of a new job are many and the adjustments you must make in order to succeed require a substantial investment of time and energy. These demands can combine to leave very little time or energy for meeting new friends or for developing new relationships. If you *are* in a relationship, these demands could distance you from your partner.

Don't expect to defeat your feelings of loneliness immediately. The first priority when you begin your new job is to perform it with professionalism, thoroughness, responsibility, and enthusiasm. However, after a few months or so, you may feel detached from those not within your operation or company and may begin to doubt your ability to attract and maintain a friendship at any level. If this occurs, take action *immediately* and lay out a plan of action! Promise yourself that you will go out at least once a week with the intention of meeting new people. Whether you go to a play, church, museum, meeting, dance, concert, health club, athletic event, or restaurant does not matter. You might even go so far as requiring yourself to meet at least two new people each week. Suddenly, you will find that you have a supportive group of friends and you will no longer feel it necessary to search nor will you feel a void in your social life.

If you are married or in a relationship, you will also find it necessary to develop a circle of friends outside of the workplace, both individually and as a couple. Most often, you will find that by pursuing some of the previously mentioned activities, you will automatically be led into new friendships which involve both of you!

Most important, do not ignore any opportunity to meet new people. You never know when or where you will meet some fantastic people with whom you can share a lasting friendship.

Financial Difficulties

If you or your family recognizes and acts on the importance of establishing and adhering to a budget, most financial difficulties can be avoided. The troubles begin when the budget is unrealistic or if you are unable to stick with it. In either of these cases, it will be necessary for you to revisit the budget to determine whether or not it is manageable. If it is, it is up to you to adjust your spending accordingly. After all, there are only two possibilities – **decrease your expenditures or increase your earnings**. Of the two possibilities, the former is much more probable at this time in your career than the latter, so do it! If your problem is discipline, financial advisors are available for you to consult with if you cannot do it alone. In fact, many social service organizations offer this as a free service.

Workaholism

When you first begin your career, you will find that you are faced with many professional challenges and that, in order to succeed as an effective and successful manager, you will need to develop new skills and refine existing skills. It is common to work at least fifty hours per week in any white-collared job, and the hospitality and tourism industry is no different. **After all, if you wanted to limit your work week to forty hours, then why did you go to college**? Most jobs that require advanced education also require increased responsibility and, along with this responsibility goes the requirement of longer-than-average hours worked per week. You might work forty hours during some weeks and sixty hours during others, as the job requires.

Unfortunately, new managers often believe that the more hours they are present at the workplace, the more they will be valued by the corporation and the better their chance for promotion. Think about this from another point of view for a moment. If you are a district manager and one of your unit managers works an average of ten hours per week more than other managers of similarly profitable units, wouldn't you begin to wonder? If you are the General Manager of Food Operations at a university and the Service Manager at your account works twenty hours per week more than the Production Manager, wouldn't you also wonder?

Do You Want To Look Like This?

In both of these instances, you would probably question the motive of the workaholics. Were the hours worked related to their ineffectiveness as managers or to the demands of the job? Most corporations now recognize that employee burn-out is expensive and undesirable and are quite aware of the fact that a balance between professional and personal lives is something to be encouraged. Effective managers are most often those who are well adjusted both at home and at the workplace.

Managers who work seventy hours per week are frequently not viewed as *superstars*, but rather as *problems*. Workaholics often expect others to work just as hard as they do and this can directly lower the bottom line by decreasing morale, increasing employee turnover, and decreasing productivity. Delegation is usually not a major strength of this type of manager, and employees will be less empowered and could feel less committed to the concept and delivery of high quality service.

Don't expect kudos for long hours unless they are absolutely necessary. In and of themselves, they won't lead to increased wages, promotions, or even good performance reviews. Furthermore, if exceptional hours are frequently necessary to be effective in your job, you need to evaluate two factors – yourself *and* your company. When you evaluate yourself, ask the following questions: Why am I doing this? Are the hours necessary? Am I in a position that is more challenging than my present skills and abilities allow? What could I do to decrease the amount of time I spend at work? As you view your operation, ask these questions: Is this a staffing problem? Can it be fixed? Should I consider another job?

Be aware that if you are always putting in sixty or seventy hour weeks, *something is wrong*! And there are only two potential problem areas – you or your employer. If the problem lies with you, you are either wasting your time or you are not effective. In the next section of this chapter, we offer some time management tools to help *you* make the appropriate changes. If the problem lies with your employer, you need to consider whether the trade-off between stress, burnout, and isolation and the rewards you gain are worth it. If they aren't, start looking!

Often, mentors can help you deal with this very real problem of workaholism. Most people have "been there" and have "done it." They learned the hard way. There is no need for you to do the same. If you do not feel comfortable confiding in a mentor or if you do not have one, you can also consult with professional counselors. You can often get referrals to good counselors from your physician or your health insurance carrier.

You could also consider joining a discussion or support group whose members experience similar destructive behaviors. Also, do not ignore the effectiveness of seminars and workshops which may help you to better learn to delegate responsibilities and develop trust in your employees. Such seminars and workshops might be offered by your company, local or regional professional associations, or area colleges.

Regardless, do not let yourself fall into the trap of workaholism. It can be one of the ultimate forms of arrogance and mistrust of other humans, or when it is enforced by your company, it is a form of slavery. There is no faster way to disassociate yourself from an atmosphere of teamwork than to assume all the responsibilities yourself. There is no faster way to professional demise than burnout, so take immediate action if you suspect that you are working too much or if your work schedule begins to adversely affect your personal life. There *is* a solution and do not be afraid to use the resources available.

Lack of Organization

Although it might sound obvious, it is necessary to strike a balance between your work life and your professional life. There is nothing that can interfere more with your quality of life than living a frazzled, frantic, and frenetic life because you are always one step behind in your schedule or because you have no time to enjoy fun, nurturing, and fulfilling activities outside of your job. Avoiding this requires organization, and organization, like anything else, is not innate. It must be developed and practiced.

Earlier, we said that successful managers are both *efficient* and *effective*. Well, guess what? Both efficiency and effectiveness are outcomes of good organization. Lack of organization will, at the very least, inhibit your ability to be successful and, at worst, destroy it. Have you ever attended a meeting where there was no agenda or focus? It is very likely that no decisions were made and time was wasted. Similarly, you might have worked a banquet where table assignments were mixed up, food timing was off, and employees were unsure of their duties. The outcome? Probably disaster! In both cases, a little bit of organization could have averted frustrating and disappointing results.

This applies to you, too. Developing skills in organization can not only head off personal and professional disaster, but can provide you with a number of rewards as follows:

- ✓ an improved professional image
- ✓ the ability to get more accomplished in less time
- ✓ a calmer and more peaceful life; and
- ✓ free time to pursue friendships, family life, or activities which you enjoy

One way to look at organizational skills is to apply a rule often referred to as the Pareto Principle. First identified by Valifredo Pareto in the early 1900s, the

Pareto Principle says that 80 percent of what is economically or socially valuable comes from only 20 percent of available resources while the remaining 20 percent of what is valuable comes from 80 percent of available resources.

Of course, the 80-20 distribution is approximate, but what it means in terms of improving your organizational skills is that you need to identify the 20 percent of your activities which result in 80 percent of your accomplishments and concentrate on organizing those. In other words, you must identify the activities which have high payoffs for you and forget about the rest.

The best way to start is to list your high payoff areas. This list should include frequently used areas which contribute substantially to your performance and are an integral part of your work flow. To make it easy, think of areas in your home or office which frustrate you and cause you to constantly lose time by searching for lost items. Make separate lists for work and home.

A work list might look like this:

- Desktop
- Telephone number file
- Top file drawer
- Computer

A home list might look like this:

- Bill drawer
- Refrigerator
- Garage
- Bedroom closet

Remember that people who spend time trying to organize *everything* are not receiving any extra value for their efforts. In fact, they are actually wasting a precious resource – time – because they spend most of it organizing. Organization is *just* a tool.

The second step is to get rid of the mess in these areas. If your desk is currently so cluttered that you lose important papers, telephone messages, and files, you need to unclutter it! If your bill drawer is in such disarray that you frequently pay bills late, you need to get it organized! To clear off your desk, throw away all junk mail and old memos. Enter important telephone numbers in your computer database, and refile the manila folders. To organize your bill drawer, sort the bills by due dates and, while you are at it, why not put some paper, a calculator, postage stamps, and a pen and pencil in the drawer?

The next step is probably the most difficult – develop a simple system to keep your high payoff areas organized. The easiest and simplest system to organize both your desktop and the constant paper flow at work is appropriately called the "4-D Method":

- ✘ **Don't open it.**
- ✔ **Discard it.**
- ✔ **Designate it for action.**
- ✔ **Direct it.**

In other words, if it is junk mail, get rid of it. If you have already marked a meeting date and the agenda on your calendar, and do not need the memo anymore, then recycle it. If a memo requires immediate attention, then act on it or put it in your in-basket to deal with as soon as possible. Finally, if a memo requires the attention of someone else, then write the person's name directly on the memo and immediately deliver it or mail it. The rule of thumb is to **rarely touch a piece of paper more than once**.

At home, the 4 Ds are a bit different regarding mail and bills:

- ✘ **Don't open it.**
- ✔ **Discard it.**
- ✔ **Date it.**
- ✔ **Do respond immediately.**

In other words, don't open unsolicited letters and junk mail. And *do not look* at unwanted magazines. Discard these items immediately. If it is a bill, verify its accuracy, return it to its envelope, write the due date on the outside of the envelope, and file it in order of its due date in your bill drawer. If it is an invitation or a notice which requires a response, answer it right away, stick it in an envelope, address it, stamp it, and mail it at your first opportunity.

There are basic organizational principles and can be easily implemented and followed. Remember:

- Identify your 20 percent areas
- Clean them up and organize them
- Develop a maintenance system to keep them organized

Figure 5.4 is an example of a check list you can use or modify to ensure that your organization is up to par. If you answer *yes* to most of the questions in this exhibit, then you are on your way to maximizing both your efficiency and effectiveness. If you answer *no* to any of the items, you have identified an area which needs improvement. Simple!

FIGURE 5.4
Am I Organized?

At Work	Yes	No
1. I have identified my work areas which I most often use.	____	____
2. These areas result in approximately 80% of my results.	____	____
3. These areas are uncluttered.	____	____
4. My system for continuous organization is simple.	____	____
5. I keep items which I most often use in easy-to-access places.	____	____
6. I have a recycling bin next to my desk.	____	____

At Home	Yes	No
7. I have identified my high payoff areas.	____	____
8. I group materials needed to complete common tasks.	____	____
9. I have taken advantage of organizing and storage aids.	____	____
10. If I use something more than twice per week, it is stored in an easily accessible place.	____	____
11. I donate clothes to charity which I have not worn in at least a year.	____	____
12. I rarely spend more than two minutes looking for a commonly used item.	____	____

Being well organized at work is critical in the hospitality and tourism industry. The pace is fast and guests, customers, and colleagues rely on you **to *deliver what you say you will, when you say you will*!** Organization at home will not only reduce stress, but will allow you more free time to enjoy your family, friends, relationships, or interests. The ultimate goal here is to **control your environment and not to let your environment control you**!

Marital, Family, or Relationship Strains

The demands of your new job combined with your desire to succeed could result in terrific strains on your marriage, family, or current relationship. It is too easy to try to be all things to all people and, in the process, to sacrifice yourself. The trick to success outside of the workplace is **BALANCE**. You need to balance your professional life with your personal life. Most important, you need to recognize that your needs for family and companionship are expected and supported.

If you are already in a committed relationship when you finish your education, chances are that your partner has already adjusted to the time constraints caused by your job and course work throughout college. This new professional period of your life might be the same from your partner's perspective and might just be viewed as a different mask.

It is extremely important that you communicate your frustrations to your partner or family during your professional adjustment period. Graduating from college was quite an accomplishment, but it also shoves you into new professional responsibilities which will probably require you to spend more time away from home. In the hospitality and tourism industry, your responsibilities are most demanding when the customer needs service. Granted, you might have planning and follow-up responsibilities, but little of that can be done at home. In college, even though you had to study, you were still in an adjacent room. Now, however, you might be in an adjacent city, state, or country, albeit on a temporary basis.

If you can openly communicate your frustrations and needs, you will have a better chance of sustaining a lasting and quality relationship. Equally important, be attentive to the frustrations and needs of your partner and family. Too often, work-related stress causes stress at home. If you can keep the lines of communication open, you can alleviate a lot of this stress.

Partners and families require attention, time, and love on an on-going basis. Your family might revel in your new position, but might still expect you to be the same as you always were when you walk through the front door after work. Be sure to *take time to nurture and enjoy your partner and/or family*. You are needed and loved just as much as you ever were, and you will probably be pleasantly surprised at their level of understanding of your struggles.

Share the joys and accomplishments of your day with them. Let them see where you work – even take them on a quick tour at a slow time if policy permits. Inform them when you are likely to be absent for a time, whether that absence is physical, emotional, mental, or a combination thereof. Most of all, *communicate and understand*! A mutually supportive and loving home environment will undoubtedly make you a more valued employee at work.

If you begin to feel strained in your personal relationships outside of work, do not ignore the strains. Plan a family get-away or a romantic dinner or weekend with your partner. If you have a hard time expressing your frustrations verbally, exchange hand-written notes then discuss the implications. Develop an action plan to address the problems and follow up on it! Maybe weekly meetings would help. Often, potentially major problems can be minimized or eliminated if tended to at their early stages. If the problems get too severe, don't be afraid to get counseling, whether alone, as a couple, or as a family. It is certainly worth the effort if you want to save your relationship and restore normalcy to your life!

Taking Care of the Body

Job-related stress at all stages in your career can result in poor dietary habits, lack of sleep, absence of physical exercise, or substance abuse. Diet, exercise, and substance abuse are detailed in Chapter 8, so they will only be briefly mentioned here. All of these dangers are very real and have been experienced by managers at all levels, from entry-level managers to CEOs.

Poor dietary habits, lack of sleep, and the absence of physical exercise can often be turned around with good time management skills and a healthy injection of self-discipline. If you find yourself skipping meals because you do not have enough time, make sure to grab some cheese or an apple, or drink a glass of milk until you have time to eat. Nutritional supplements such as vitamins can help replace some nutritional deficiencies, but they can never substitute for real food. Remember, your body needs calories, protein, and carbohydrates to perform at its peak.

Poor sleeping habits can also be caused by poor time management but, more often, are a direct result of stress. The first case is easy – change your schedule so you can get the sleep you need. This varies among individuals, but most people require between six and eight hours of sleep each day. Remember, you do not have to accomplish your entire life's plan at once, and without sufficient sleep, chances are that you will actually accomplish little of any quality.

Lack of sleep caused by stress is more difficult to fix and requires additional measures. Perhaps meditation before bedtime can help. Maybe you are eating or exercising too close to bedtime. It is always best to explore your personal habits *before* assuming that you have a medical or psychological problem. If you cannot determine the cause for your sleeping problems and have taken all the steps you can think of to alleviate them, it is time to visit your physician or therapist. Mild sedatives can help induce sleep, but they should only be used as a temporary measure since they can be addictive. Also, certain non-addictive herbal medicines will help induce sleep. Your body could have forgotten what a good night's sleep really feels like and might be fighting it. Maybe it just needs a little outside prodding to get it back on track.

The absence of exercise is also common when you begin your new career. You might feel too tired when you get home, or feel that you do not have the time to exercise. First, you must realize that exercise comes in many forms, from yoga to weight-lifting. Luckily, each of us is unique.

The trick is to find something that maintains your interest and that you truly enjoy doing. If you do not enjoy your aerobics class, you will find that you never seem to have the time to make it to the gym. Perhaps a home exercise plan which increases your flexibility and strength would be better. If you enjoy high-impact activities, then you will probably quickly lose interest in your weight-lifting regiment. Perhaps it would be best if you joined a community softball team. The possibilities are endless and lack of time is no excuse! A moderately paced two-mile run only takes twenty minutes. A two- or three-mile walk requires only about ten to twenty minutes more. Total weekly time investment? About one or two hours! You could get your physical exercise and simultaneously use the time to meditate, plan your next day, or listen to a novel via cassette on a WalkMan. An added plus? Exercise helps you sleep better!

Substance Abuse

Unfortunately, substance abuse is common in the hospitality and tourism industry. Many managers have been through rehabilitation – do not permit yourself to join the fraternity.

It is easy to say: "Whatever you do, do in moderation." However, the reality is that many hospitality and tourism managers live their lives in direct opposition to this maxim. The pace is not moderate and neither are the demands of the job, the hours worked, or the customers' expectations. In many ways, this industry is one of indulgence. We serve alcohol and deal with customers who are partying, celebrating, or vacationing. Finally, the ideal of service is *exceeding* expectations and this automatically negates the concept of moderation.

Enough cannot be said regarding the dangers of substance abuse. It can devastate relationships, divide families, ruin careers, and ultimately kill. It is no joke. Substance abuse takes many different forms, from the use of tobacco to the overuse of alcohol to dependency on prescription medications to the consumption of illegal drugs. The ultimate penalty for all of these is death, although suffering always comes first. By the way, the suffering is never limited to you alone, but is shared by all those around you, both at home and in the workplace.

No longer is it shameful to admit to a substance abuse problem. In fact, most people know when someone is affected before the abuser is ready to admit it. Instead, you will be respected for your actions and will often be supported in full by your professional colleagues, personal friends, and family. Even if you aren't, your life and career are at stake, so take action anyway. Consult the employee assistance program at your corporation, see your doctor, and/or join a support group.

In a few short words – *substance abuse kills*. If you think you need help or if those close to you think you need help, do not hesitate. Many options are available and many are reasonably priced or even free. It is life . . . or death. The choice is yours.

BALANCE, BALANCE, BALANCE

This chapter outlines the potential joys and frustrations you could face as you begin your new professional life. The key to all of it can be summed up in one word – *balance*. Corporations are rapidly realizing that a balanced manager is more productive and effective in leading and motivating work teams. Some corporations even include *balance* in their managers' performance evaluations.

The following managers agree with the importance of achieving a balance between personal and professional lives and offer some suggestions and insights.

Choose an Organization Which Will Help You BALANCE!

"When I graduated from college, I worked for a few corporations that did not recognize the importance of the personal lives of their managers. The company I'm with now supports balanced employees, and gives us tools to develop that balance.

My work goals are clear and attainable, and result in a less stressful work environment. Granted, some days are more hectic and stressful than others, but having a daily, weekly, and monthly plan at work reduces frustrations and increases work-related predictability, at least to some point. And, less stress at work means a better life outside of work!

No longer can corporations expect their managers to be married to their jobs. Too many other things in life are important, too. Be sure to find a company that supports your development in *all* areas and contributes to that balance."

Jodi Barnard
Quality Assurance Manager
Ritz-Carlton Cleveland
Cleveland, Ohio

Balance is Everything!

"When managers start out, they often think that they need to prove themselves by spending long hours at work, and by volunteering for virtually every committee and project. After time, many realize that this type of work behavior can *burn them out*. No one's relationships should fail due to the demands of their job, no one's health should suffer, and everyone should have enough free time to enjoy hobbies, sports, and other interests.

Most of all, you need enough time for your family. Your partner needs your love and understanding. You need to share and explore together, and it is difficult to do this if you are stressed. Your children will grow up faster than you can believe, and you need to be a part of this growth. They require your love, support, and attention. It is important that you take an interest in their lives and that you support their activities by your attendance whenever possible.

I have worked for various hospitality firms over the years, and have always tried to balance my personal life with my professional life. Although the balance got upset at times, it always seemed to get back on track. It takes some effort on your part, but it is well worth it!"

Robert Cady
Regional Director of Human Resources
Bally's Health & Tennis Corporation
Ft. Lauderdale, Florida

Although it may seem as if you have to be everything to everyone, you do not. First, be everything to yourself and your family or partner. You will find that the rest follows with some perseverance, direction, enthusiasm, ethics, and experience. It can all mesh, and it will.

ADDITIONAL READINGS

The 10 Natural Laws of Successful Time and Life Management, Hyram W. Smith; Warner Books, (New York, 1994).

Bonnie's Household Budget Book, Bonnie Runyan; St. Martin's Press, 4th Edition (New York, 1992).

Deadly Choices: Coping with Health Risks in Everyday Life, Jeffrey C, Harris; BasicBooks (New York, 1993).

The Wall Street Journal Guide To Understanding Personal Finances, Kenneth M. Morris & Alan M. Siegel; Lightbulb Press (New York, 1992).

What You Can Change . . . And What You Can't, Martin E. P. Seligman; Fawcett Columbine (New York, 1993).

PROFESSIONAL DEVELOPMENT

"Knowledge and power are synonymous."

Francis Bacon

Imagine this! Years of study are over. You have been through endless interviews, written tons of thank you notes, and your efforts have been successful. You have landed a professional job with your dream company. Good-bye, college! Hello, world!

About two weeks into your new job the thought comes to you – I'm still learning! You no longer have the burden of classes and exams but you are very busy. There are performance expectations regarding your daily activities and your mind feels as if it is on information-overload!

No matter how much work experience you have had, there is still a lot to be learned – procedures, policies, details of your job, organizational values and culture, and, like it or not, organizational politics. You are learning about what is expected of you and you might be trying to develop a management style that suits you. So, even though school is finished, you are still in a learning mode and failure to learn will cost you more than a grade.

Learning on the job can be similar to school in some ways, but mostly it's different and more varied. There is less structure, and more of the responsibility rests on your shoulders. Sure, there may be seminars and training sessions. You might even participate in a lengthy formal training program. However, a lot of what you gain in terms of knowledge comes about solely because of your effort.

You learn the specific tasks of your job by observing others and trying them out for yourself. You learn about the business and its culture by investigating, observing, and asking questions, or by reading company manuals or trade journals. You may also find that your boss or some other senior manager will spend time talking with you, and in some cases, act like a coach – praising you when you excel and suggesting ways to improve when your performance could be better.

By now you should have begun to realize two things. First, this period of your professional career is indeed a *new beginning* and, second, it's a lot like the phase you just *ended* – you are still in a stage of preparation. The only difference is that there is less structure, and most of the responsibility for making your professional life viable rests on *your* shoulders.

True, you have a job but you are also building a career. Remember the difference – you *earn a living* from a job. You trade time, effort, and skills for wages. For many people, that's all their work is about – a trade off of some part of themselves for money. A job is separate from an individual, and you can, if you choose, put very little of yourself in your job. In fact, you can virtually separate the two if you try really hard.

A career, by contrast, is much more than a job, or even a series of jobs. Why? Because a career includes your purpose in life, your freedom to exercise and develop judgment, the degree to which you value yourself, and, to some extent, your entire sense of identity. Careers develop over many years, require a substantial investment of self, and have to be crafted or built! The rest of your professional life is about career building, and a major component of career building is called *professional development*.

WHAT IS PROFESSIONAL DEVELOPMENT?

In broad terms, professional development is an organized process designed to improve your effectiveness and performance as a manager, both today and in the future. On another level, it is a process of grooming yourself to meet the challenges of the future and to prepare yourself for positions of greater responsibility.

Before we go on, it's probably useful to clarify a few things. To begin with, professional development is a process and not an event or even a series of events. It is something you will engage in (or at least need to engage in) over the entire span of your career and it requires planning and flexibility.

The benefits of professional development spill over into other aspects of your life. Maturity of judgment, an enhanced sense of self-worth, and a clearer sense of your identity are not only going to make you a better person, they are going to put you well on the road to becoming **who you are**. That, according to the philosopher Freidrich Nietzche, is the purpose of life.[9]

Why Develop Professionally? Because It's Part of Who You Are!

In line with this, the benefits of professional development accrue not only to you but also to the company you join, the business community as a whole, and ultimately to society. At this point you might be asking, "If my company benefits and society benefits, then whose responsibility is professional development?"

9   Irvin D. Yalom, *When Nietzsche Wept: A Novel of Obsession* (New York: New York, 1992).

The answer to that is rather complex. Many large companies and even some smaller ones, for that matter, have management development programs to groom and develop managers. They want improved performance *now* and they want a stable group of polished and talented managers to assume senior positions as the business grows or as senior positions become available. To that end, they try to select talented employees in the first place and provide developmental experiences such as cross-training, coaching, and training to improve the performance and promotability of their managers.

This is an essential task for all organizations. However, it is also an essential task for you and it is too important a task to place solely in the hands of someone else. That is why we use the term *professional development* as opposed to *management development.*

Professional development serves your career and is, therefore, your responsibility and **yours alone**. Sure, you can take advantage of management development programs, but you have to realize that management development programs are designed to directly serve the organization's needs, and only *indirectly* to serve yours. This means that you bear the ultimate responsibility for designing and carrying out your *own* plan of professional development.

There is also another, more compelling reason to develop a carefully planned professional development program for yourself. There is a trend away from long-term employment with one organization. Some call this the "new employment contract." Under this contract, companies do not promise long-term employment or any kind of loyalty for that matter. Instead, they promise opportunities for professional development and learning which, if you take advantage of them, will enhance your success with that company or some other company should either you or your present employer decide to separate.

A WORD ABOUT SUCCESS

In many respects, career building is about success – but not success in the way you might conventionally define it in terms of salary or position. Rather, success as we use it here means being successful at performing your job and in building your career along the lines which you envision.

The distinguished management theorist, Peter Drucker, says that managers achieve success by being both efficient and effective.[10] Efficiency, he says, is concerned with *doing things right* – following proper procedures, managing the resources under your control, scheduling wisely, etc. Effectiveness, by contrast, focuses on *doing the right things*. This means making the right decisions, being entrepreneurial, being visionary, and implementing strategies to achieve your vision. Some managers are either efficient or effective, but in the modern business environment, successful managers must be both.

The message to aspiring managers should be clear. You are not born with these qualities, nor can you acquire them overnight. Instead, you develop them through experience, effort, trial and error, and learning.

The notions of efficiency and effectiveness may seem simple, but they are exceptionally complex. To become the success that your potential demands, you must invest time and effort in acquiring and developing a vast array of skills. Acquiring, in this case, means learning, and developing means working toward mastery.

Take, for example, learning to swim. You first learn the strokes, and you master the sport, to one degree or another, only with practice. You wouldn't compete in a swim meet after one lesson or even after ten. Competitive swimming requires knowledge, ability, conditioning, and practice. Mastery comes only after a lot of hard work.

Changing Roles

Your reliance on particular skills will shift as you progress in your career. Perhaps you might have studied corporate finance in college. After you completed the course, you had a sense of how finance operates in the business world. However, unless you are in a position which directly relates to finance, there is precious little chance that your first few jobs will require you to use much of what you learned in your finance course. But, if you think about the position or role you might hold five or ten years from now, knowledge of finance might be essential to your profession.

Take a look at Figure 6.1. Notice how your role changes as you move up the

[10] Peter Drucker, *Management: Tasks, Responsibilities, and Practices* (New York: Harper & Row, 1973), p. 45.

organizational ladder. You will probably start as a Stage 1 or 2 manager when you graduate from college. Each step up the ladder requires greater dependence on some skills and diminished reliance on others. For example, a Stage 3 manager is going to rely heavily on human relation skills. A Stage 4 manager will still need to exercise human relations skills, but might find that problem solving and decision- making skills are more critical for success.

FIGURE 6.1
Stages of Professional Development

Organization Members		Organizational Roles
Seasoned change agent	STAGE 5	Promotion to higher responsibility
The experienced manager becomes a change agent	STAGE 4	Managing managers, wider span of control, multi-unit or increased responsibility
The junior manager becomes a seasoned manager	STAGE 3	Preparing to manage managers and facilitate change
The lead employee becomes a junior manager	STAGE 2	Developing management skills, conceptual ability, human relations skills
The promising employee becomes a lead employee	STAGE 1	Learning operations skills, wider experience, more responsibility

We acknowledge our debt to Professor Tom Powers and the School of Hotel and Food Administration, University of Guelph, Ontario, for the use of this figure.

A number of years ago, Professor Tom Powers of the University of Guelph performed a major study of chain restaurant firms.[11] The purpose of that study was to identify management development needs of these organizations. Among other things, he concluded that successful unit managers had a significant chance of failure when they were promoted to multi-unit management. The reason the risk of failure was so high was because these newly promoted managers didn't realize that their multi-unit management role was substantially different than their unit management role. The skills that made them successful unit managers were insufficient to make them successful multi-unit managers. The multi-unit managers who made it, according to Powers, were those who realized that they needed to acquire and exercise different skills in their new roles.

SKILLS OF SUCCESSFUL MANAGERS

So, what are these skills and how does the need for them shift as you move along your career path? Actually, *skills* is too narrow of a term. Some organizations might use the word *competencies*, but what we are really talking about are skills, ability, and knowledge. For the purpose of our discussion, we will use the word *skills*. The skills you will need as you grow in your profession can be fitted into five broad categories:

- Technical
- People
- Business
- Conceptual
- Personal

Let's explore what is included in each of these categories.

Technical Skills

Technical skills are the skills that are related to your job. For a travel agent, these might include knowing how to manipulate the SABRE or the APOLLO reservation system. For the restaurant manager, these might mean learning culinary skills or table service skills. For the front office supervisor, these could involve learning the reservation system and in-house accounting procedures.

[11] Thomas F. Powers, *Hospitality Management Development for the 1980s,* **Cornell Hotel and Restaurant Administration Quarterly**, 1980 (20) , pp. 39 - 47.

Technical skills are very important because they are at the center of a particular company or industry. They must be learned and mastered to a certain degree by *all* managers directly involved in operations. By doing this, you will be better able to understand the operations you manage, and you will be better able to lead the employees you supervise. This is because you will gain increased credibility by demonstrating these skills.

People Skills

People skills are at the heart of our industry. We serve our customers individually and directly, and hospitality and tourism operations are labor intensive – that is, they require more people than other industries to get the job done. Under the category of people skills we include things such as customer service skills, employee relations skills, the ability to motivate others, supervisory skills, and knowledge of employment law. Some of these are innate. For example, you might have a natural tendency to be personable or persuasive. Still, even natural abilities can be more polished and made stronger. Other people skills, by contrast, must be learned and practiced. Like technical skills, people skills are essential for managers involved in hospitality and tourism operations.

Although we deal with travel, guests, good food, fine wines, and accommodations, hospitality and tourism managers are above all business people. Technical skills relate to our products, whereas business skills relate to the *reason for the existence of our company*. Traditionally, hospitality managers have relied heavily on technical and people skills, but in the complex environment of today, a solid grounding in business is ***critical***.

One reason for this is due to the flattening of organizational structures by eliminating layers of middle managers. This means that quite a few business decisions previously made by middle managers are now being made at lower levels of the organization. In a sense, unit level managers and even department heads are being called on to run their own business! Business skills include knowledge and ability in marketing, accounting, finance, entrepreneurship, production, and operations management as they apply to service industry.

In line with this, Shangri-La Hotels and Resorts, a major Asian hotel chain and one of the leading hotel operators in the world, recently implemented a business management program for all of its middle level managers. Plans are to put all managers involved with operations through this program in the future. The program is lengthy, thorough, and comprehensive. It covers, interestingly enough, finance and managerial accounting, operations management, marketing, and entrepreneurship. The program is designed to be "generalizable." That means that it goes beyond the way Shangri-La does things and teaches from a general perspective. Similarly, Allegro Resorts, the leading international, all-inclusive resort chain based in the Dominican Republic, is developing a series of intensive three-day seminars to accomplish similar goals.

Conceptual Skills

Conceptual skills relate to problem solving, planning, decision making, and strategizing. They also involve seeing the big picture. Obviously, these are developed, refined, and re-developed over a long period of time. Nevertheless, managers at all levels require some degree of conceptual ability. Since the hospitality industry is fast becoming a mature industry, tomorrow's senior executives will be selected from those who have well-developed conceptual abilities. Why? Because in mature industries, competition is intense and leaders need to be good problem solvers *and* strategists.

Personal Skills

Personal skills cover just about everything else. They run the gamut from etiquette to presentation skills and from grooming to organizational skills. Identifying your weaknesses in this area and correcting them will serve you well throughout your career. In part, you will acquire and polish your personal skills as you mature. However, like other skills, you also have to put effort into developing these.

CHANGING ROLES MEAN CHANGING SKILLS

As Figure 6.2 clearly points out and as we have previously discussed, your move up the management ladder will require a shift in the skills you will rely on most. For example, as a front line manager you are charged with making operations work, leading a work team, and making things happen for customers or guests. The skills you need to be successful are in the technical and people categories.

As you move up to middle management, however, your work changes. For the first time, you will begin to manage mangers, you will have more responsibility for bottom line results, and you will have more problem solving responsibilities.

You are, therefore, less reliant on technical skills and more reliant on people skills. Similarly, you start to need more sharply honed business and conceptual skills.

FIGURE 6.2
Changing Roles and Changing Skills

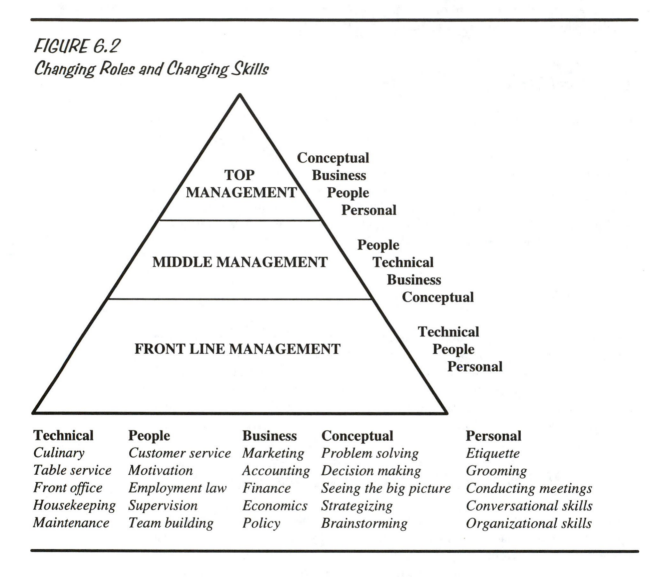

Technical	People	Business	Conceptual	Personal
Culinary	*Customer service*	*Marketing*	*Problem solving*	*Etiquette*
Table service	*Motivation*	*Accounting*	*Decision making*	*Grooming*
Front office	*Employment law*	*Finance*	*Seeing the big picture*	*Conducting meetings*
Housekeeping	*Supervision*	*Economics*	*Strategizing*	*Conversational skills*
Maintenance	*Team building*	*Policy*	*Brainstorming*	*Organizational skills*

When you reach the top levels of management, your work changes again. You may be tasked with planning and major decision making. You must have the big picture perspective to do this. Therefore, you will be more reliant on conceptual skills. Also, your business, personal, and people skills will need to be more refined than ever before.

Finally, it is important for you to be aware that, at every stage of the game, you must have *improved* your skills in each of the appointed categories. The business skills that work for you as a middle manager probably won't be adequate at the top levels of management. Similarly, the people skills you employed as a front line manager must improve as you move into middle management. This brings us back to our point that professional development is a continuous and career-long process.

ASSESSING YOUR DEVELOPMENT NEEDS

Self-assessment of skills, interests, and values is a continuous process. This also applies to ascertaining your development needs. The checklist presented in Figure 6.3 is designed to help you identify areas of strengths or weaknesses. With regard to skills development, you can use it to assess your strengths and weaknesses now, and we'll show you how to use it to make a professional development plan later.

First, however, we need to issue a series of warnings:

1) This will *not* be the *only* check list you need to complete. You should probably do one *at least* once a year starting right now!

2) In order to properly fill this out, you need to have a sense of where you want to go – front office, travel, conventions and meetings, contract food service, catering, food and beverage, restaurants, culinary, etc. This way you can identify the job specific technical skills you will need to develop.

3) The list is thorough but it can't possibly cover everything. Particularly in technical areas, you will need to fill in some blanks which are provided.

4) You have to be absolutely honest! One place to start in assessing your strengths is to list the areas in which others affirm you and to then list the skills which made these affirmations possible. The reverse also works! You can list the areas in which you may have been criticized and see what skills you might need to work on. Then, with a little introspection, you should have a good sense of yourself and that can be put to use in taking this inventory.

5) You might also consider adding a fifth column entitled "overdone." Sometimes, as we will discuss in Chapter 7, too much of a strength can be overpowering and a detriment.

Review the following list of developmental areas and then check the response which most clearly represents the degree to which you believe you hold the skill or ability listed. Note that you will have to fill in the skills for the specific job you aspire to.

FIGURE 6.3
Professional Development Inventory

H = *High*   **M** = *Moderate*   **W** = *Weak*   **N** = *Not at all*

AREA						AREA				
TECHNICAL	H	M	W	N		*BUSINESS*	H	M	W	N
Job Specific Skills						1. Marketing Knowledge				
1.						2. Sales Skills				
2.						3. Business Law				
3.						4. Accounting				
4.						5. Finance				
5.						6. Entrepreneurship				
6. Word Processing						7. Operations Management				
7. Spread Sheets						8. Total Quality Management				
8. Desk Top Publishing						9. Other				
9. Knowledge of POS Systems						10. Other				
10. Food Knowledge						11. Other				
11. Beverage Knowledge										
12. Equipment Knowledge						*CONCEPTUAL*				
13. Maintenance						1. Industry Knowledge				
14. Sanitation						2. Strategic Thinking				
15. Safety						3. Problem Solving				
16. Culinary Skills						4. Decision Making				
17. Service Skills						5. Quantitative Analytical Skills				
18. Understanding of Tourism						6. Conceptual Analytical Skills				
19. Knowledge of Lodging Systems						7. Planning				
20. Other						8. Organizing				
21. Other						9. Other				
22. Other						10. Other				
						11. Other				
PEOPLE										
1. Leadership						*PERSONAL*				
2. Supervision						1. Business Etiquette				
3. Public Relations						2. Social Etiquette				
4. Motivation						3. Personal Grooming				
5. Employee Selection						4. Business Dress				
6. Training						5. Social Poise				
7. Performance Appraisal						6. Public Speaking				
8. Customer Service						7. Conversational Skills				
9. Knowledge of Employment Law						8. Personal Organization				
10. Coaching						9. Conducting Meetings				
11. Delegation						10. Making Presentations				
12. Conflict Management						11. Foreign Languages				
13. Change Management						12. Communication				
14. Managing Diversity						13. Other				
15. Recruiting Employees						14. Other				
16. Other						15. Other				
17. Other										

PLANNING YOUR PROFESSIONAL DEVELOPMENT PROGRAM

Whether you know it or not, you have already begun the process of professional development. This process began when you chose to pursue a career in hospitality and tourism. Through the process of socialization and maturation, you developed a sense of work values and interests as well as a sense of a desired lifestyle. As you observed the world of work, you probably came to believe that these values, interests, and life-style considerations could best be fulfilled by a career this industry.

Now you are engaged in a set of activities such as attending classes and gaining practical work experience that you believe will help you launch a successful career. In other words, you have both **developed and acted upon a professional development plan**. As we have said repeatedly, you will continue to do that throughout your career, and only the methods available to achieve your goals will become more varied. This brings us to a critical observation about planning for professional development.

A plan for professional development starts with goals! Sure, some people get lucky and stumble into a career, but most of us have to carefully craft our careers and set goals. As we told you in Chapter 2, you must temper goal setting with an honest and thorough evaluation of your interests, abilities, life-style goals, and work ethic.

For example, if you find that you place a high value on raising a family and being involved in community affairs and you don't want to relocate from your home town, it is doubtful that you could achieve a long-term goal of becoming a general manager of a large hotel within, say, ten years. Your personal interests and values have limited your ability to achieve this goal. If you set this as a goal for yourself, it would be an exercise in self-deception and a set up for failure. If, on the other hand, you are willing to delay starting a family, limit your activities away from the job, and make a few geographic moves, your chance of achieving this goal will increase. There are still at least four other factors that will have influence on whether or not you achieve your goal:

- Your ability
- The effort you put into preparing yourself for future positions
- Supply and demand
- Luck

We think these words speak for themselves so we won't bore you with an explanation of the obvious!

Developing the Plan – The First Steps

As we explained earlier, your plan starts with goals and objectives. Initially, you should set goals for no more than five years into the future because circumstances have a way of changing.

Let's say you are in your second year of college. If you started a plan today and are attending a four-year institution, you would be planning for the third year after your graduation. It's also quite reasonable to simply plan for the first job you want following graduation. The point is, however, that you need to set a reasonable time frame so that your plan is actionable, so you can take the appropriate action to carry it out.

Once you have set your goals it is important, once again, to do some self-assessment. Remember the inventory you filled out in Figure 6.3? Now is the time to do some more work with that inventory.

Obviously, you can't work on all areas at the same time and all the items listed don't necessarily apply to your short and intermediate term goals. Take a look at Figure 6.4. It lists the same skills as were listed in Figure 6.3, only the responses are different.

Reflect on the goals you have set for yourself and make a decision as to whether or not the skill or ability is *critical, important, somewhat important*, or *not important* to achieving the goals you have set for yourself. Then mark the appropriate response. Be selective, however, because you have limited time to work on these areas. On the other hand, don't be too selective because this will render your plan ineffective.

Make a list of the skills and abilities you marked as either critical or important; compare these to your responses to the skills inventory in Figure 6.3. To what extent do you already possess this skill or ability? After this comparison, you can make a list of the areas on which you need to focus in the near future.

FIGURE 6.4
Developmental Needs Assessment

C = Critical   I = Important   S = Somewhat Important   N = Not Important

AREA TECHNICAL	C	I	S	N	AREA BUSINESS	C	I	S	N
Job Specific Skills									
1.					1. Marketing Knowledge				
2.					2. Sales Skills				
3.					3. Business Law				
4.					4. Accounting				
5.					5. Finance				
6. Word Processing					6. Entrepreneurship				
7. Spread Sheets					7. Operations Management				
8. Desk Top Publishing					8. Total Quality Management				
9. Knowledge of POS Systems					9. Other				
10. Food Knowledge					10. Other				
11. Beverage Knowledge					11. Other				
12. Equipment Knowledge									
13. Maintenance					*CONCEPTUAL*				
14. Sanitation					1. Industry Knowledge				
15. Safety					2. Strategic Thinking				
16. Culinary Skills					3. Problem Solving				
17. Service Skills					4. Decision Making				
18. Understanding of Tourism					5. Quantitative Analytical Skills				
19. Knowledge of Lodging Systems					6. Conceptual Analytical Skills				
20. Other					7. Planning				
21. Other					8. Organizing				
22. Other					9. Other				
					10. Other				
PEOPLE					11. Other				
1. Leadership									
2. Supervision					*PERSONAL*				
3. Public Relations					1. Knowledge of Business Etiquette				
4. Motivation					2. Knowledge of Social Etiquette				
5. Employee Selection					3. Personal Grooming				
6. Training					4. Business Dress				
7. Performance Appraisal					5. Social Poise				
8. Customer Service					6. Public Speaking				
9. Knowledge of Employment Law					7. Conversational Skills				
10. Coaching					8. Personal Organization				
11. Delegation					9. Conducting Meetings				
12. Conflict Management					10. Making Presentations				
13. Change Management					11. Foreign Languages				
14. Managing Diversity					12. Communication				
15. Recruiting Employees					13. Other				
16. Other					14. Other				
17. Other					15. Other				

If you have done a thorough and selective job you should have a list of between 10 and 20 skills that you will want to develop over the next three to five years. Your next task is to develop a plan, but, before you tackle that, it is important to have an idea of the various methods you can use to build these skills and abilities.

The Professional Development Model

Figure 6.5 details the components of professional development planning. We have already written at great length about setting goals and self-assessment. So, we will turn our attention to the remaining components.

FIGURE 6.5
The Professional Development Model

GOALS
Personal   Professional
Short-Term   Long-Term

ASSESSMENT
Personal   Professional
Abilities   Skills
Values   Interests

EXPERIENCE
Lateral Job Rotation
Progressive Responsibility

MENTORING AND COACHING

TRAINING
Job Specific
Skill Specific

EDUCATION
Seminars
University Programs
Industry Programs
Masters Degrees

The last four components of the model point the way to actually acquiring the skills you need to make you a more effective manager *now*, as well as to help you to achieve your short- and intermediate-term goals.

➡ **Experience**

Experience is perhaps the greatest teacher of all. It helps you to learn technical skills, it provides you with a laboratory for developing characteristics such as leadership style, and it allows you to try on decision making and problem solving skills.

Notice that you must manage two aspects of your experience. You need to gain exposure to a variety of different jobs on one level so that you can learn and practice technical skills and gain a wider perspective. At the same time, it is necessary to ensure that you seize opportunities, such as promotions, which allow you to assume greater responsibility.

Experience is important, but it is not the only teacher. Experience must also be supplemented by the processes of mentoring, training, and education.

➡ **Mentoring**

Mentoring involves sponsoring, teaching, counseling, and sharing of experience by a person who has been around longer than you or who is above you in the organization hierarchy. While sometimes mentors will find you, more often than not, you must seek them out and engage them in the process of mentoring. This means identifying someone you admire and asking for advice or information. You can't just do this once or twice; you need to do it frequently. At the same time, you will need to work on building a *relationship*. This doesn't mean you have to be good buddies, but it does mean frequent and substantial interaction with that person. You may find that some people will rebuff your efforts on this, but most will be flattered.

➡ **Training**

Training can be either formal or informal. A great deal of training comes about in the form of on-the-job training or through supervision by higher level managers. More often than not, however, this informal type of training is insufficient by itself. It must be supplemented by more formal and focused training so that you can learn the skills you need quickly and efficiently. Training is short term and it is directed at developing specific skills or abilities. Also, it is most often directly related to the organization in which it occurs. Training, for example, might focus on how to use a new reservations system that is specific to your hotel.

➡ Education

Education, by contrast, has many more forms. While the transfer of skills and knowledge in training is specific and direct, education has broader goals. The purpose of management education, as we see it, is four fold:

1) to impart knowledge;

2) to improve higher order skills in general areas such as marketing, organizational behavior, or strategic planning, to name a few;

3) to change attitudes; and

4) to enhance your ability to identify and deal effectively with change.

Education builds on training and experience, and the extent to which its purpose is achieved depends on factors such as the depth and breadth of your experience, your level of previous education, your intellectual capacity, and your willingness to devote time and effort to the process.

Education can take many forms and, while the following list is not exhaustive, it can give you an idea of the possibilities:

◆ Seminars

◆ University and community college continuing education courses

◆ Distance learning through industry associations such as the Educational Foundation of the National Restaurant Association or the Educational Institute of the American Hotel and Motel Association

◆ University-sponsored management development programs

◆ Masters degree programs

Your choice of educational programs will depend on your needs at specific times in your career. Masters degrees, for example, aren't immediately useful for people without some substantial experience. More often than not, people who obtain a masters degree immediately after their undergraduate years fare no better in the entry level hospitality job market than those with a bachelors degree.

At least in hospitality and tourism, it is better to use a masters degree for a specific purpose. For example, after working for a few years in operations, you may find that you have developed an interest in human resources or marketing.

At this point, a masters degree would provide you with knowledge to pursue a different career path within the industry. Similarly, a masters degree at some other point in your career might be useful to enhance your business and conceptual skills in order to prepare you for increased responsibility.

Another option is to participate in a certification program offered by trade or professional associations in your industry segment. Certification programs often require a combination of experience, study, service, and passing an examination.

Certified hospitality managers are allowed to use designation letters like FMP (Food Management Professional) or CCM (Certified Club Manager). The value of certification programs varies, but such programs have been growing rapidly over recent years and it is likely that they will become more important and more valuable in the future.

An example of this is the CCM designation. To become a Certified Club Manager, managers must meet rigorous educational, experiential and service requirements, *and* pass a 400 question exam. Only about 70% of the first-time takers pass this exam, but the effort is worth it.

According to the Club Managers Association of America (CMAA), club managers with the CCM degree earn on average $8,000 more per year than those without it! Appendix 6.1 lists various certifications in our fields and Table 6.1 lists the names and addresses of certifying associations.

Table 6.1
Certifying Associations

American Culinary Federation (ACF)
10 San Bartolla Rd.
St. Augustine, FL 32084-3466
(904) 824-4468

American Dietetic Association (ADA)
216 W. Jackson Blvd.
Chicago, IL 60606-6995
(202) 289-3100

Dietary Managers Association (DMA)
400 E. 22nd St.
Lombard, IL 60148
(312) 932-1444

**Educational Foundation of the
National Restaurant Association (EF of NRA)**
250 S. Wacker Dr., Ste. 1400
Chicago, IL 60606
(312) 715-1010

**Educational Institute of the American
Hotel & Motel Association (EI of AH&MA)**
1407 S. Harrison Rd.
East Lansing, MI 48826
(517) 353-5500

**Hospitality Sales and Marketing
Association International (HSMAI)**
1300 L St., NW, Ste. 800
Washington, DC 20005
(202) 789-0089

**Hotel Catering and Institutional
Management Association (HCIMA)**
191 Trinity Rd.
London SW17 7HN England
01-672-4251

**International Association of
Conference Centers (IACC)**
243 N. Lindbergh Blvd., Ste. 315
St. Louis, MO 63141
(314) 993-8575

**International Association of
Hospitality Accountants (IAHA)**
P.O. Box 203008
Austin, TX 78720-3008
(512) 346-5680

**International Food Service
Executives Association (IFSEA)**
1100 S. State Rd. #7, Ste. 103
Margate, FL 33068
(305) 977-0767

Meeting Planners International (MPI)
1950 Stemmons Hwy., Ste. 5018
Dallas, TX 75207-3109
(214) 746-5222

**National Association of Food
Equipment Manufacturers (NAFEM)**
401 N. Michigan Ave.
Chicago, IL 60611-4267
(312) 644-6610

**National Executive Housekeepers
Association (NEHA)**
1011 Eastwind Dr., Ste. 301
Westerville, OH 43081
(614) 895-7166

National Tour Association (NTA)
P.O. Box 3071
Lexington, KY 40596
(606) 253-1036

**Professional Convention
Management Association (PCMA)**
100 Vestavia Office Park, Ste. 220
Birmingham, AL 35216
(205) 823-7262

Putting the Plan into Action

If you have followed our recommendations, you should now have a list of several key development areas. Now, you will have an opportunity to plan *how* you will actually develop these skills and abilities.

Keep in mind that if you have two or three more years of school ahead of you, you can still start your professional development plan now. Colleges and universities have quite a few tools available to help you. These tools include work experience, courses, faculty and industry mentors, pre-professional organizations, and so forth.

Start Your Professional Development Plan!

Take the list of important skills that you identified in Figures 6.3 and 6.4. Make a chart or plan similar to the one below to help you develop those areas you feel are important to achieving your goal but which you think you need to develop more fully. It may seem silly to put this in writing but doing so enables you to think more clearly and it allows you to check on your progress. It's much akin to a daily "to do" list.

After you have identified the areas you want to work on, think about what options or actions might help you develop that skill or competency and write them down. Don't limit your thinking and don't keep your list small because, at this stage, you are merely brainstorming. When you have written your list of developmental choices, choose the one, two, or three actions that are most appealing and which make the most sense for you and write them down also. Finally, include some method for monitoring your progress. We have chosen the date completed as a way to do this but a simple check mark would work just as well.

For example, you might aspire to be an events coordinator at a convention center after graduation. You have already gained some experience working at a convention center and have had a hand in coordinating a few small events but you have targeted, for example, crowd control, sales ability, and leadership as areas that you need to know more about or as skills you want to strengthen. Your plan might look like Figure 6.6.

FIGURE 6.6
Skills/Competency Development Plan

Skill/Competency	Developmental Options	Action Choices	Completion Date
Crowd Control	A. Read fire codes B. Attend fire code seminar C. Interview experienced event coordinator D. Interview security manager E. Attend traffic management seminar	1. Attend fire code seminar 2. Interview experienced event coordinator 3. Attend traffic management seminar	___/___/___ ___/___/___ ___/___/___
Sales Ability	A. Intern in sales department B. Find sales coach C. Read book on selling techniques D. Take selling course E. Listen to sales tapes	1. Intern in sales department 2. Take selling course	___/___/___ ___/___/___
Leadership	A. Read books on leadership B. Take a course in leadership C. Observe effective leaders D. Get leadership experience in student organizations	1. Read books on leadership 2. Observe effective leaders 3. Get leadership experience in student organizations	___/___/___ ___/___/___ ___/___/___

While this partial development plan is designed for a student who is at the early stages of career planning, it is useful for *all* stages of your career. There will be more development opportunities and choices available to you and the action plan will be more complex, but the basic premise is the same. You start with an inventory of where you are now, decide what skills to work on, identify alternative opportunities, then choose the best ones for you.

A WORD ABOUT TECHNOLOGY

To compete successfully in the future, managers in the hospitality and tourism industry must be both competent and comfortable controlling information technology. Technology means computers, telecommunications, and information storage systems.

Managers in the 21st century will be effective only if they understand technology, and its impact on consumer trends and organizations. This means a great deal more than simply knowing how to use spreadsheets and word processing systems. You must include in your professional development plan a way of understanding *how* current and future technology will fit into existing operations and *how* it will change marketing, organizational, and financial planning.

This doesn't mean that you have to be a technological specialist, however, it does mean that you have to understand it and make use of it. Futurist Alvin Toffler has observed in his recent book, *Powershift*, that information drives modern organizations more than money or hierarchical position.[12] Powerful and effective managers become so because they are able to understand, control, and manage knowledge. Knowledge, he says, comes about from selective use of the information brought about by advancing technology.

A FINAL WORD

We have made rather strong statements about your need to continuously develop, implement, and redevelop professional development programs over the course of your career. But, *don't just take our word for it*. Read what other recent graduates say about their own professional development plans.

[12] Alvin Toffler, *Powershift* (New York: Bantam Books, 1990).

I Saw the Writing on the Wall

"For a long time, I thought I had made it. I started in the hotel business when I was 16 years old, as a bell person. Nine years later, I found myself in the rooms executive position at the Tucson Hilton East. I felt I should have been happy, but I wasn't. I was concerned about my future. I wanted to be a general manager in a luxury resort. I knew that this wouldn't happen until I did two things: get some experience in a luxury corporate property and complete my degree.

With that in mind, I started taking some courses and when an opportunity to join the Hyatt Corporation came around, I took a position as the front office manager for the Hyatt Regency in Bellevue, Washington. This was a step backward but it fit my plan. After two years at the Hyatt, I quit and spent two years finishing my college degree. I supported myself by working as a truck loader for United Parcel Service.

When I graduated, it dawned on me that I needed luxury resort experience if I was to realize my goal. With that in mind, I began looking for positions. I finally settled on my current position because it afforded me the experience I needed with a company I liked. I'm pleased with the way I handled this and I have no regrets."

Kevin Johnson
Assistant Director, Front Office Operations
The Pointe Hilton Resort on South Mountain
Phoenix, Arizona

I Needed To Put the Final Pieces in the Puzzle

"I pretty much grew up in the hotel business. I started in my teenage years and gained hands on experience. Later, I gained management experience in both rooms and food and beverage. Educationally, I had some college but no degree, and I felt I needed to fill in some knowledge gaps particularly in the area of business management.

After serving as an assistant general manager for two hotels, I realized that formal education of some type was necessary. I did some research and found a year-long management development program for hospitality professionals which was offered by a local university. It suited my time schedule, and it focused on business administration, including finance and accounting. It was just what I needed.

Since completing the program, I have served as General Manager at two of my company's major properties. My educational experience not only gave me the knowledge I needed; it increased my confidence."

> *Ric Rabourn*
> *General Manager*
> *West Coast Silverdale Resort*
> *Silverdale, Washington*

Luck and Planning

"When I started college, I had no idea about what I wanted to do for a career. I had worked in construction, but had little other experience. After transferring to a state university, I noticed that it had a hospitality management program. Since I had always had an interest in food, I checked it out and decided to try it. I loved it!

As a student, I got both rooms and food and beverage experience in hotels. Also, I spent sometime managing a small, independent restaurant to gain management experience. The program director became my mentor and had a great influence on my choices of work experiences. In my senior year, I decided that I wanted to go into teaching, so I planned on getting an MBA degree and, eventually, a Ph.D.

After completing my MBA, I decided to return to the field before going on for more education, because I wasn't sure if I wanted to teach.. I was hired into Sheraton's training program for MBA graduates. Through a stroke of luck, the resident manager's position came open after I had been in training for six months. Since no one was available to fill the position, I took over on a temporary basis. I was given the title of Executive Assistant Manager. Shortly after that, I became the permanent Resident Manager and held that position for 2 ½ years.

I was then given the opportunity to become an operations analyst at Sheraton's corporate headquarters in Boston. I reported directly to the President of ITT Sheraton North America, Richard Hartman. I learned a great deal about the hotel business, its operations, and financial issues while in that position.

I have since moved back into operations. I believe my program of professional development included luck, education, seizing opportunity, and learning all I could from each job I had."

Stuart Wilging
Resort Manager
The Phoenician Resort
Scottsdale, Arizona

I Believe an MBA Will Enhance My Life

"I returned to school at age 49 after a career as a singer and a mother. My children were grown and I wanted something meaningful to do. While I was in college, I managed to obtain an internship with Marriott Management Services and this led to a permanent position after graduation. I have had several positions since then and have taken advantage of professional development opportunities provided by Marriott and elsewhere.

Education and training make me a better manager. In fact, since I am a food service manager at a university, I plan to take advantage of my location and work toward an MBA degree. I have had four years of management experience and an MBA now makes sense because I can relate experience to coursework. I believe the MBA will enhance my personal and professional life."

Teri Youngers
Assistant Manager
Fountains Cafe
Pacific Science Center
Seattle, Washington

We hope that these four real-life stories will help you to see that professional development is a planned and purposeful activity which is employed by successful managers. **Start your program now!**

American Dietetic Association (ADA)
RD	Registered Dietitian	DTR	Dietetic Technician, Registered
FADA	Fellow of the American Dietetic Association	RD, CS	Registered Dietitian, Certified Specialist

American Culinary Federation Educational Institute (ACFEI)
CPC	Certified Pastry Chef	CC	Certified Cook
CWPC	Certified Working Pastry Chef	CSC	Certified Sous Chef
CEC	Certified Executive Chef	CCC	Certified Chef de Cuisine
CCE	Certified Culinary Educator	CEPC	Certified Executive Pastry Chef
CMPC	Certified Master Pastry Chef	CMC	Certified Master Chef

Convention Liaison Council (CLC) — CMP — Certified Meeting Professional

Club Managers Association of America (CMAA)
MCM	Master Club Manager	CCM	Certified Club Manager

Dietary Managers Association (DMA) — CDM — Certified Dietary Manager

Educational Institute of American Hotel and Motel Association (EI)
CFBE	Certified Food & Beverage Executive	CHA	Certified Hotel Administrator
CEOE	Certified Engineering Operations Executive	CRDE	Certified Rooms Division Executive
CHHE	Certified Hospitality Housekeeping Executive	CHRE	Certified Human Resources Executive
CHTP	Certified Hospitality Technology Professional	CHSP	Certified Hospitality Sales Professional
CHS	Certified Hospitality Supervisor	CHT	Certified Hospitality Trainer
MHS	Master Hotel Supplier	CHE	Certified Hospitality Educator

Educational Foundation of the National Restaurant Association (EF)
FMP	Foodservice Management Professional	ServSafe	Food Safety and Sanitation Certificate
ServSafe	Responsible Alcohol Service Certificate	ServSafe	Employee and Customer Safety Certificate

Hotel, Catering and Institutional Management Association (HCIMA)
MHCIMA	Member HCIMA	FHCIMA	Fellow HCIMA

Hospitality Sales and Marketing Association International (HSMAI) — CHSE — Certified Hospitality Sales Executive

Institute of Certified Travel Agents (ICTA) — CTC — Certified Travel Counselor

International Association of Exposition Managers (IAEM) — CEM — Certified Exposition Manager

International Association of Hospitality Accountants (IAHA) — CHAE — Certified Hospitality Accountant Executive
CHTP — Certified Hospitality Technology Professional

International Food Service Executive Association (IFSEA) — CFM — Certified Food Manager
CFE — Certified Food Executive

International Special Events Society (ISES) — CSEP — Certified Special Events Professional

National Association of Catering Executives (NACE) — CPCE — Certified Professional Catering Executive

North American Association of Food Equipment Manufacturers (NAFEM) — CFSP — Certified Foodservice Professional

National Executive Housekeepers Association (NEHA) — CEH — Certified Executive Housekeeper

National Tour Association (NTA) — CTP — Certified Tour Professional

Professional Convention Management Association (PCMA) — PCS — Professional Conference Specialist

Canadian Professional Certifications and Designations (National)

ACCES	Alliance of Canadian Travel Associations/Canadian Institutes of Travel Counsellors (ACTA/CITC) Canadian Educational Standards System		
Certificate	Travel Counsellor Entry		
ACTC	Access Certified Travel Counsellor	ACTM	Access Certified Travel Manager

Canadian Restaurant and Foodservices Association (CRFA)	CFM	Certified Foodservice Manager
Canadian Food Service Executive Association	CFSEA	Certified Food Service Executive
Canadian Federation of Chefs and Cooks (CFCC)	CDC	Chef de Cuisine
Hotel Association of Canada (HAC)	CRDE	Certified Rooms Division Executive

CHHE   Certified Hospitality Housekeeping Executive

National Apprenticeship Designation

Red Seal   Cook

Canadian Professional Certifications and Designations (Provincial)

Awarded by Alberta Tourism Education Council (ATEC), Manitoba Tourism Education Council (MTEC), Northwest Territories Tourism Training Group (MTTTG), Ontario Tourism Education Council (OTEC), Pacific Rim Institute of Tourism (PRIT), Saskatchewan Tourism Education Council (STEC), Tourism Industry Association of Nova Scotia (TIANS)

Accommodation Sector

Director of Sales and Marketing	ATEC
Sales Manager	ATEC, MTEC, PRIM, STEC
Housekeeping Room Attendant	ATEC, MTEC, OTEC, PRIM, STEC
Guest Services Attendant	ATEC
Front Desk Agent	ATEC, MTEC, OTEC, PRIM, STEC, TIANS

Food and Beverage Sector

Beverage Services Manager	ATEC, MTEC, PRIT, STEC
Maitre D'Hotel	ATEC
Host/Hostess	ATEC
Wine Steward	ATEC
Bartender	ATEC, MTEC, PRIT, STEC, TIANS
Food and Beverage Server	ATEC, MTEC, OTEC, PRIT, STEC, TIANS
Cook Helper	Blue Seal - Provincial Apprenticeship Designation, Ont.
Pastry Cook	Blue Seal - Provincial Apprenticeship Designation, Ont.
Baker	Blue Seal - Alberta, B.C., Newfoundland, N.S., Ont.

Adventure Tourism Recreation Sector	Outdoor Guide (Core)	NWT-TTG
Travel Trade Sector	Local Tour Guide	ATEC, MTEC, PRIT, STEC, TIANS
Events/Conferences Sector	Special Events Coordinator	ATEC, MTEC, PRIT, STEC
Transportation Sector	Taxicab Driver	ATEC, MTEC, PRIT, STEC
Tourism Services Sector	Tourism/Visitor Information Counsellor	ATEC, MTEC, PRIT, STEC, TIANS
	Reservations Agent	ATEC, MTEC, PRIT, STEC, TIANS

Adapted with permission from The Council on Hotel, Restaurant, and Institutional Education, CHRIE Survey - 1994.

MANAGING YOUR CAREER

Once you have made a successful transition, you will have to put considerable effort into managing your career. Management, in this case, simply means paying attention to your career and yourself. We're talking about getting to know yourself and what you want, maintaining and enhancing your overall well-being, learning from your mistakes, acting ethically, and anticipating the future.

LESSONS

As your career moves along, your work can provide you with many valuable lessons. However, as in most situations, you have a choice. You can ignore these lessons or you can embrace them. If you choose to ignore them, you might get by, but chances are good that your career will not be as rewarding or fulfilling as it might have been. For some, this is OK. On the other hand, if you attend to these lessons, you will have an opportunity to not only improve your performance, but to achieve satisfaction and fulfillment beyond what you ever expected. You should be aware, however, that learning from your experience is much more difficult than remaining oblivious. Learning requires honest self-evaluation, acknowledgment of your mistakes, and, most of all, it requires **ACTION**.

WELL-BEING

No one can be effective on the job or happy in their life without maintaining a certain level of overall well-being. The hospitality and tourism industry requires *energy* and, unless you maintain your physical health, you won't be energetic. But, physical health, while important, is only one aspect of well-being. Mental and emotional wellness are ***crucial*** to personal and professional effectiveness and most would agree that each of us has a spiritual side that needs attention as well.

ETHICS

The days of stepping around or blurring ethics are gone. Both society and business are becoming increasingly aware of ethics and have come to expect ethical behavior on the part of everyone from public servants to employees in responsible positions as well as less responsible ones. This is probably due to ethical abuses on the part of government officials and corporations in the past, as well as the large number of new ethical dilemmas that technology and modern society pose.

It's not enough to simply do the right thing anymore, because what constitutes the right thing is not always clear. Being ethical requires an understanding of the various philosophical underpinnings of ethics, as well as careful examination of situations to determine if they present any ethical dilemmas.

In the hospitality and tourism industry, this might range from deciding whether or not to serve an intoxicated person to fairness in a hotel management contract. It might also include evaluating the trade-offs between highly profitable mass market tourism development and less profitable low-impact tourism development.

LOOKING AT THE FUTURE

Change of course is inevitable and it seems that, for now, both society and business are changing at unprecedented rates. Looking to the future to anticipate and understand change will help to provide career-minded professionals with information to ensure both corporate and personal effectiveness.

CONCERNING THIS SECTION

This section focuses on essential areas of career management. Chapter 7 discusses self-evaluation to help you to identify your weaknesses, capitalize on your strengths, and learn from your mistakes. Chapter 8 focuses on physical, mental, emotional, and spiritual health. Chapter 9 explores various ethical theories and shows you how to identify and act from your own ethical framework. Chapter 10 examines four major forces that are likely to affect the hospitality and tourism industry in the next century and, thus, your career.

CHAPTER	
7	# THE LESSONS OF EXPERIENCE

"Always do right – this will gratify some and astonish the rest."

Mark Twain

At this point, you have your eyes on a bright future in the hospitality and tourism industry. Your college education, you believe, will well prepare you for success. After all, it costs enough money and you have certainly invested enough time! Your interests throughout college may have been relatively focused – professional clubs, social groups, honorary societies, intramural or collegiate sports, chorus, or student political organizations. Even if you worked throughout college, sustained a relationship, or raised a family, the demands on your time were probably somewhat predictable from week to week. Chances are you even experienced some type of normalcy and followed some semblance of a schedule.

Get ready for a change!

CHANGING INTERESTS, VALUES, AND SKILLS

Upon graduation, you will operate in an entirely different world – one which will be both unique and strange to you. Maybe even scary. Feelings of apprehension and self-doubt are normal; changes are to be expected.

Regardless of your age in college, you might be a peer leader – one who heads up your small group projects, for example. You might be everyone's friend – the one with the contagious laugh and fun-loving attitude. On the other hand, you might be the perennial bookworm – the one who spends most evenings or weekends with your nose in the books, or the dedicated partner – the one who foregoes evening and weekend collegiate events for quiet time at home. Most likely, you have a certain vision of yourself by now. Your interests, whether in power, people, humor, education, or home life, have been relatively well defined by you, your peers, your partner, or your family.

You may think you are what you are and can never change, and you may think your personal and professional interests will always revolve around the same core interests as they do now. This is not likely to be the case as you continue throughout your professional career.

This first major stage in your new professional career is an ideal time for self-discovery and experimentation. You can break out of the mold you have been in and will be in the perfect position to begin to expand your life experiences. Professionally, this will start upon graduation. Personally, it will be your choice.

Many graduates who scorned the cell-phone carrying executives who chased the small white ball all over the green grass find themselves taking golf lessons so they can play in hotel or restaurant scrambles. Some who previously bought clothes that were made only of 100% cotton now find themselves donning silk ties or suits. Some who swore they would never eat anything that hid itself in a conical shell are now savoring escargot. Some who abhorred any song without a driving bass beat are now listening to Vivaldi. Prepare for it, if possible. Look forward to it. It is inevitable!

Changing Interests

Changing interests are part of life's passage. Think of how boring life would be if you still ate the same foods as you did when you were ten, you still wore the same hair style as you did in high school, you still thought the same thoughts you had in your first year of college, and you still had the same goals as you did last year. Change is part of growth. It is inevitable unless, of course, you choose not to grow.

The end of college life represents the beginning of a new life. This change does not have to be difficult or depressing. It can be an exhilarating time in your life, a time to take new risks and to explore. A recently published work, *Transitions*, explores such changing periods in lives. The author, William Bridges, identifies three passages – Endings, The Neutral Zone, and The New Beginning.[13] The Ending stage is actually an opportunity to begin anew. The Neutral Zone, the next stage of a transition, is characterized by feelings of disconnectedness to people and to the past. The final transitional stage, Bridges describes, is The New Beginning, in which a person discovers and delights in external and internal stimuli which combine to permit growth and change.

Applying *Transitions* to this time in your life, The Ending, represents the end of your college days; The Neutral Zone represents the period when you will settle into your new job or when you accept greater responsibilities in your current position; and The New Beginning represents the point when you feel empowered and excited about this new chapter in your life. **No stage is to be feared**. They are all natural stages of personal and professional development, whether you are ready or not!

Perhaps the most difficult part of change is reconciling the changes within yourself and explaining them to your friends and family. When your interests, values, and skills change, it is difficult to reconcile who you were with who you are now. No longer are your actions predictable, and no longer are your thoughts conventional. You may find yourself doing and saying the things your parents did – you know, those irritating things. You may find yourself exploring new schools of thought. You can choose either or a combination of both – embracing and re-enacting the past or creating a totally new future.

These changing interests, values, and skills will continue throughout your life, yet will seem to be most pronounced at the college-to-career transition stage. The basic process of adaptation and acceptance will be the same throughout your life transitions, but the content of or reason for the change will probably differ. For example, you may have always desired to work in a resort, but after five years in resort management, may realize that you now want to manage condominiums or become an executive chef in a small fine dining facility or, for that matter, become a poet or an artist. These changes are natural. They will continue throughout life as your experiences expand, your goals shift, your priorities reshuffle, and your emotional and spiritual needs mature.

---

13 William Bridges, *Transitions: Making Sense of Life's Changes* (New York: Addison-Wesley, 1993).

Changing Values

Changing values are closely connected with changing interests in that their occurrence is inevitable. Values represent the importance you attach to a specific way of thinking. First, you must identify exactly what your personal values are! Next, you must attempt to closely match your values with all activities in your life and with your personal and professional goals. Finally, you must be aware of changing values over time and must make adjustments to your personal and professional plans in accordance with these changes.

The identification of your values is often initially difficult and tedious. It requires introspection, usually at a depth to which most of us are not accustomed. A good starting point is to identify your interests. These interests can be categorized in two major categories: **personal** and **professional**. Next, the interests should be broken down into descriptive components; that is, you should attempt to identify the major elements of each interest.

An inventory of personal inventory may include tennis, hiking, learning a different language, reading, cooking, traveling, and investing in unique art. An example of a break-down of each activity into its major elements follows in Figure 7.1.

FIGURE 7.1
Personal Interests Inventory

TENNIS
Physical exertion, mental challenge, competition on an individual basis

HIKING
Physical exertion, affinity for outdoors, desire to be alone, need to be connected with nature

LEARNING A DIFFERENT LANGUAGE
Mental challenge, desire to understand other cultures, empathy

READING
Desire to expand vocabulary, escapism

COOKING
Creativity, attention to health

TRAVELING
Affinity for a certain level of risk, desire to experience different cultures, need to divert attention

INVESTING IN UNIQUE ART
Taste for the aesthetic, importance of investing, interest in living surroundings

Common themes run throughout the elements of each of these personal interests. These themes represent certain values. Most likely, a person with these interests would value mental challenge, physical fitness, and individuality. This person probably also values change and growth on both a mental and spiritual plane.

If this person's professional life does not mesh with his personal values, then internal conflict may result. Internal conflict causes stress and anxiety. Although perfect congruency is virtually impossible, you should attempt to closely match your activities with your value system. The closer this match, the better the chance for success and self-fulfillment!

Changing Skills

Thankfully, every person's skills change over time. If you had only the skills now that you had ten years ago, it is unlikely that you would even be in college. You certainly would not have the career opportunities you have now. Skills can be continually enhanced and improved by a number of methods. As before, the best way to start on this road to development is to first identify your skills. Next, you should set realistic goals as to how you want these skills to mature or change.

Perhaps the easiest way to assess your current skills is to list the areas in which others have recognized you and then list the skills which made these recognitions possible. Next, you should refer to your interest and value assessment. List the skills that permit you to embrace each interest and to participate in each activity. Chances are these skills will be quite similar, and represent your current inventory of professional and personal skill strengths.

These might include good physical coordination, excellent command of languages, and need for action. Again, these skills should be as closely matched to your professional life as possible. For example, a person with the skills we just listed might not excel at a career that requires confinement to a desk. Awareness of the impact of your skills upon your career success is imperative. At the least, it can help to minimize personal and professional struggles.

The Need for Continual Self-Assessment

Self-assessment of changes in interests, values, and skills should be on going. Ideally, it should be done at least once a year. The tools we listed previously should help you in the identification process. Your self-assessment should be recorded and referred to periodically, particularly when you decide to assess how you have changed.

An additional tool you could employ for self-assessment would be to write yourself a letter on a regular basis, say, on every birthday. This letter should contain the elements described previously, as well as any other observations or thoughts you wish to include. For example, you might describe important events in your life and how they affected any decisions you made. You might include the names of friends who have been important in shaping your life. You might also include any personal and professional disappointments you have experienced. Reading past letters will accentuate the importance of changes in your life, especially when you compare these changes to your current situations.

Try to identify the reasons *why* these changes occurred. Some changes just happen, some are influenced by your environment, and some are influenced by other unidentifiable sources. The identification of the *why* can often offer insight into the interests, values, and skills upon which you wish to concentrate.

Most important, remember that changes are natural. You should acknowledge these changes and nurture them. After all, varied and meaningful experiences will help to maximize your completeness as an individual.

ACCEPTING YOUR LIMITATIONS AND CAPITALIZING ON YOUR STRENGTHS

Perhaps the most humbling experience in life is acknowledging personal and professional weaknesses. We all know the adage that to err is human, but rarely do we accept that "human" in ourselves.

The acknowledgment of weaknesses occurs at two levels – the overt level, or what we actually know, and the covert level, or what we do not know or choose to hide. Joseph Luft aptly described this phenomenon as the *Johari Window*.[14]

Applying *Johari's Window* to the acknowledgment of mistakes will offer some insight into your personal and professional behavior. Figure 7.2 shows that some weaknesses are acknowledged by both the individual and others (cell 1).

[14] Joseph Luft, *The Johari Window,* **Human Relations Training News,** 5 (1), 1961, pp. 6 - 7.

For example, your quick temper may often be manageable but might surface during a stressful banquet in which the kitchen is unusually slow. In this case, your weakness would be obvious to you *and* to your work team as well.

FIGURE 7.2
Johari's Window

2 Known to Self Unknown to Others	1 Known to Self Known to Others
4 Unknown to Self Unknown to Others	3 Unknown to Self Known to Others

Sometimes, you might know your weaknesses, but may choose to conceal them from others (cell 2). For example, a new manager may know that she is not comfortable with delegating authority. Although she is aware of this, she effectively hides it by consciously forcing herself to empower employees whenever possible. Other employees may never notice her hesitation to delegate and empower, and may view her as an effective motivator and team-builder.

Cell 3 represents weaknesses that are unknown to the individual but are clear to others. Here, you might not know that you have the habit of cutting people off in mid-sentence. However, this habit might be clear to your colleagues and other employees. They could see you as someone who does not value the opinions of others and who does not listen.

Finally, some personal and professional weaknesses may not be known to either the individual or others (cell 4). Although these might ultimately affect your personal and professional development, you cannot actually address any weakness until it manifests itself in the form of an action, as in cells 1, 2, and 3.

Humans have an uncanny talent for denying weaknesses. Most believe weaknesses will go away if they are just ignored. While weaknesses might remain, the method in which you manage them can change. When you can learn more about how your mistakes are perceived by others, you can effectively reduce cell 3 by attempting to minimize these weaknesses. Furthermore, when you can admit and even show your weaknesses to others, you can reduce cell 2 with the help of colleagues and other members of the work team. The result is that the opening up of your *self* will improve communication processes and result in fewer mistakes and misunderstandings previously caused by your individual weaknesses.

Is a Weakness Always a Weakness?

Some perceived weaknesses are actually sheep in wolves' clothing. In other words, they are not actually weaknesses in their effect. Is empathy a weakness? What about compassion? Is an ethical person weak?

Too often, those starting a career confuse personal strengths with professional flaws. Look at the following example.

> *You are an assistant banquet manager in a full service resort. Your lead line cook missed work the past two days without calling in. However, he shows up for work today, the day of a banquet for 800. When you discuss his absences with him, he admits that he was going through severe depression since his spouse left him three days ago. He could not eat or sleep, and work was the last thing on his mind.*

As a new manager, would you follow the corporate call-in rules and fire him? Would you show compassion, give him a written warning, and refer him to counseling? Would you say you understand and leave it at that? These decisions are difficult under any circumstance, but are most difficult for the new manager.

Although there is no correct solution to the above scenario, it poses some interesting philosophical and behavioral dilemmas on the part of the manager. Is sympathy in this case a weakness? When does compassion turn from a strength into a weakness?

Is a Strength Always a Strength?

Similarly, what you consider a strength might not always be an asset when it comes to fruition. For example, you may consider your ability to interact with people as a strength. However, you may realize that people often walk away from you at social events, even just after a short introduction. Your gift of gab may be too much of a gift! It might be that the very strength you take pride in can actually turn against you.

Another example of a strength-turned-sour can occur when a new employee is self-confident and assured. This self-confidence can help the new employee assume more responsibilities than the average person, which could result in an early promotion or monetary rewards. On the other hand, this self-perceived strength could be viewed by some to be a weakness – arrogance. This perceived arrogance could result in a lack of understanding between the new employee and other employees. More seasoned employees could view the new employee as a 'lone ranger,' greedy, or uncooperative. They could intentionally exclude the new person and could ultimately make the work place stressful for all parties.

Also remember that *any* strength can be overdone and can turn into a weakness. For example, if planning is one of your strengths, be careful not to become so myopic that you can never operationalize your plans. If analysis is one of your strengths, be careful that you do not spend so much of your time analyzing that you forget the other aspects of your job as a manager. **Remember that managerial balance is most important** and that your strengths should *add* to that balance and not tip the scales in either direction.

THEN HOW CAN I ACCEPT MY WEAKNESSES AND CAPITALIZE ON MY STRENGTHS?

The most effective way to capitalize on your strengths is to position yourself to do so. This does not necessarily mean that you should showcase your strengths to your fellow employees and to management, but that you should use them as a tool for success. Be cautious, though – strengths can only be maximized if you recognize, and work within the limitations of, your weaknesses.

It has been said that one person's strength is another person's weakness. This saying has some truth and certainly some relevancy to your professional career. It is not the strength alone that can turn into another's weakness, though. It is that strength *combined with* individual traits, skills, and experiences that can differentiate the effects of strengths between people. Most corporate presidents, general managers, and department heads surround themselves with people who possess strengths they do not. Similarly, they surround themselves with people whose weaknesses are not the same as their own.

The previous assessment tools should help you to adequately evaluate your individual strengths and weaknesses. Now, position yourself by matching your strengths and weaknesses with your career path *and* personal life to best realize your potential.

THE PITFALLS OF SUCCESS

Success, by its conventional definition, is the goal of many college students. However, the quest for professional success can take a toll on one's health, mental stability, and personal relationships. In the end, many ask themselves, "Has it really been worth it?" Some of these dangers, along with ways to deal with them, were discussed in Chapter 5. Others will be discussed in Chapter 8.

If you are just beginning your professional career, success at an early stage may be the outcome of your knowledge, skills, and abilities, or it may be due to pure luck. Most likely, it will be the result of some combination of both. Regardless, early career success carries with it some potential threats. Your ego may be unrealistically inflated and could ultimately lead to professional and personal devastation. Also, early success often carries with it a certain lifestyle which is not always easy to manage or keep in perspective. Finally, early career success may lead to unrealistic expectations regarding your future. You may think that since you were the youngest general manager in the history of your corporation, you will necessarily become the youngest vice president. This may or may not be true. Perhaps your true talents lie in operations, not in corporate strategy making.

Keeping the Ego Intact

Regardless of your definition of success, you will probably know when you have achieved "it." You know the expression, "Never forget your roots?" Well, don't! The reasons for your success are numerous and complex, but necessarily include support from your family and friends. You may think that your years in the Young Republicans or as a chaperone for your child's class field trip taught you nothing but perhaps they helped you develop leadership skills. You may think that your short-lived stint in the school band was worthless, but perhaps it helped teach you discipline and, hopefully, the appreciation of music. You may have destroyed that high school football jersey or that soccer coach tee shirt, but perhaps it helped teach you responsibility and perseverance. You may laugh at that picture you drew years ago that hangs in your parent's living room but perhaps it helped foster your creativity. All these former parts of your life may seem irrelevant now, but their importance cannot be overstated.

Remember the feeling of pride you had when your football team won their homecoming game by 24 points, no matter how long ago that was? Is that feeling any different from the feeling you should have when your employees wrap-up an overwhelmingly successful banquet? Remember the feeling of accomplishment you had when you recited a Shakespearean soliloquy with only a few stutters? Is that feeling any different from the feeling you should have when you conclude a lucrative sales call that ends in a booking? Remember the feeling of satisfaction you had when you baked your first cake and it didn't fall? Should that feeling be any different than the feeling you have when you or one of the chefs prepares an exquisite dish that becomes the trademark of your restaurant?

The moral to the story is that the pitfalls of success can often be avoided just by remembering that you have a history which helped formed who you are now.

Self Esteem Is Important!

Self-esteem, or your belief in **you**, is an important part of personal and professional maturity. You need not be arrogant, but you should recognize your strengths. You need not be stubborn, but you should stand by your beliefs. Self-esteem cannot be developed overnight. In fact, most struggle their entire lives to achieve a level of belief in self. Although it might be difficult to believe that you are extremely capable and have a bright professional future, **believe it**! Often, the repetition of self-affirming phrases can help, and will lead to affirmation of you by others. Try repeating a phrase such as "I like myself, I am worthy of my position, and I have a promising future" every day before you go to work. It might sound a bit absurd at first, but soon you will begin to believe it!

The Life Style Danger

Most often, money and prestige accompany professional success. Money and prestige are difficult to manage *whenever* they come in one's professional career, but they are undoubtedly more difficult to manage when they come early.

You may have been used to driving a dilapidated manual car with bald tires and now find a BMW in your garage. You may be used to shopping for clothes at garage sales and now find Evan Picones in your closet. You may be used to splurging on a bottle of Chablis and now find your wine collection stocked with vintage reds.

Money Isn't Everything, Is It?

A drastic change in your financial status can make the transition from college student to hospitality or tourism executive even more difficult, particularly if it happens quickly. The best advice is to remember that money is *only* green ink on white paper. It serves as a medium of exchange of goods and services for other goods and services. Nothing more, nothing less. Granted, more money can afford you an "easier" life, but can it really? It all depends on your perspective.

You will retire some day and will require a certain level of resources to pay for health care, housing, and other needs and wants. This requires sound financial plans as outlined in Chapter 5. Also, good health and continually increasing levels of productivity, at any age, are not guaranteed. A realistic view of money can help you plan for these situations. More important, it can result in a healthy and ethical attitude toward material possessions.

A Job Title Is Everything, Right?

The attainment or drive for prestige is the other potential danger associated with success. Professional prestige is commonly tied to job titles. Remember that job titles are just that – titles. Rarely do titles accurately describe a job. Never do they fully describe a career. Job titles are stagnant and dormant. They describe a position, *not* the individual in the position. It is important to realize that a job title does not "make" a person. Neither can it destroy a person.

Most people are automatically stereotyped by their job title, since many believe that it is the ultimate measure of prestige. How many times have you been introduced to someone at a social event? They are introduced my their name first. Then, a remarkable thing occurs – their job title immediately follows. It is as if they are *only* permitted to retain their name as long as it is tied directly to their professional position. Would it be wrong to introduce a person or yourself by name only? Would this de-emphasize the importance of prestige? Would it increase the emphasis on individuality and open doors to real communication without false pretenses? Try it.

LEARNING FROM MISTAKES

Life experience is the best teacher and the best vehicle for growth. A big part of this growth through experience occurs because of mistakes that you made or that someone else made. Mistakes cannot be viewed as professional or personal failures. Instead, they should serve as a guide to improvement. The key is to admit your mistakes. Once you can acknowledge that you have erred, you have admitted your human fallibility and you have taken the first step to real growth.

Realistically, it is not prudent to admit all of your mistakes to everyone. The admission could make you seem too self-deprecating, could blur your focus on self-fulfillment, and could ultimately limit your opportunities for success and happiness. However, within reason, the acknowledgment of mistakes is important, particularly when these mistakes affect others.

It is natural that you will make more mistakes when you first begin your job or are promoted to a new position. To you, the environment will be unknown and the decisions you make will be ones you have never made before. These situations combine to create an environment in which errors in personal or professional judgment are common. Do not wallow in despair. Instead, use the opportunity to improve yourself. Let mistakes renew you, invigorate you, and better you!

Following are three scenarios in which rising managers have made professional mistakes. In each case, the manager used this mistake as a developmental tool. Note the variety of scope and outcome of each mistake.

Take Time To Think and Calm Down!

"In college, it is acceptable and even expected to fly off the cuff. When you're in management, though, it is very different. Employees often test you, particularly when you are young. The hardest lesson I learned, and am *still* learning, is to take time to think about my response to a problem before I react, rather than reacting too quickly. Only if you can recognize this as a weakness can you make an effort to correct it and to modify your behavior accordingly."

Ginger Rolli
General Manager
Cooker Restaurants
Florence, Kentucky

In this case, the rising manager realized the implications of her propensity to make decisions too quickly. She knew enough to recognize this as a weakness in herself that could affect the quality of her restaurant operation and is taking steps toward change. Only because of her ability to acknowledge her mistakes, however, can she take the first step toward self-improvement.

Customers Need To Believe They Are Always Right!

"When I first started out in institutional food service management, I learned the hard way: The customer is always right! How did I learn this? A customer *knew* she was right, but I knew she was wrong, so I attempted to explain to her *why* she was wrong. Needless to say, my knowledge and logic did not impress her and she became extremely angry. I learned quickly that it is far better to smile and validate the customer's beliefs than to give explanations or even excuses."

Kathy Sanders
Assistant Food Service Director
ARAMARK
University of North Carolina
Charlotte, North Carolina

This manager learned quickly that the customer's beliefs must be recognized and heard by management. Most often, customers do not want to hear *why* something happened – they just want it fixed or want to blow off steam. Maintaining a smile and a closed mouth in these circumstances is difficult at first, but you will soon realize that it is necessary for the continued success of your operation *and* for your continued promotability as a manager.

Communicate, Communicate, Communicate!

"One of the mistakes I made early in my career was forgetting the importance of communication between line and staff employees. I was working at the front desk when a dissatisfied guest wanted a room change. We were extremely busy, and the guest insisted on speaking with a manager. I gave the guest the name of our Front Office Manager, but I neglected to tell the manager that the guest was on his way to see her. I forgot one of the most important rules of business – good communication. It is important not to put any other employee in a situation in which he or she is unprepared."

Adam Hentz
Evening Housekeeping Manager
Ritz-Carlton Buckhead
Atlanta, Georgia

The mistake made by this manager is a quite common mistake to make during your first years. During college, communication between you and your friends, you and your professors, and you and your internship employer is quite different. The communication between you and your friends is understandably quite informal. Some of it may even be based on a mutual understanding, with no verbal exchanges taking place. The communication between you and your professors was probably information based. That is, you sought information or advice, depending on whether you were discussing your class or your career. Although the communication between you and your internship employer was at a different level, there was probably not a need for it to be complete and on going.

Communication in the workplace, however, is at an entirely different level. You must be aware of the ramifications of *not* communicating problems or concerns when appropriate. Failure to do so could result in difficulties throughout your career. Upper-level management may be wary of your loyalty, judgment, or thoroughness. Fellow employees may feel threatened by your non-communication. They may misread it and think that you are withholding information to make yourself look better to upper level management at the expense of the operations.

The best rule of thumb is to make certain that everyone in your work area is aware of any problems that have recently occurred or are about to occur. This will make you a trusted colleague and employee. Remember, there are enough daily surprises in the hospitality and tourism industry. You need not be the cause of any more.

Mistakes Can Only Occur Through Action

It is important to realize that mistakes can only occur through action. In other words, the fact that you erred was due to the fact that you were achieving or producing. If you were doing nothing at all, you might be guilty of laziness or omission, but you certainly could not be accused of actively making a mistake.

Most important is to learn how to recognize these mistakes as part of professional growth. You must not dwell on them, but must use them as learning mechanisms. After all, mistakes are part of life and a way to ultimate success.

KNOW THYSELF – BE THYSELF

Know thyself – be thyself. These two phrases are so important to professional and personal fulfillment, yet are so often misunderstood or ignored.

Know Thyself

Before you can become who you are truly meant to be, you first need to know who you are now. You have already inventoried your interests, values, and skills. You have developed some goals on a number of levels. How do these combine to define *you*?

At this point, you need to try to detach yourself from you. That is, you need to look at yourself through objective eyes. It is extremely easy to deceive oneself, at least as viewed through conscious actions. To fully know who you are, you now need to pry into the real person behind the overt actions and words – the real you.

Remember how simple life was when you were very young? You knew who you were, within the limitations of age, and you knew what was expected of you. Although those carefree days are gone, the simplicity you felt then can be felt again. This simplicity can often lead to success as you will see later. There is no best way to get to know your real self – different methods work for different people. Some find the solace of nature conducive to self-discovery. Some find that small group interactions help. Some might wish to employ a counselor. Some might use books in their search for their true self.

Although it is far beyond the scope of this book to fully explore these different methods, it is sufficient to let you know that they are there. Peruse bookstores or libraries, open the newspaper, or glance at the Yellow Pages. Many successful professionals have struggled in their search for self-discovery, so do not feel alone. The experience itself can be extremely rewarding. The outcome can be unbelievably enlightening and fulfilling.

Be Thyself

You should have enough information by now to have a pretty good idea of the real you. Now, the trick is to *become* you!

So often in business, rising managers believe that they need to act a certain way in order to get noticed and, therefore, promoted. These actions often emulate those of a family member, a mentor, or an upper level manager. You must remember that the way people act is certainly not the sole determinant of their promotability. Moreover, if you start to observe the personalities of general managers or company presidents, they are not alike. You will find that all have mastered certain skills such as the ability to quickly interpret financial statements and the ability to make relatively quick decisions, yet their overall personalities and interests vary greatly. So do their management styles, since these are the result of many experiences, traits, values, abilities, beliefs, and skills.

It is not necessary to behave gruffly if you are inherently sensitive. It is not necessary to make forceful decisions if you are the type who prefers to weigh different options first. It is not necessary to assume the traits of a "type-A" personality if yours, in fact, more closely resembles a "type-B" personality.

The most important rule of thumb is to *be yourself*! Have faith that others will respect you and, yes, even like you just the way you are. Everyone knows that we are but human and have a certain combination of strengths and weaknesses. You will find that your strengths will be admired by others and, most pleasantly, that your weaknesses are quickly forgiven, if noticed at all.

It is often difficult for people to truly believe that they can be successful just by being themselves. Think about the alternative – who else would you become? To alter who you truly are, if this is even possible, would be deceitful to others and would be the ultimate denial of yourself.

Although it is often necessary to temper certain behaviors in certain situations, it is not necessary to alter your true self. For example, if you have always had the propensity to laugh a bit too loud and a bit too much, you might want to control that laughter a bit in corporate meetings. However, that same laughter might endear you to friends and might be your personal trademark to your employees and to your colleagues. Similarly, if you have always had a habit of procrastinating, you should attempt to meet deadlines at work without putting undue pressure on others and on yourself. Some of the skills you developed to deal with your constant procrastination, however, may make you invaluable in times of workplace disasters when quick decision-making and actions are imperative. You might be just the one to take charge in a hurricane emergency. You might be a perfect choice to draft the renovation proposal that the owners just informed your general manager they will need by tomorrow.

If you totally hid these parts of the real you, certain opportunities might never present themselves. More important, if you attempt to change yourself to fit into a certain mold, how can you be certain that the mold you chose is actually desirable? Can you be *truly* fulfilled if you know that you made a conscious decision to live a lie, that is, to become someone who you are not?

You are acceptable *just as you are*. In fact, you are *more* than acceptable. You are unique, and that uniqueness will undoubtedly enhance your corporation and its employees. Part of your worth comes from your combination of perceptions, experiences, and values. That combination is yours alone and should be protected and nurtured.

Self-deceit and self-denial are dangerous to your professional career and to your personal life. Believe in who you are! Have faith in yourself! Most of all, as stated in the previous chapter, become who you are! You will be more dependable, more promotable, and, most of all, more fulfilled.

ADDITIONAL READINGS

Career Fitness, Peter D. Weddle; Codell & Davies (New York, 1994).

Do What You Are, Paul D. Tieger & Barbara Barron-Tieger; Little, Brown and Company (Boston, 1992).

Do What You Love, The Money Will Follow, Marsha Sinetar; Dell Publishers (New York, 1987).

The Three Boxes of Life and How to Get Out of Them, Richard N. Bolles; Ten Speed Press, 2nd edition (Berkeley, California, 1981).

Zen and the Art of Making a Living, Laurence G. Boldt; Penguin Corporation, 2nd edition (New York, 1993).

CHAPTER 8

LIVING A HEALTHY LIFESTYLE

"The artist is nothing without the gift, but the gift is nothing without work."

Emile Zola

We've discussed professional development at length. However, it is important for you to realize that professional and personal development go hand in hand. You can't fully develop professionally unless your personal life is running smoothly – the ups and downs of your professional life have substantial influence on your personal life. What this means is that you have to develop both your personal and professional sides and you can't ignore one at the expense of the other.

Personal development involves attaining a certain amount of self-awareness and striving for self-improvement. It is a continuous process which is not geared toward mastery, but is partially focused on maintaining personal wellness by living a healthy lifestyle. In concrete terms, this means you need to be remain healthy *and* maintain your peace of mind.

MAINTAINING YOUR PHYSICAL HEALTH

Maintaining your physical, emotional, mental, and spiritual health is necessary for you to be at your best for your friends, family, partner, and career. It requires discipline and on-going attention, but will ultimately make your life much fuller and, probably longer. Not only will you feel better, you will be more tolerant and less anxious and, needless to say, you will probably improve your job performance. Total health is never guaranteed, but at least you can view it as a challenge, and take the necessary steps to make it happen.

We briefly touched on wellness in Chapter 5. In this chapter, however, we will discuss in detail three key aspects of maintaining your health – exercise, diet and nutrition, and avoiding the misuse of substances such as alcohol or drugs. Think of them as a package deal. Good practices in two areas are sabotaged by poor practices in the other. If you jog daily, follow sound nutritional practices, and drink a liter of vodka every day, you will not enjoy physical well being.

Our goal here is to provide you with solid information and some practices to help you maintain and augment your health. At first, these practices might seem overwhelming, but with some effort and attention, they can become healthy habits which will last for a lifetime.

Exercise, Exercise, Exercise

The benefits of exercise are numerous, and range from lower blood pressure to weight control. Exercise is also an excellent stress-management tool since it works to burn off feelings of frustration, anxiety, and helplessness. Furthermore, exercise helps bring your body into sync with your mind. You will find yourself thinking clearer, your memory improved, and your logic more astute.

Exercise takes many forms. Some like to work out at home while some like to frequent a gym or a health club. Some prefer to exercise inside while others prefer to exercise outside. Some prefer extensive and exhaustive routines while others prefer moderate routines. The important thing to remember is that exercise plans are as individual as eating habits and hairstyles. Some routines may fit your lifestyle whereas others may not.

It is important for you to find some form of exercise which you enjoy and which can become a part of your daily routine. Common excuses for not exercising include not having enough time or not being athletic. This really doesn't work, because an exercise routine does not necessarily mean that you have to run a five-minute mile or bench press an amount equal to your body weight. A regular plan of exercise can be as simple as a brisk walk through a park or reserve, stretches on your living room floor, or the Chinese art of Tai Chi. Numerous video tapes are available which feature nearly every type of exercise plan you can imagine – check them out! Figure 8.1 lists various exercise options which can be done alone. The list is by no means exhaustive, but it just might spark some interest for you.

FIGURE 8.1
Exercise Options

Option	Suggested Duration or Distance per Session
Bicycling	At least 5 miles
Climbing stairs	20 minutes
Golf (no carts allowed!)	9 or 18 holes
Jogging	At least 2 miles
Hiking	At least 2 miles
Rollerblading	At least 3 miles
Stretching	30 minutes
Swimming	20 minutes
Tai Chi	Variable
Walking	At least 3 miles
Weight lifting	30 minutes

You can mix and match options from this list. In fact, a balanced program of exercise calls for a *combination* of aerobic, flexibility, and strengthening exercises. For example, you can do 10 minutes of stretching every day, 15 to 20 minutes of jogging three times weekly, and lift weights for 15 to 20 minutes four times weekly. This means a minimum time investment of 25 minutes per day or about 3 hours per week. Not much of an investment when you consider that you have 168 hours available each week. Alternatively, some sports such as tennis or rollerblading, if regularly practiced, can satisfy all three requirements.

Although most of the activities listed in the previous table can be done alone, some enjoy them even more if they do them with another person. Jogging with a friend can help you maintain your pace and motivation, hiking with a partner might make you feel safer, and bicycling with your family could double as a family outing.

Most often, developing an *individual* exercise routine is best since you can do it at your own pace, within your own time schedule, and can stick to your workout even when you travel. Obviously, there are also many activities that you can perform in a group or in a league, such as field hockey, soccer, softball, rowing, or volleyball. These, too, are great forms of exercise and might just help you meet new friends as well! Handball, racquetball, and tennis are also excellent forms of exercise, but all three require both appropriate facilities and a reliable and interested partner.

Regardless of the exercise routine you choose, you must take care not to injure yourself. You might be surprised at the variety of injuries that can occur – everything from a dislocated shoulder to shin splints. You might also be surprised at how easily and often exercise-related injuries occur.

Exercise Is Necessary for Your Well-Being!

The best way to avoid injuries from happening is to learn how to do the exercise correctly, to adequately warm up beforehand and cool down afterwards, and to give your body time to recover between workouts. The way to get the most out of exercising is to stop while you still feel good and are not too sore. "No pain, no gain" is out of vogue, particularly for the amateur.

Before beginning a new exercise program or sport, you need to determine your current level of fitness. The Cooper 12-Minute Walking/Running Test, shown in Table 8.1, can help.

TABLE 8.1
Cooper 12-Minute Walking/Running Test (Distance in Miles Covered in 12 Minutes)

Fitness Category	Gender	Age				
		20-29	30-39	40-49	50-59	60+
Very Poor	Men	<1.22	<1.18	<1.14	<1.03	<0.87
	Women	<0.96	<0.94	<0.88	<0.84	<0.78
Poor	Men	1.22-1.31	1.18-1.30	1.14-1.24	1.03-1.16	0.87-1.02
	Women	0.96-1.11	0.95-1.05	0.88-0.98	0.84-0.93	0.78-0.86
Fair	Men	1.32-1.49	1.31-1.45	1.25-1.39	1.17-1.30	1.03-1.20
	Women	1.12-1.22	1.06-1.18	0.99-1.11	0.94-1.05	0.87-0.98
Good	Men	1.50-1.64	1.46-1.56	1.40-1.53	1.31-1.44	1.21-1.32
	Women	1.23-1.34	1.19-1.29	1.12-1.24	1.06-1.18	0.99-1.09
Excellent	Men	1.65-1.76	1.57-1.69	1.54-1.65	1.45-1.58	1.33-1.55
	Women	1.35-1.45	1.30-1.39	1.25-1.34	1.19-1.30	1.10-1.18
Superior	Men	>1.77	>1.70	>1.66	>1.59	>1.56
	Women	>1.46	>1.40	>1.35	>1.31	>1.19

Adapted with permission from Kenneth H. Cooper, *The Aerobics Program for Total Well Being* (New York: Bantam Books, 1982).

This test not only indicates your current level of physical fitness, but can give you a measuring stick to gauge your progress. You will know if your exercise routine has been effective when you performed at the *fair* level when you started and, six months later, perform at the *excellent* level.

Some people should get permission from their doctors before beginning an exercise routine. You should see your physician if you:

➡ have heart trouble or high blood pressure;
➡ have frequent pains in your heart or chest;
➡ have a bone or joint problem; or
➡ fall into the Very Poor, Poor, or Fair category of the Cooper test.

Your doctor will be able to suggest certain exercises to increase your endurance and strength within the limitations of your current health problems.

After you know your current fitness level and have the blessing of your doctor if you need it, learn about the exercise or sport you intend to try. Buy or borrow some books or talk to friends or professional trainers. You might find that what you *thought* was appealing about a certain type of exercise is actually a turn-off. For example, you might have always thought of bicycling as your preferred form of exercise, but find out that maintaining a bike requires more time than you wish to spend. You might also find that the exercise or sport is too expensive for you to begin at this point in your professional career.

You should also consider the safety of certain outdoor activities such as jogging, walking, or hiking. If you cannot find a safe area around your neighborhood to exercise outside, then either drive to a safer area to work out or choose another activity.

Once you decide on an exercise or sport, do some strengthening and flexibility exercises before you actually begin your program. And remember – **GO SLOWLY**. Many health clubs and universities have professional trainers who can help you get started on an exercise plan and can instruct you on how to do it correctly. Also, many books are available and provide the same information, but be careful. Sometimes photographs are not as effective as hands-on instruction.

Most of all, remember that exercise is not just a hobby – *it must become part of your life*. It takes a little discipline at first, but soon you will find that you feel empty and even lethargic without it. The benefits from exercise can be felt almost immediately, and these good feelings can continue throughout your life.

Eat Smart, Feel Good

The demands of your job might make it difficult for you to eat the way you know you should. Without fuel, the body cannot continue to function at its best and it tends to tire much faster. Remember the four basic food groups: meat, fish, poultry, and legumes; milk, yogurt, and cheese; fruits and vegetables; and breads and cereals? Well, times have changed and so has the way nutritionists look at dietary needs. More and more people are reducing or eliminating their intake of red meat. There is an increased emphasis on moderate use of salt and sugar and lighter meals with reduced fat content. The increased attention to nutrition and its profound effect on health has resulted in revised dietary guidelines as shown in Figure 8.2.

FIGURE 8.2
Daily Dietary Guidelines Food Pyramid

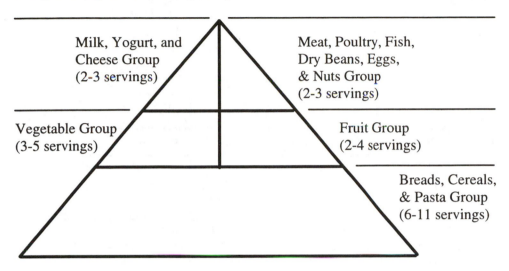

Adapted from The Dairy Farmers of Washington, 1995.

You needn't think about these guidelines as being restrictive because you can be as creative with them as you want to be. Many dishes combine food groups including pasta with vegetables, stir-fry, and even pizza. There are many good cookbooks which can help you plan meals and even menus. But, pay attention to your cooking *process* in order to maximize the benefits of the foods you eat. Keep in mind that certain vitamins – most often B-6, B-12, C, niacin, riboflavin, and thiamin – can be destroyed by excessive boiling, so steam your vegetables, cook them in just a small amount of water, or eat them raw.

Potential Medical Benefits, Too!

Many foods are claimed to have medical benefits in addition to nutritional ones. Traditional views of nutrition have changed and there is a renewed interest in the healing power of food. The trend is away from diets and toward a personalized approach to nutrition. It is also toward the positive effects of a healthy diet, and how certain foods are *friendly* and have health-boosting potential.

Table 8.2 lists foods believed to reduce the chances of certain diseases and disorders. It is important to note that these foods *alone* will not necessarily heal you or prevent certain diseases. You still need to visit your physician and continue treatments, medications, or vitamin supplements as prescribed. Healthy and preventive eating habits are just part of the total picture of good health.

TABLE 8.2
Healing and Preventive Foods

Disease or Disorder	Suggested Vitamin or Mineral	Best Food Source(s)
Acne	Zinc	Lean beef, crabmeat, oysters, pork
	Vitamin A	Broccoli, cantaloupe, greens
Anemia	Iron	Veal, beef, scallops, beans
	Vitamin C	Broccoli, greens, fruit juices, oranges
Cancer	Vitamin A	Broccoli, cantaloupe, greens
	Vitamin C	Broccoli, greens, fruit juices, oranges
	Fiber	Bread, potatoes, broccoli, bananas
	Calcium	Milk, cheese, yogurt
	Vitamin D	Sardines, tuna, salmon
High blood pressure	Calcium	Milk, cheese, yogurt
	Potassium	Spinach, beans, tomatoes, winter squash
	Polyunsaturated fats	Fish oil, polyunsaturated vegetable oil
Insomnia	Tryptophan	Turkey
Osteoporosis	Calcium	Milk, cheese, yogurt
	Vitamin D	Sardines, tuna, salmon
	Phosphorous	Artichokes, cottage cheese, pasta
Skin Wounds	Vitamin C	Broccoli, greens, fruit juices, oranges
	Zinc	Lean beef, crabmeat, oysters, pork
Ulcers	Linoleic Acid	Polyunsaturated vegetable oil

Compiled from Patricia Hausman & Judith Benn Hurley, *The Healing Foods* (New York: Dell Publishing, 1992).

One of the biggest contributors to heart attacks, strokes, and other cardiovascular and circulatory problems is a high blood cholesterol level. Table 8.3, adapted from the American Heart Association guidelines, shows where to draw the line.

TABLE 8.3
Acceptable Cholesterol Levels

Age	Acceptable Range (milligrams of cholesterol/deciliters of serum)
0 - 19	120 - 180
20 - 29	125 - 190
30 +	130 - 200

Cholesterol screening is an inexpensive and widely available test. It's worth a trip to your doctor, clinic, or health fair to check it out. If you are above the acceptable range according to your age, take immediate action. Some actions you can take include seeking medical advice, modifying your diet, and exercising.

High blood pressure is another health danger faced by people of all ages. Unlike many other ailments, high blood pressure often has no symptoms. Prevention, rather than treatment, is "the key" and while some people have a predisposition to this condition, there are a number of things you can do to ward off elevated blood pressure or to reduce it if it is outside of the acceptable limits. These include quitting smoking, exercising regularly, and reducing your consumption of alcohol, caffeine, and sodium. Your best bet, however, is to see your physician.

Sources of Calories

Not only are food, but the *sources* of nutrition bear equal weight. For example, if you are an "average" person for whom a 2,000 calorie a day diet is appropriate, according to the United States Department of Agriculture, your diet should reflect the following amounts of fat, cholesterol, carbohydrates, sodium, protein, and fiber:[15]

- ✓ 65 grams of total fat
- ✓ 20 grams of saturated fat
- ✓ 300 milligrams of cholesterol
- ✓ 20 - 30 grams of fiber
- ✓ 300 milligrams of carbohydrates
- ✓ 2,400 milligrams of sodium
- ✓ 50 grams of protein

[15] Calculated from Cream Style Corn can, 1996.

You are probably wondering how you can determine if you are getting 300 milligrams of carbohydrates or exceeding 2,400 milligrams of sodium. Perhaps the best way to calculate food content is to consult food labels or books. Also, some restaurants, particularly in the quick service segment, provide charts with nutritional information.

If you suspect that your diet deviates from established norms or if you are concerned about ensuring a healthy diet, you might want to keep a log or record of your daily food intake and compare it with food labels or nutritional guides to determine whether your diet meets the nutritional guidelines. If you find you are outside of the guidelines, you should strongly consider changing your eating habits. Particular areas of concern are insufficient fiber intake and excess fat, cholesterol, and sodium intake. The former can eventually lead to colon and rectal problems and the latter to cardio-vascular problems.

Water Is the Source of Life

Finally, do not forget the importance of water to the healthy functioning of your body. Seventy percent of your body is made up of water and it serves many functions from hydration to carrying nutrients through the bloodstream. You should drink eight or more glasses of water every day in order to maintain the appropriate balance of water in your body. Excessive perspiration caused by an increase in physical activity or just by your nature warrants an even greater intake of water.

Avoidance of Substance Abuse

In Chapter 5, we pointed out that substance abuse was dangerous. It can destroy relationships, divide families, ruin careers, and eventually kill. This section will focus specifically on alcoholism and drug abuse. We talk about the nature of both, how they harm you, and what to do if you or someone you know is a victim of alcoholism or drug abuse.

Alcoholism

Excessive drinking and alcoholism represent a substantial danger for employees in the hospitality and tourism industry. Long hours, a fast pace, and easy access to alcohol make the overuse of this substance highly tempting. The conventional wisdom holds that overuse of alcohol is common in the industry. However, there is a difference, as we will point out, between excessive drinking and alcoholism. Sometimes they go hand in hand; sometimes not.

Most experts agree that alcoholism is a primary disease, *not* a bad habit or a personal weakness. An alcoholic can never be cured, but can enter a state of remission in which the effects of alcoholism are arrested. Alcoholism is also a progressive disease if left untreated. It involves the compulsive use of alcohol for which the abuser develops an abnormal tolerance, an increasing psychological and physical dependence, and severe discomfort upon withdrawal.

Recent studies indicate that the tendency toward alcoholism might be hereditary.[16] One study involved sets of identical twins who were separated at birth and whose biological parents were both alcoholics. One twin was adopted by a couple who abstained from alcohol use entirely, and the other remained with the alcoholic parents. The results were surprising: Sets of twins become alcoholics at the same rate regardless of their environment. This is strong evidence that alcoholism has its roots in genetic make-up rather than the environment.

Other studies show that alcoholism tends to occur in certain families at a rate above the national average. Recent research has indicated differences between the metabolic rates of alcoholics and non-alcoholics, providing further evidence that alcoholism may be genetically based.[17]

White-collar alcoholics are not always easy to identify. An estimated ten to eleven percent of people who drink suffer from alcoholism, and the disease is not selective based on people's career choices.[18] White-collar alcoholics do not introduce themselves as alcoholics, nor do they carry around a brown paper sack with a bottle inside.

[16] James Milam & Thomas Ketcham, *Under the Influence* (New York: Bantam Books, 1981).

[17] *Ibid.*

[18] *Positive Action for Lawyers: A Professional Alcoholism Program* (California State Bar: March 1, 1978).

Alcoholics come in all shapes and sizes and have various drinking patterns ranging from daily drinking to social drinking. According to the American Psychiatric Association (APA), three major patterns of drinking emerge: regular intake of large amounts of alcohol; regular drinking limited to weekends; and drinking binges with long periods of sobriety in between.[19]

Although the physical dependence combined with the mental obsession usually becomes evident over time regardless of the alcoholic's efforts to hide the addiction, some are able to hide their disease for many years.

The term *functional alcoholic* is often used to describe the person who conceals the disease from colleagues, family members, partners, and even physicians up until an early death from an accident, heart attack, cirrhosis, or suicide. They are often perfectionists and workaholics with a low tolerance for change. Upon the death of the functional alcoholic, most will be surprised to learn of the real cause of death – they mistook workaholism for ambition and perfectionism for a character trait.

According to a researcher, alcoholics structure more and more of their lives around drinking as the disease progresses. Feelings of paranoia are strong and almost constant, and alcoholics take great pains to obtain, conceal, and protect their supply of alcohol. Alcoholics have been known to fill their coffee mugs with vodka-laced coffee, to mix gin with their morning orange juice, and to bolster soft drinks with whiskey. Although these actions represent the extreme, addiction to alcohol, depending upon the person, can be as subtle or as simple as reliance on alcohol to reduce stress. However, as we will discuss later, stress *does not* cause alcoholism.

It is important to understand that the use of alcohol or even the excessive use of alcohol does not necessarily mean that a person is an alcoholic. As we said earlier, alcoholism is a disease and has been commonly defined as such since the 1950s. However, the symptoms are not as clear cut as in most other diseases.

For example, alcoholism has been the subject of thousands of research studies. In fact, a Web search using the keywords *behavior* and *alcoholism* produced 40,000 matched before we trimmed it down. However, several things are clear.

[19] Anonymous, *Diagnostic and Statistical Manual of Mental Disorders* (4th Ed.) (Washington, D.C.: American Psychiatric Association, 1994).

First, there is a new and developing view of alcoholism. Second, alcoholism *does* negatively affect behavior and performance. Third, even though many people give "lip service" to the disease concept, alcoholism is often regarded as a personal failing or weakness. The APA does not necessarily define alcoholism as a separate disorder. Rather, it lumps it in with dependence on a variety of substances. While the specific symptoms of these dependencies may vary according to the substance used, dependency on any substance can and most likely will lead to "clinically significant impairment or distress including behavioral change."[20]

E.M. Jellinek, a pioneering researcher, was one of the first to define alcohol as a *progressive disease.* By that, he means that it starts with subtle behavioral changes such as increased drinking and (obviously) more hangovers. It then spirals downward and includes various behavioral problems such as problems at work, dysfunctional relationships, drunk driving, acting in a deranged manner, and, finally, a complete breakdown of rational structure. [21]

The important thing to remember here is that we are not preaching against the sins of alcohol. Being an alcoholic is not a moral weakness nor is it shameful. It just is. You don't become an alcoholic because of stress or because of difficult times. After all, "everyone is at some biological risk for developing alcoholism. However, a person who has a higher biological risk has a lower trigger."[22]

The lesson? Alcoholism can mess up your life. You can recover and, for whatever reason, the conventional wisdom says that people in the hospitality and tourism industry are more prone to this disease than others.

[20] Anonymous, *Diagnostic and Statistical Manual of Mental Disorders* (4th Ed.) (Washington, D.C.: American Psychiatric Association, 1994).

[21] E.M. Jellinek, *The Disease Concept of Alcoholism* (New Haven, Connecticut: Yale College and University Press, 1960).

[22] Anonymous, *Coping with Alcoholism,* February 13, 1996 (World Wide Web address: http://wso.villans.edi/peerh/drugs/alcohol/alcoism.html).

The following questionnaire in Figure 8.3 should be answered honestly and completely. Checking *yes* does not necessarily mean that you are an alcoholic, but does raise some warning flags.

FIGURE 8.3
Drinking Habits Questionnaire

	Yes	No
1. Have you ever awakened the morning after drinking and found that you could not remember part of the previous evening?	____	____
2. Do you often find it tough to stop drinking when you want to?	____	____
3. Does your family or partner ever worry or complain about your drinking habits ?	____	____
4. Do you ever get into fights after drinking?	____	____
5. Have you ever missed classes or work because of your drinking?	____	____
6. Do you or your friends think your drinking is not "normal"?	____	____
7. Do you ever drink before noon?	____	____
8. Have you ever gone to anyone for help about your drinking?	____	____
9. Have you ever been arrested because of drunken behavior?	____	____

If you think you have a drinking problem, there are various forms of help available. The choice of treatment should be based on professionally determined needs of the patient *and* on the patient's ability to pay. Alcoholics should seldom select their own treatment plans since they often select the "easiest" one or the treatment plan least likely to succeed in a continued attempt to feed their disease.

Treatment plans vary according to their cost, the time commitment required, and their intensity. Outpatient treatment programs, including Alcoholics Anonymous, may involve as few as two or three one-hour meetings or sessions per week. These programs are often less intensive than other treatment plans, but are effective for many alcoholics. On the other end of the spectrum are inpatient treatment plans. Some require hospitalization for twenty-eight days, and a few require two to four months of daily therapy.

Regardless of the treatment plan selected, the alcoholic must continue some form of counseling or support – usually for life. Again, the addiction to alcohol is incurable; relapse often occurs when any treatment plan is stopped.

Virtually all treatment plans are confidential and are reported to an insurance company only if the patient chooses to use insurance as a form of payment. Most important, alcoholics seeking treatment *must* discuss their plans with their employer who might otherwise view the person's time away from work as a frivolous vacation.

Although many firms recognize that alcoholism is an illness and a common one at that, some are still unable to understand that alcoholism is a disease. Unlike someone with cancer or high blood pressure, an alcoholic often denies that there is any problem or tries to minimize its impact on his behavior, and this makes it tough.

Only with open communication in a non-threatening environment can an alcoholic face her disease head-on and get the treatment she meets. Families and partners must also be involved with the treatment plan, and groups such as Al-Anon exist to counsel, support, and educate those closely involved with the alcoholic and can provide tools for families or partners to understand the disease and its effect on them.

Figure 8.4 highlights some common misconceptions about alcoholism. These misconceptions, identified by Alcoholics Anonymous, must be addressed before attitudes can change and treatment is supported and encouraged by employers, family, and friends.

FIGURE 8.4
Common Misconceptions about Alcoholism

- Alcoholics have the power to control their drinking. After all, it is a habit supported by choice.
- Those close to alcoholics can reason with them and successfully appeal to their sense of pride, ambition, fear, and even life.
- When others speak to alcoholics, they are speaking with a rational and logical human.
- Alcoholics are more receptive to advice when they are drunk.
- Once treatment is over, alcoholics can resume normal activities and will not need on-going support since their drinking has stopped.

As Figure 8.4 shows, the stigma that accompanies alcoholism is still alive and well. Only education can change attitudes, and, thankfully, that is already beginning. Strong lobbying efforts, led by Mothers Against Drunk Drivers and other groups, have influenced many state legislators to adopt stricter penalties and mandatory treatment for those who drive under the influence of alcohol.

Numerous firms have adopted employee assistance programs which include treatment for alcoholism in the array of services offered. Many hospitality and tourism firms include alcohol awareness as part of their on-going training for managers.

As attitudes toward alcoholism change and its status as a disease becomes more understood and accepted, fewer families and relationships will be devastated, more careers will be salvaged, and many more lives will be saved.

Drug Abuse

Experts define alcohol, caffeine, and nicotine as addictive drugs, but in this section, we are referring to prescription and illegal drugs *other than* alcohol, caffeine, and nicotine. Drug abuse takes on the same characteristics as alcohol abuse with only two differences – addiction to prescription drugs often occurs under the care of a physician and addiction to illegal drugs *is illegal*.

Tranquilizers such as Valium, Librium, Atavan, and Xanax are often prescribed to reduce or mask feelings of anxiety. Anxiety often stems from stress and frustration, and the fast pace and demanding nature of work in hospitality and tourism can lead to plenty of stress and frustration.

Anti-anxiety drugs are often prescribed by physicians and psychiatrists without sufficient warning to the patient regarding the dangers of addiction and the difficulty the patient will have getting off these drugs. Addiction to prescription drugs is extremely common and follows the same pattern as alcohol addiction, but is even *less* likely to be noticed by colleagues, family members, and partners.

Addiction to illegal drugs involves a number of different issues in addition to the addiction itself. First, obtaining the drug necessarily involves secrecy due to the danger of arrest. Second, the use of these drugs requires concealment. Finally, the sale, purchase, or use of an illegal drug can result in the loss of jobs, fines, or imprisonment.

The illegal drug most commonly by professionals is cocaine, which when inhaled produces a euphoric twenty- to forty- minute high and temporarily increases the blood pressure, pulse, and body temperature. The use of cocaine among white-collar professionals has more than doubled in the past decade, in spite of its high cost and warnings regarding the dangers of addiction.[23]

Regular cocaine users often experience financial difficulties as their dependency on the drug increases, as well as depression when they are deprived of the drug. This depression can be severe, and some users try to battle it by continuing their use of cocaine or by using prescription "uppers" or illegal amphetamines. Others try to ignore the depression as a way to deny their addiction.

Crack cocaine has recently emerged in the United States, and its use is increasing at an alarming rate. "Crack" results in heightened euphoria, and a more severe and longer-lasting state of depression than regular cocaine does. Crack more rapidly assaults the cardiovascular system and constricts blood vessels, and can lead to a heart attack or stroke, even for the first-time user.

Other commonly used illegal drugs are marijuana and hashish, both of which are ingested by inhaling smoke. Marijuana is extracted from the hemp plant, and hashish is basically marijuana in a more concentrated form. Both drugs slow the pulse rate, numb the senses, and cause prolonged lethargy.

The dangers of illegal drug use, even occasionally, cannot be overly stressed. Illegal drugs are expensive and physically dangerous, and treatment for addiction to such drugs is frequently not supported by employers. The criminal activity that surrounds the use and abuse of illegal drugs not only jeopardizes the user, but the user's family, friends, and partner as well.

Treatment for the addiction to prescription and illegal drugs is much the same as for the addiction to alcohol. Many programs are covered by health insurance plans, and offer both inpatient and outpatient services as mentioned in the previous section. Drug addicts have a separate support group, Narcotics Anonymous, which is modeled after Alcoholics Anonymous. Nar-Anon can offer support and education for the families or partners of drug addicts, and can help them cope with the devastating effects that the abuse has had on them.

[23] Raymond P. O'Keefe, *The Cocaine Impaired Lawyer,* **Dickinson Law Review**, 1988 (92), p. 615.

EMOTIONAL WELLNESS

Emotional health is often taken for granted unless it is challenged by crises. Very often, your emotional health is affected by your relationship with your family, friends, or partner. You must remember that ups and downs are part of being human and that spurts of uncontrollable laughter or tears are our way of surfacing these emotions.

However, if you find that you are on a constant emotional roller coaster, you can take a number of actions to find the source of your emotional unbalance. Counseling is probably the best way to explore the real source. But, even with counseling, you will need supportive relationships to act as a sounding board, to provide feedback on your progress, and to help you access your inner energy.

We have all recently heard that those who are in supportive relationships tend to live longer than those who live more isolated lives. We have also heard that people who own pets live longer and recover from heart attacks and other ailments faster than those who have no dogs or cats. Finally, we know that pregnant women with strong support systems experience fewer complications in childbirth than those who lack support. Obviously, supportive relationships offer many benefits, and can positively affect your emotional stability.

Recognize the importance of relationships to your emotional health! Develop a strong and mutually supportive network with your partner, close friends, parents, siblings, other family members, mentor, or people with common interests. If your current network is weak or unpredictable, you might find your emotional highs and lows even more extreme than they could be. In addition to developing a network, you might want to consider getting a pet – it might be just the thing you need!

Remember that you will end up giving the people in your support network the same calmness and strength they give you – it is a *two-way street* with benefits for everyone!

MENTAL WELLNESS

Stress and even anxiety are to be expected at certain times in your career and will be more pronounced during transitional stages such as the one you will soon enter. And while these feelings are normal, elevated symptoms can indicate a more severe mental disorder or illness, one which requires medical attention. In fact, one in four Americans will suffer from a mental illness at some point in their lives.[24]

We suspect that the most common forms of mental illness in hospitality and tourism managers are depression and anxiety disorders, both of which are frequently triggered by stress. However, stress is often not the primary cause, and the removal of stress, while it may be helpful, will not always provide a cure. Without treatment, both of these disorders can lead to personal and professional damage and even to hospitalization or suicide.

Depression is a common disorder which strikes many people at some point in their lives. It is a medical disorder and should not be confused with "being down" or "having the blues" because of some temporary set back or loss. Rather, symptoms of depression include an inability to concentrate, changes in sleep patterns, atypical outbursts of anger, and unexplained weight loss or gain, to name a few. These symptoms are often ignored, misunderstood, or in some cases, even misdiagnosed.

In our industry, many people mistake depression for job burn-out and attempt to cure it by taking a few days off. The fact is, however, that if a person is clinically depressed, a few days off from work will have no effect on the disorder.

Depression is one of many mood disorders. Current medical thinking suggests that most mood disorders are biological illnesses and perhaps genetically based. Medication is almost always the mainstay of any treatment plan. For this reason, you cannot ask a person with a mood disorder to snap out of it or to stop behaving in destructive ways. He needs medical attention. Similarly, if *you* feel any of the symptoms of depression, you should seek medical help immediately. Modern medication can often eliminate symptoms of depression in as little as two or three weeks and, unlike tranquilizers or anti-anxiety drugs, they are not addictive.

Anxiety disorders are also common. Symptoms vary, but they often include a tightness in the chest, unexplained fear, shortness of breath, insomnia, or an elevated pulse rate. Like depression, anxiety disorders can have a severe effect on work performance and personal relationships. There are many causes for anxiety disorders, but frequently they are triggered by stress or major life changes such as divorce or failure at work. Treatment includes counseling and sometimes medication.

[24] Anonymous, *Myths about Mental Illnesses,* **American Psychiatric Association Newsletter** (Division of Public Affairs, September 1987), p. 2.

Another common disorder, psychosomatic illness, can also be caused by stress. Common symptoms are gastrointestinal, cardiovascular, or muscular problems which are often complained of, but left untreated. Less frequent but more severe is paranoia disorder in which the person experiences delusions of grandeur or schizophrenia and the body ceases to function normally. In both of these cases, hospitalization is usually recommended.

The good news is that all of these diseases are treatable through counseling, medication, and/or hospitalization. Don't ignore the signs if you or those close to you suspect that you have a mental disorder. The stigma surrounding many mental illnesses is thankfully lessening and both inpatient and outpatient treatment is available.

SPIRITUAL WELLNESS

Most of us want to maintain our physical and emotional well-being, but we have a spiritual side as well and, in our opinion, this needs attention, too. The point of this section is to introduce the notion of spiritual growth and development and to discuss, in a general way, why it is important and how to go about it.

A word of warning – we need to distinguish between religion and spirituality because they are not necessarily the same thing. Religion is based on a set of beliefs stemming from a particular notion of theology and involves practices and points of view which are organized around those beliefs. Most religions use traditional elements of song, prayers, dances, and rules.

Spirituality, on the other hand, promotes inner peace through an appreciation for one's surroundings, the recognition of commonality and the depth of the human experience, and the nurturing of the soul. It is not necessarily based on a particular theology and may have no holy book or set of rules. It is often viewed as a combination of philosophy, sacredness, and even mythology and has been practiced in many cultures in many forms for thousands of years.

The practice of religion can be part of the search for spiritual wholeness or growth but, in our opinion, it is not the only way to spiritual wholeness. In fact, many Americans are seeking alternatives or supplements to organized religion. For example, most bookstores and libraries have extensive "new age" collections, and discussion groups, support groups, and even communities which focus on spiritual matters are commonplace.

In the United States, a good way to understand spirituality is to think of the Native American tradition. Native Americans have traditionally honored spirits of the earth and sky, among others, and still retain many traditions to acknowledge these spirits. They also recognize the goodness, strength, and eternalness of the spirit outside of the body. Their spiritual practices involve ritual, of course, but mostly they are reflected in attitudes and a way of life.

Take Time To Grow

Spiritual growth requires introspection, imagination, open mindedness, and discipline. Spirituality requires a person to study the nature and depth of life without preconceived ideas regarding how things should be or how people should behave.

It is also important to realize that religion and spirituality can go hand in hand. They do not necessarily conflict, but can actually *support* each other. Most traditional religions believe in internal goodness, as does spirituality. Both recognize the importance of the soul to the mutual happiness of humans. And both require study to formulate a strong system of internalized beliefs.

The need for recognition and connection to the spiritual comes about as a result of our need to feel a connection with our fellow human beings, the world, and the universe. Also, we need spiritual connections to understand the reasons for existence and to come to peace with or accept things we don't understand, such as love, goodness, or even evil. Finally, for some of us, the spiritual search helps us come to terms with forces or powers which we believe to be of a higher order than ourselves.

TYING IT ALL TOGETHER

The hospitality and tourism industry, as well as most others, is beginning to recognize the importance of **total health** to employee job performance and job satisfaction. Increased attention to physical, mental, emotional, and spiritual health and wholeness is becoming commonplace.

If you continually work to strengthen your body, mind, and soul, and treat them as irreplaceable and even sacred, chances are that you will experience a lifetime of good health. If you slip, though, remember that many avenues are available for assistance. Use them!

ADDITIONAL READINGS

Care of the Soul, Thomas Moore; HarperCollins Publishers (New York, 1992).

Healing the Shame that Binds You, John Bradshaw; Health Communications, Inc. (Deerfield Beach, Florida, 1988).

Keep It Simple, Hazelton Foundation; Harper & Row Publishers (San Francisco, California, 1989).

The Power of 5, Harold H. Bloomfield & Robert K. Cooper; Rodale Press (Emmaus, Pennsylvania, 1995).

CHAPTER 9

RECOGNIZING AND EMBRACING ETHICS

"There is nothing so strong or safe in an emergency of life as the simple truth."

Charles Dickens

Although the term *ethics* may sound like something only lawyers or religious people would be concerned with, you will find that, as a member of the business community, you will probably face ethical dilemmas on a daily basis. In order to function effectively and achieve peace of mind and emotional well-being, you will need to develop and internalize some sort of ethical code. Notice, we *said develop and internalize*! This is because we contend that ethics are more than a set of imposed rules and that each of us has to reason out our personal beliefs which set our individual ethical standards. In the following sections, we discuss the notion of ethics, the philosophical foundations of ethics, and how ethics are practiced on various levels.

The focus on ethics has increased over the past few years. It is expected to continue to grow as society becomes more aware of situations that call for ethical judgment and of their societal importance. The media has highlighted many examples of unethical governmental and corporate behaviors that include manipulation of financial data and legal data, denial of health risks caused by the use of certain products, and disregard for environmental responsibilities. These extend, as well, to the arena of day-to-day operations. In our industry, violations of operational ethics include lack of attention to food safety, overcharging to take advantage of a certain group or situation, and disregarding the welfare of employees.

Government and business organizations, however, are not the ones who violate ethics. Individuals can also engage in unethical behaviors. Common personal ethical violations include misusing company resources, deflating income or inflating deductions on annual tax forms, and misrepresenting educational background or work experience in order to get ahead in a career.

There are many definitions of ethics, but most include a reference to moral behavior of some kind. However, the real question is: What is moral and what is not? The word *moral* refers to culturally defined beliefs about what is right and wrong. Accordingly, morals vary from culture to culture, person to person, and generation to generation. Understanding ethics is complicated because notions about ethical behaviors stem not only from personal beliefs, but are influenced by law, societal norms, corporate cultures, and many other factors.

THREE THEORIES OF ETHICS

We said earlier that ethics are not just a set of imposed rules. Rather, they are reasoned out on the basis of a particular philosophy or set of theories about the nature of humans and society. All have deep historical roots and we would be remiss if we did not explain the philosophy underlying the three main ethical theories which influence our culture – utilitarianism, the Golden Rule, and positive versus natural law.[25] All three are discussed below.

Utilitarianism

Utilitarianism was first put forth by English philosopher and economist John Stuart Mill.[26] The utilitarian view of ethics assumes that people will act in accordance with Utility and, therefore, will follow a rule called the Greatest Happiness Rule. According to this Rule, individual actions are *wrong* or *unethical* if they result in unhappiness and cause an individual to feel pain or to be deprived of pleasure. Actions are *right* or *ethical* if they promote happiness and cause an individual to feel pleasure or to be free of pain.

[25] Mortimer D. Schwartz, Richard C. Wydick, & Rex R. Perschbacher, *Problems in Legal Ethics* (St. Paul, Minnesota: West Publishing, 1992), p. 5.

[26] John Stuart Mill, *Utilitarianism* (Great Books of the Western World: Encyclopaedia Britannica, 1990).

Utilitarianism assumes that individuals can maximize the welfare of the entire society solely by acting in a way that results in their own greatest happiness. However, the utilitarian principle requires people to be impartial regarding happiness; that is, they must value their happiness as highly as they value the happiness of everyone else's, and act in accordance with these values. The theory suggests that individual paths to happiness and fulfillment be joined with the whole and that individuals work toward a collective good. The utilitarianistic view of ethics sets a very high standard for humanity – a standard that most say is virtually impossible to achieve.

In a perfect world, people *will* maximize their own happiness and maximize the happiness of others at the same time. However, the world is never perfect. For example, what if someone values money and money makes her happy according to the Rule? She might deceive others in order to make more money, and that deceit could cause great unhappiness for those she manipulates. But, according to the Rule, she "gained her happiness." The undesirable effect of her gain on others does not factor into the Rule.

Do her ethics according to the Greatest Happiness Rule allow others to experience their Greatest Happiness? Of course not! What if another person maximizes his happiness by beating another candidate out for a promotion? Granted, *his* happiness is maximized, but what about the person who did not receive the promotion? The point is that the balance required by the Rule is hard to achieve.

Economist James Rachels is the best known critic of utilitarianism and identifies three major problems with the theory of utilitarianism.[27] First, he challenges the assumption that actions can be judged solely by their consequences and that the *reason* for the action can be completely ignored. For example, Rachels claims that, according to utilitarianism, a gift given from one person to another would be judged as a "good" act regardless of the motives of the giver. To Rachels, a person who gives a gift and expects nothing in return should be ethically distinguished from one who gives a gift in exchange for future favors from the receiver (often referred to as bribery).

Rachels also questions the basic assumption of the Rule – that everything can be measured solely by the amount of happiness it produces or does not produce. Finally, he doubts that one person's happiness can receive the same weight

[27] James Rachels, *The Elements of Moral Philosophy* (New York: McGraw-Hill, 1986), pp. 90 - 103.

as another person's happiness – more likely, we value consequences differently and feel different gradations of happiness.

Rachels' arguments are provocative, but do not diminish the importance of utilitarianism to the study of ethics. Because by its very nature, ethics represent the *ideal* and variation from the ideal is part of being human. In other words, utilitarianism assumes that all actions are driven by a desire to achieve happiness and pleasure for as many as possible. We admit this theory has many flaws, but at least it associates individual actions with larger consequences. We think that we can all acknowledge that the consequences of most actions will affect other people and the importance of this effect cannot be ignored.

The Golden Rule

You are no doubt familiar with the Golden Rule in one form or another. Basically, it says that we should treat others as we treat ourselves. This seems simple but, like many simple things, if you think about it in depth, it becomes complex. It is in this complexity that you can use the Golden Rule to develop and act upon a code of ethics. Not surprisingly, the Rule has religious roots that span almost all major faiths. H.T.D. Rost, a teacher of comparative religion, offers the following list of examples:[28]

➡ **Christianity**
In everything, do unto others what you would have them do unto you, for this sums up the law of the Prophets.

➡ **Hinduism**
Do not to others what ye do not wish done to yourself; and wish for others too what ye desire and long for, for yourself. This is the whole of the Dharma, heed it well.

➡ **Buddhism**
All shrink from suffering, and love of life; Remember that thou too are like them; Make thine own self the measure of the others, and so abstain from causing hurt to them.

➡ **Taoism**
To those who are good (to me), I am good; and to those who are not good (to me), I am also good; and thus (all) get to be good.

[28] H.T.D. Rost, *The Golden Rule: A Universal Ethic* (Oxford: George Ronald, 1986), pp. 28, 39, 43, 49, 103.

➡️ **Confucianism**
What you do not want done to yourself, do not do to others.

➡️ **Islam**
None of you believes until he wishes for his brother what he wishes for himself.

Applying the Golden Rule to ethics requires that individuals act according to their *own* standards and do not push their individual tastes or lifestyles on others. For example, if you prefer to play loud music in the middle of the night, the Golden Rule does not insist that you do it to benefit your neighbors since you presume they like it, too. Rather, it requires that you apply your own standards to them, which forces you to question *your* preferences. Would *you* like for them to make noise when you are trying to sleep? Probably not, so follow the Rule and turn down the music.

The Golden Rule has a lot of credibility, apparent from its importance to most major religions and cultures. It requires that individuals apply standards, not actions or beliefs, to their neighbors, customers, and colleagues. These standards, or guides for actions and behaviors, must be the same standards which individuals want applied to them, regardless of the circumstances or the reasons behind the standards. The action itself must be ethical, and then, according to the Golden Rule, this ethically-based action will result in an ethically-based outcome.

Positive versus Natural Law

Another way to view ethics is to think about the difference between positive and natural law. *Positive law*, based on legislative acts, judicial decisions, and executive orders, gives society behavioral guidelines and, more importantly, includes penalties for violations of the law. Its primary purpose is to maintain social order.

On the other hand, the higher order of *natural law*[29], first described by 13th century philosopher and theologan Thomas Aquinas, has no identifiable basis. It does not include specific rules or penalties. Rather, natural law requires only that people, regardless of their culture or religious beliefs, treat each other with respect and conform to their *nature*, meaning mental, moral, and physical

[29] Anonymous, *Natural Law* (Great Books of the Western World: Encyclopaedia Britannica, 1973).

constitutions. It involves much more than the Golden Rule; it stresses individual responsibility and mandates that every person act as a caretaker of both nature and society. It also presumes that every person is governed by rational needs and logical thoughts.

From the point of view of positive law, ethics can be mandated by rules and, accordingly, can be enforced. Enforcement, or course, requires the development of penalties for ethical violations. For example, we know that shorting your restaurant on the nightly cash deposit and keeping it for yourself is ethically wrong. It is *also* defined as theft or embezzlement by positive law and carries with it a punishment of a fine or imprisonment. Cheating on a test is also ethically wrong and is included in the policies of most colleges as a violation of student code. The penalty for cheating can range from failing the test to academic suspension to dismissal. In both of these instances, it's pretty clear that these actions go against the mandate of natural law as well.

Other ethical violations are based wholly on natural law and carry no specific positive law penalties with them. For example, restaurant managers who choose not to support a recycling program in their establishments are wasting natural and valuable resources and are contributing to the increasingly serious waste disposal problem. In many states, though, the manager does not violate any positive laws.

Many hotels regularly overbook, or sell more hotel rooms than are actually available, in an effort to fill the hotel. Overbooking is often legal as long as hotels attempt to keep overbooking in line with industry standards and provide the guest with other lodging options. However, the hotel has a responsibility to the guest to provide lodging at *that* facility. The guest may have had practical or sentimental reasons for choosing the hotel in the first place and was probably inconvenienced and disappointed by the overbooking practice.

The point of this discussion is to make the case that the bases for ethical behavior are not simply rules and regulations. The rules that come from positive law are insufficient by themselves to help you to develop and act on a code of ethics. You also have to rely on your internalized sense of right and wrong which comes from natural law.

ABSOLUTE ETHICAL BEHAVIORS

Certain ethical behaviors are absolute! Some major ethical concerns for the hospitality and tourism industry contain elements which can be viewed according to all three theories of ethics – utilitarianism, the Golden Rule, and positive and natural law.

Quality

➡ **Utilitarianism**
A utilitarianistic view of ethics would require individuals to provide quality products and services that would result in the greatest amount of happiness for the largest number of people. That happiness could be measured by the financial success of the operation or by levels of customer and employee satisfaction.

➡ **The Golden Rule**
Ethics regarding quality would require providers to deliver the same quality of products and services they would want to receive. Here quality would be measured by standards, not by specific activities.

The Bad and the Good

➡ Positive and Natural Law

Under positive law, operations have a legal obligation not to misrepresent their product or service. Under natural law, they have an obligation to fulfill the expectations of their employees, customers, and owners.

Safety

➡ Utilitarianism

Ethical acts regarding safety under the utilitarianism principle would require the service provider to provide a level of safety that results in the greatest happiness for all. This happiness could be measured by increased revenue from repeat business, the satisfaction the provider received from the guest's service experience, or the feelings of the provider in assuring guests a safe environment.

➡ The Golden Rule

Ethical standards under the Golden Rule would require that service providers offer all guests, customers, and employees the same level of safety *they* would like. These standards might include adequate locks on hotel rooms, sufficient warnings to travelers going abroad, or appropriate floor coverings in the kitchen area.

➡ Positive and Natural Law

Positive law requires a certain level of safety for the guest or customer. This includes providing the guest with a reasonably safe facility in which to sleep, serving the customer food which is properly handled and prepared, and reasonably warning the tourist about dangers of traveling to certain countries. Natural law mandates that operators exert *more* than reasonable care to provide safe lodging, food, and travel, and might include hiring an extra security guard or installing more lights in the parking area than the law requires.

Individual ethical codes are based on combinations of the above theories. These codes differ from person to person, but all require some level of responsibility to society, whether that responsibility stems from individual actions or intent or from actions which better the whole of society.

ETHICS OF PROFESSIONAL ASSOCIATIONS

Many professional associations have adopted codes of ethics. Some of these codes are voluntary for members; others must be signed before joining the association. An example of a code of ethics for an association is the one adopted by the International Association of Auditorium Managers (IAAM) which states that the manager should:

- ✓ Strive for continued improvement in the proficiency and usefulness of service.
- ✓ Maintain the highest ideals of honor and integrity in all public and personal relationships.
- ✓ Emphasize friendly and courteous service to the public and recognize that the function of the building is at all times to serve the best interests of the public.
- ✓ Exercise fair and impartial judgment in all Association and professional business dealings.
- ✓ Maintain the principle of fairness to all.
- ✓ Have a firm belief in the dignity and worth of service rendered by the building and have a constructive, creative, and practical attitude.
- ✓ Refrain from any activity that may be in conflict with the interest of the employer.

If you read the code closely, you probably noticed that the IAAM supports ethical practices in the personal *as well as* the professional lives of their member managers. You should also know that the code is entirely voluntary. As a preface to the code, the IAAM states that "the Association believes that certain ethical practices *should* govern the conduct of every professional manager in the Association." Again, this type of voluntary compliance is common in the codes of ethics of professional associations. Associations recognize that their membership is culturally diverse and has different experiences and beliefs, so the code serves only as a guide, not as a requirement for membership.

If the professional association to which you belong requires your signature as a statement that you accept their code of ethics, be sure to read the code carefully. Sometimes, your promise involves a commitment to adhere to ethical standards in your personal life as well as in your professional life. Some association members resent this control over their personal choices, however, and therefore adherence to these types of codes is often voluntary as you have seen in the case of the IAAM.

Ethical professional practices supported by associations often include standards for quality assurance and honest financial reporting. Most service-based professional associations aim their codes of ethics at three groups: the customers, the employees, and the owners.

An example of an ethical standard for *customers* might read: "We will provide our customers with consistent and high quality service limited only by our available resources. We will acknowledge every complaint in an expedient manner in an attempt to meet or exceed guest expectations."

An example of an ethical standard for *employees* might read: "We will treat our employees as well as we treat our customers because we believe that happy customers are a direct result of happy employees. We will adequately train employees for every position in which they work and will offer them reasonable benefits and wages."

Finally, an example of an ethical standard for *owners* might read: "We will honestly disclose all financial information to potential investors and include projections that are developed to the best of our abilities. We will provide our investors with a reasonable return based on our available resources and will not unnecessarily waste our revenue-generating assets."

ETHICS OF PROFESSIONS

Some professions support their own codes of ethics. For example, the medical profession has long supported the Hippocratic Oath and the legal profession has its own well-developed ethical standards. Violations of these codes can result in various penalties ranging from a private reprimand to removal from the profession.

The hospitality and tourism industry has lagged in the development of profession-specific codes of ethics. Often, mandatory professional codes are associated only with professions which require licenses to practice and, to date, the only hospitality and tourism profession which requires a license to practice is a dietitian. In most states, dietitians may not work in their field until they pass a licensing examination which includes the acknowledgment and signing of a code of ethics which has been in effect since 1989. The Code applies to Registered Dietitians, Dietetic Technicians Registered, and American Dietetics Association (ADA) members. Violations of the Code can result in censure (written reprimand), suspension of ADA membership, suspension of professional registration, expulsion from the ADA, or permanent revocation of credentials. Parts of the Code are listed below:

- → The dietetic practitioner conducts himself/herself with honesty, integrity, and fairness.
- → The dietetic practitioner maintains confidentiality of information.
- → The dietetic practitioner assumes responsibility and accountability for personal competence in practice.
- → The dietetic practitioner promotes or endorses products in a manner that is neither false or misleading.
- → The dietetic practitioner accurately presents professional qualifications and credentials.
- → The dietetic practitioner accepts the obligation to protect society and the profession by upholding the Code of Ethics for the Profession of Dietetics and by reporting alleged violations of the Code through the defined review process.

Some predict the development of profession-specific codes of ethics in the hospitality and tourism industry, regardless of whether the individual professions within the industry require licensing or not. The difficulty of this, of course, is enforcement, for if a license is not required to work in a certain profession, how can a person who violates professional ethics be disciplined? These codes will almost certainly have to be on a voluntary basis, at least until (and if ever) certain professions within the industry are licensed. The point is that *true professionals* will always develop and apply a code of ethics whether or not their profession has a formal one.

REALISTIC ETHICS: WEIGHING RIGHT AND WRONG

Ethical situations surface daily in operations, regardless of one's profession. Some ethical dilemmas have a right response and other dilemmas clearly have a wrong response. Note that the easy ethical questions are often supported by law. For example, many industrialized countries have codes, statutes, or case law to guarantee a basic level of food safety. These are straightforward and common across most cultures:

? Should the food your operation serves be properly handled and prepared? **Of course.**

? How many security guards should you hire for a concert or a sporting event?
Hire the necessary staff based on past experience and industry standards.

? Should you inform the tour group you just booked of the safety precautions they should take when visiting a politically volatile country?
Most certainly.

Other ethical responses are not as easy to discern and develop, and these seem to bring about the most confusion and debate. The most obvious examples of ethical dilemmas are cultural in scope. For example, it is unethical and often illegal to accept a bribe in some countries, but it is a recognized cost of doing business in others. It is unethical to accept tips for service in some nations, but it is expected and even built into the wage structures in others. Employment discrimination is permitted in certain countries, while others have laws against it. "Buying a job" is often the best road to success in some countries and is even supported by law, whereas the same behavior is discouraged in others and the legal penalty for such actions can be severe.

Other ethical dilemmas are not necessarily culturally based, however, and create some interesting and difficult professional situations. The most difficult ethical dilemmas experienced by hospitality and tourism managers are caused by the clash between responsibility to the guest, responsibility to the employee, and responsibility to the owners. The triad goes like this: customers and guests expect the highest value for their dollar spent, owners expect a high level of profit, and employees   expect and require reasonable working conditions and

The "Right" Decision Is Not Always Obvious!

benefits. It might be easy to say that you always try to exceed customers' expectations, deliver a high level of profit to your owners, and treat your employees fairly, but that can be difficult to achieve and may put you in a precarious operating situation!

Difficult situations in ethics are often caused by the following:

- conflicting values and expectations
- the lack of training and education
- the absence of an ethical code or quality statement
- confusing or nonexistent job descriptions
- no articulated quality of service standards
- lax hiring and promotion practices
- advertising campaigns which are difficult to adhere to
- economic or political instability

We can offer no real solutions for these tough situations. Most important is that you recognize these as real problems and know that you will have to make some decisions which are rarely clear and often difficult. As a guideline, Stephen Hall, the Executive Director of the International Institute for Quality and Ethics in Service and Tourism, proposes a five-step test for ethical decision making:[30]

1) Is the decision legal?
2) Is the decision fair?
3) Does the decision hurt anyone?
4) Have I been honest with those affected?
5) Can I live with my decision?

Yet even these guidelines can be difficult to follow. For example, is the decision fair to whom? How fair does the decision have to be? Many decisions knowingly or unknowingly hurt someone, so should you balance the amount of hurt between the people affected?

COMMON TRAPS TO AVOID

By now, you are probably aware of the ethical and moral traps lurking within the hospitality and tourism industry. When late hours are part of the routine and

[30] Stephen S.J. Hall, *Ethics in Hospitality Management* (East Lansing, Michigan: The Educational Institute of the American Hotel & Motel Association, 1992), p. 13.

alcohol and hotel beds are always around, personal integrity can be challenged. Many seasoned managers will warn you – "never, ever play where you choose to earn your pay." Regardless, affairs and sexual liaisons within this field are unfortunately quite common and their dangers merit discussion.

The Personal Issues

For a moment, discount the legal battles you might face if you were to proposition a subordinate, colleague, or customer and think about other ramifications. If you have a partner, how would he feel if you had sexual relations or a romantic encounter with someone else? What about the partner of the person with whom you had an affair? Even though you will probably spend more time with your fellow managers than you do with your partner, you must be careful not to blur the boundaries of either relationship. Keep your work life professional and keep your home life personal.

Remember – few people come out of sexual relationships in the workplace unscathed. As you have probably noticed by now, many firms directly address this potential problem by forbidding workplace relationships between employees at different levels within the organization. Sometimes, if a relationship begins between people in the same organization, one person is asked to leave the firm or transfer to another division or department.

Keep your eyes open to such dangers. You might think you are impervious to temptation, but you are only human. So, stay out of compromising situations – not only for your career, but for those you love.

The Legal Issues

By now, all of you have read about laws that ban sexual harassment in the workplace and probably have a general idea of what it means. Don't worry, though, if you are still a bit confused – the definition of sexual harassment is somewhat fuzzy. In an effort to help clarify which words or actions constitute sexual harassment, the Equal Employment Opportunity Commission set forth the following:[31]

---

31 Title VII of 1964 Civil Rights Act as interpreted by the Equal Opportunity Commission.

"Unwelcome sexual advances, requests for sexual favors, and other verbal or physical conduct of a sexually explicit nature constitute sexual harassment when:

(1) such conduct is made either explicitly or implicitly a term or condition of an individual's employment;
(2) submission to or rejection of such conduct by an individual is used as the basis for employment decisions affecting such individual; or
(3) such conduct has the purpose or effect of reasonably interfering with an individual's work performance or creating an intimidating, hostile, or offensive work environment."

Items (1) and (2) above refer to *quid pro quo* sexual harassment, which literally means "something for something" in Latin, whereas item (3) refers *to hostile work environment* sexual harassment. Both types of harassment carry legal penalties ranging from damage awards to the injured to dismissal for the offender.Those who think they can get away with requesting sexual favors or demeaning an employee based on gender are very much mistaken.

We are not suggesting that you adopt a no-fun attitude at the workplace, only that you respect your fellow workers and treat everyone in a professional and equitable manner. Although food and lodging operations often involve close employee-to-employee, employee-to-guest, and guest-to-guest interaction, this interaction need not be threatening to anyone. Use your common sense. Even though you might think that you are just teasing, your words could be misconstrued by someone else.

You can be a compassionate and caring manager without sacrificing mutual respect and basic dignities. Investigate any harassment complaint immediately and thoroughly. Often, sexual harassment is clouded by misunderstandings since one person's interpretation of a statement might be the exact opposite of the sender's intended message. Do your best to create an open and straight-forward work environment and, most of all, make sure that *you* follow these standards.

Most firms post their policies stating their intolerance of sexual harassment, yet many have ignored the importance of work force training. Many consultants are available to train employees at all organizational levels and many professional organizations offer seminars in developing and maintaining a harassment-free workplace. Suggest training for your firm's employees if you see some questionable actions recurring or hear derogatory jokes or remarks. Prevention is the key here – for the future of your firm *and* for your continued success.

A CONFUSING NOTION!

It should be clear by now that ethics can be confusing. They are limited by culture, affected by life experiences, molded by beliefs, and are rarely clear cut. However, if you always consider standards of mutual treatment, you should experience a bit more peace regarding the consequences of your decisions.

AN ACCOUNT WITH AN UNHAPPY ENDING

"When I graduated from college in the early '80s, I was hired by a food service firm as a Service Manager. Although I loved my job, every time my regional manager came to visit, my love turned to abhorrence. His favorite pastime, after he reviewed our profit and loss statement, was to call the General Manager and me into the main office, close the door, and tell jokes. One day, these jokes took a sharp turn and became sexually- and racially-biased. I left the office immediately because I refused to tolerate his behavior. He actually looked puzzled!

Although I was too afraid to say anything to the Vice President, my resignation letter dated exactly one month later read:

'. . . I can no longer work for a company which so blatantly supports racially biased and unethical behavior. Perhaps with training this can be rectified, but I am not willing to wait. . . .'

Unfortunately, this occurred before much attention was paid to ethics and there was really no recourse. Thankfully, times are changing."

Anonymous

ADDITIONAL READINGS

Body and Soul, Anita Roddick; Crown Trade Paperbacks (New York, New York, 1991).

Credibility, James K. Kouzes & Barry Z. Posner; Jossey-Bass Publishers (San Francisco, California, 1993).

THE FUTURE OF THE INDUSTRY: IT IS NOW!

"Give me a lever long enough and a prop strong enough, I can single-handed move the world."

Archimedes

Throughout this book, we have discussed the hospitality and tourism industry and how *you* can be an important part of it. However, your success is not solely dependent on your preparation, fit to the industry, and knowledge, skills, and abilities.

As we said in Chapter 1, it is also heavily influenced by forces outside of your control which shape the future. You can choose to work with these forces and have a better chance at success, or you can choose to ignore them and take your chances.

We are quickly heading into a new millennium and, like it or not, a lot of changes are coming. We chose four major forces which we feel will drive most of the future changes in our industry: 1) shifts in worker *and* customer demographics; 2) the use and advancement of technology; 3) the recognition of tourism as an important economic stimulus; and 4) the effects of globalization on the environment.

CHANGING DEMOGRAPHICS

Demographic changes are caused by population shifts, social policy changes, and other important factors such as war or famine. Some changes are temporary and some are permanent, yet *all* will have a profound effect on your career. Changing demographics will alter both the worker *and* the customer base in the hospitality and tourism industry and will change everything from who we hire to how we operate.

Shifting Worker Demographics

As we said at the beginning of this book, the majority of jobs in the future will lie in the service, technology, and health care industries. This means, of course, that the hospitality and tourism segment of the service industry will offer many people some great career opportunities.

However, what about the *supply of workers*? Will there be enough people to fill the positions? What about the *quality of the workforce*? Will they be adequately educated and trained? Will they be prepared for the sophistication of the industry since the demands of the industry will require a better prepared and more committed workforce than in the past? Finally, what about the *faces of the workers* as diversity becomes fused into every organization, whether small or large? Let's examine these questions.

Will There Be Enough People To Work?

Like many other industrialized nations, the United States has experienced numerous baby booms of varying degrees, most often at the end of a war or a recession. This type of boom is cyclical and often predictable – and it is happening again!

An increase in the number of births during a certain period in time has a direct effect on the size of the workforce as these boomers come of age. Usually, the boom is preceded by a dry period – that is, there is an actual shortage of workers and the unemployment rate is very low. When the boomers reach eighteen, however, the number of workers available per job is higher and unemployment rates can increase. Think about it – a large workforce requires more jobs to maintain a low level of unemployment, right?

Will the Workforce Be Ready?

Experts are quite divided regarding the preparedness of the workforce for the next century. Some believe that the workforce will have to be better educated in a general way so they can be flexible as the workplace continues to evolve. Others believe that job-specific skills that are easily transferable will be the most essential for career success. Regardless, we feel that a *combination* of education and training is ***the only way*** for a professional to remain competitive.

Education and training programs are becoming increasingly essential since more and more workers have become displaced for several reasons such as:

- technological changes, which make the skills of some workers obsolete or which replace workers entirely

- outsourcing, which allows companies to decrease operating costs by having specialty companies perform certain functions such as payroll, marketing, advertising, and purchasing
- relocating certain corporate functions, or for that matter, entire corporations, to take advantage of lower taxes or lower labor costs in another region or country

Many displaced workers are choosing to join the hospitality and tourism industry since this industry is predicted to grow and offers better chances for job security as well as advancement. After all, no machine can replace the smile of a skilled server or the fine touches of an experienced chef. No computer image can replace the sensations a traveler feels when entering a rainforest for the first time – smelling the foliage, seeing the magnitude, and hearing the sounds of the water dripping off the leaves.

Our entire industry is based on customer contact and, lucky for you, ***that*** can never be replaced by a machine, outsourced to another organization, or moved to another location. Imagine saying to a guest, "If you go to our property in North Dakota, we can give you a smile and good service. Sorry, we don't have that here in California!"

So, what does this mean for you as a future manager? Well, it means that you had better get all the education and training possible – throughout your career. Why? Because change is escalating, and competition is demanding a workforce committed to life-long learning. It also means that you had better hire people who view education and training as their responsibility and accept it as a way of life. As you mature in your career, you have a responsibility *to develop a team that is at the cutting edge* with respect to their skills and knowledge.

What Will the Workforce Look Like?

The last employment-related change we will mention involves the ethnic, cultural, and physical make-up of the workforce of the future. As you have already noticed (at least, you better have noticed!), the lines between cultures are becoming blurred. Spanish and Vietnamese are now the languages of instruction in many primary and secondary schools in the United States. More and more of our governmental leaders are second-generation citizens. Cuisine has become so internationalized, one would be hard-pressed to find a city without a Mexican

The Workforce of the Future Will Look Very Different

or Thai restaurant. The lines between people with or without disabilities are also becoming blurred as people with different abilities are entering the workforce like never before.

All of this means that, in the future, a majority culture will no longer exist – at least not like we know it now. The workforce will be diverse – hopefully to the point where diversity is no longer noticed or even discussed!

Shifting Customer Demographics

The changes in the demographic make-up of customers will likely be very similar to that of the worker base. This means that customers will no longer fit a predictable mold.

For example, menus that cater to a wide variety of tastes and preferences will become commonplace. This is already happening in many arenas. Japanese breakfast buffets are commonly available in many large hotels in major cities. On the other side of the Pacific, Asian hotels cater to the tastes of western business people.

North American cuisine itself has borrowed from many countries and regions, and a variety of ethnic and neo-ethnic restaurants abound. For example, Mediterranean cuisine is currently very trendy and tapas bars are mushrooming. As for other preferences, vegetarian restaurants are becoming increasingly popular and one hotel chain, the Ritz Carlton, makes macrobiotic foods available to its guests.

Similarly, tourist packages will offer a variety of new experiences, destinations, and adventures. Take, for example, an Arizona vacation that includes golf on the first day, hiking the red rocks on the second, and skiing near Flagstaff on the third. Similarly, imagine an African trip that starts with shopping and sightseeing in Johannesberg, and doing a photo safari the next day. This is followed up by a ten-day, 2,000 mile motorcycle jaunt through Zimbabwe and Zambia that includes the danger of isolation, the beauty of Victoria Falls, and the excitement of viewing crocodiles on Lake Kairiba. While these trips may sound personally exciting, putting together packages such as these requires a new view of tour *packaging as well as* creativity on the part of tour promoters and travel agents.

Finally, facilities will offer a wider variety of accommodations for people with all types of abilities. This will not be a matter of simple compliance, but a matter of maximizing revenue. First, this customer segment is growing and will continue to grow as people live longer; and second, this segment can and does travel extensively. Thus, accessibility simply makes *good business sense*!

This means that hospitality and tourism businesses will do more than widen doors or put Braille numbers on hotel room doors. It means going *beyond* the letter of the law and *pursuing* a viable market segment. This will require not only structural changes, but attitudinal changes as well.

The need for the Americans with Disabilities Act shows that this has not been a common attitude in the United States in the past. Interestingly enough, however, in certain countries like Lithuania, consultants have identified impediments to access as a barrier to tourism and businesses have taken steps, without legislation, to court this market. We see this as the future in North America as well.

This will be an exciting time of change. As we said before, diversity will probably no longer be a goal of most organizations when they become naturally diverse. After all, why state a norm as a goal?

TECHNOLOGY AND YOU

Everybody knows that technology is expanding at unprecedented rates. We all know what a struggle it is to keep a computer working fast enough or hold enough information. The tourism industry now uses global distribution systems to take care of everything from hotel reservations to airline ticketing anywhere in the world. Even presentations lacking the pizazz of multi-media are now considered boring and old-fashioned. What does this mean for you? Plenty!

You need to keep abreast of what is happening on the technology front so that you can keep your skills current; properly use the information that modern technology permits you to access; and anticipate impacts, opportunities, and changes brought about by technology.

The skills aspect is obvious. If technological changes require you to develop new skills, then you had better get busy learning them. However, keep in mind that skills related to technology are **only tools** that will help you perform better. They are not an end unto themselves. Basically, technology will do one of two things: provide us with more and better quality information; or help us to provide better services and products for our guests.

For example, hotel efficiency used to be measured by computing the overall occupancy and the average daily rate per room sold. In recent times, however, the industry has used a concept called REVPAR (revenue per available room) to measure their efficiency because it gives a valuable comparison between actual and potential revenue. With advanced property management systems, a hotel's performance is likely to be measured by *total* sales per room, and not just by a comparison between actual and potential room revenue.

The effects of technology can be felt throughout the entire system. In many hotels, front office workers no longer post charges to guest accounts since the property management systems do this automatically. Guests can check themselves in and out simply by inserting a credit card into a machine. Servers no longer have to go into the kitchen to place their food order with the chefs – their hand-held computers deliver this information through wireless transmission. Guest history reports can be generated easily and show the spending patterns of the guests as well as room preferences. Also, travelers can check in on a flight and book their seat assignment via a machine and a credit card – and never have to wait in line (unless there is a line at the machine)!

Modern technology already enables us to do all of these things, and the future promises even more opportunities to use information. Information, *if you can get it*, can be used to improve anything from the profitability of food outlets to mini-bar offerings, and it certainly provides us with a powerful marketing tool!

Remember to keep an eye on technology-related opportunities. Not so long ago, satellite and other telecommunications technology were supposed to make a significant dent in lodging revenues and business travel. While technology has proven useful for short meetings and some educational purposes, most businesses have found that it is *not* a substitute for face-to-face interactions, and *hotels* have discovered that the ability to link with other sites actually *increases* their conference and meeting business!

TOURISM AS AN IMPORTANT ECONOMIC FORCE

Since the end of World War II, most countries have opened their doors to inter-country travel. Tourism, in its purest sense, means traveling for either business or pleasure, and can have many benefits for the destination spot including:

- ✓ larger governmental "coffers" since taxes are collected at the local level
- ✓ real estate development
- ✓ increased employment opportunities
- ✓ more investment opportunities for both firms or individuals

Although spin-off effects on related businesses make it difficult to accurately measure the total monetary benefits enjoyed by the destination, there is no doubt that tourism is profoundly important to the economic health of industrialized nations as well as developing nations.

Tourism and Industrialized Nations

Tourism within and between industrialized nations has become a way of life as transportation systems have matured, cultures have become blurred, and organizations have become global. Traveling has become so easy, there is little reason *not to* explore other areas of the world! Also, international and domestic business travel has become increasingly necessary. Lower airfares, extensive train and bus services, and automobile access have made it possible for most people to travel – and more often than ever before.

Air Travel Is Now the Norm

Take a look around you when you go to the airport – it is busy, if not chaotic, with people of all ages and from all over the world scurrying about to catch their flights. The excitement of travel is **contagious**!

Industrialized nations, as well as states, provinces, and regions, are promoting themselves as destination spots on television, radio, and the Internet in great numbers. Obviously, there is intense competition to get a piece of the tourism "pie" by presenting their locations in a unique and attractive way. They are all working to change the balance of tourism trade in *their* favor – that is, they hope that travelers will spend more money in their area than their residents will spend elsewhere. This means, of course, that tourist destinations will continue to develop marketing tools, expand products, and deliver a higher level of service.

This competition is good for you in a personal and professional sense. Not only can you learn about and visit more places, you can feel secure in having chosen the hospitality and tourism industry as a career field!

Tourism and Developing Nations

The story of tourism in developing nations is often entirely different. Many developing nations have realized that tourism is a major, *if not the only*, attraction for foreign investment – and at a monetary cost which is significantly lower than, say, manufacturing or high-tech industries.

For example, for a country to start its own automobile production facility, it would have to have access to raw materials and trained labor, and would have to develop an efficient distribution system. The dilemma? If developing countries had access to these things, they would no longer be termed *developing*! Therefore, many of these developing countries are looking toward tourism as an economic jump-start.

Not only will the host country enjoy higher tax revenues and employment levels, it will experience an influx of foreign currency into a system where currency is probably worth little or nothing on the international market. Its citizens can enjoy a higher standard of living, and the increased revenue from tourism can fund more educational and training opportunities. It can also support an improved infrastructure – roads, airports, utilities, and banks – to attract foreign investment in other industries.

The drawback to the development of tourism in such countries is serious – environments and cultures can be raped in exchange for improved economic health. Unwitting and even unscrupulous investors can ruin pristine lands, ancient cultures, indigenous foliage, and unique wildlife in a matter of years.

Ecotourism, which was briefly discussed in Chapter 1, has grown in importance and can balance the need for tourism revenue with the protection of the local culture and environment. Furthermore, although only a few treaties currently exist which protect developing countries from the negative effects of tourism, more are expected in the future.

In short, most agree that tourism is a major economic force and will grow in importance as travel becomes even easier and more affordable. Tourism is no longer the glamorous and "fluff" industry it once was – it is now as integral to the economic well-being of countries as their production and manufacturing facilities once were – actually, even more so!

EFFECTS OF GLOBALIZATION AND THE ENVIRONMENT

The effects of both globalization and environmental concerns on the hospitality and tourism industry are profound. As travel continues to increase and cultures begin to meld, a number of important questions will arise. Will individual cultures eventually fade away? Will the increase in the number of travelers threaten the environments of the destinations? How can you, as a responsible hospitality manager, protect cultures and environments from the potential dangers of tourism?

Thankfully, there is a new and powerful trend in tourism that addresses these important issues. Ecotourism, the newest buzzword in travel, goes by many different names such as ecotravel, nature-based travel, cross-cultural exchanges, adventure travel, reality tourism, and low-impact tourism; but it all means the same thing – travel with a conscience.

The idea behind ecotourism is that once travelers see a rainforest or an ancient tree, they will want to preserve it. According to Lisa Tabb, the publisher of *Ecotraveler Magazine*, ecotourism is a "marriage of adventures, discovery, and environmental responsibility."[32]

Ecotourism differs from conventional tourism in that it respects and sustains the environment as well as local cultures. Travelers can explore, study, interact, and discover cultures and environments around the world. The most popular eco-sites, respectively, are in Central America, South America, Canada, the

---

[32] Anonymous, *The Color of Ecotravel*, **DiveTravel** Magazine, August 20, 1996 (World Wide Web address: http://www.divetravel.com/Ecoltrav.html).

United States, the Caribbean, Antarctica, Australia, and Africa.

The activities vary from place to place. Ecotourists can kayak in the quiet waters of a river in Colorado; they can camp in the wilderness in Australia; they can build solar ovens in Kenya; or they can work to save the rainforests in Brazil. There are many opportunities for the socially responsible traveler, and many more are becoming available all the time.

Check the Internet for fun, and you will see how large this segment of tourism really is. To give you an idea, consider that ecotourism grossed $335 million of the $3.5 trillion spent on tourism in 1995. That's a decent market share for a new concept, wouldn't you agree?

Increased consumer awareness and concern has forced many hotels to adopt environmentally friendly practices such as recycling paper, glass, plastics, and other products; installing water saving devices in guest rooms and kitchens; treating and reusing wastewater from guest showers and laundry; and reventing heat from the laundry facilities for use elsewhere in the hotel. It is even common for guests to choose whether to have their linen and towels washed daily.

Third world countries will, hopefully, include ecotourism as a major consideration as they write their economic development plans. Rather than destroying the habitat and the culture in the interest of increased revenue from tourism, residents can enjoy a **higher sustainable standard of living**. The long-term effects are positive ones for the travelers and local inhabitants alike!

Like with many good ideas, the implementation of ecologically friendly practices can be difficult. We have to remember that, at its core, tourism is a business and, while some countries like Costa Rica have had success with this type of travel, this is not always the case. As we said in Chapter 1, mass market tourism is much more profitable than low-impact tourism, and even airlines are reluctant to offer service to destinations that don't generate volume. As a result, low-impact tourism often *follows* mass market tourism.

Still, keep your eyes on this important trend. Hotel and tour rating systems for eco-conscious travelers are now being developed. Travelers will soon be better able to distinguish between sophisticated operations and those which are not yet as sophisticated. As a future hospitality and tourism professional, your knowledge of and participation in socially and environmentally responsible travel could eventually be as important to your career as your understanding of the profit and loss statement!

THE FIT FOR THE FUTURE

The future of the hospitality and tourism industry is bright and exciting. You are embarking on a career in an industry that promises to thrive as demographics change, technology advances, and people become more aware of the economic, social, and ecological effects of travel. Tourism has become increasingly recognized as an industry that is important to the wealth and health of individuals, states, regions, and nations. As the effects of globalization continue to shape the future, this industry will offer even more challenges and prospects.

This industry is not for everyone, but *for those who fit*, the hospitality and tourism industry can be personally rewarding – economically, mentally, emotionally, and spiritually. As we said in the beginning of the book, a career is not just a job. It can drive many things in your life including your lifestyle, the amount of free time you have, the area in which you live, your interests and activities, and your health.

For now, the rest is up to you. Yes, many people will help you along the path and affect your life in many different ways. However, the choices are always yours and the consequences of these choices are also yours. Prepare thoroughly, develop continually, act responsibly, reason carefully, and *enjoy yourself*!

ADDITIONAL READINGS

Job Shift, William Bridges; Addison-Wesley Publishing (Reading, Massachusetts, 1994).

The Leader of the Future, Editors: Frances Hesselbein, Marshall Goldsmith, & Richard Beckhard; Drucker Foundation Future Series (New York, New York, 1996).

Managing Diversity, James Walsh; Merritt Publishing (Santa Monica, California, 1995).

Managing in the Next Millennium, Mike Johnson; Butterworth-Heinemann, Ltd. (Oxford, England, 1995).